MACROMEDIA Flash .NET

Pallav Nadhani
Gregg Wygonik
David Neal
Todd Yard
Chris Bizzell
Graeme Bull

Flash .NET

© 2002 friends of ED

First Printed November 2002

Trademark Acknowledgements

friends of ED has endeavored to provide trademark information about all the companies and products mentioned in this book by the appropriate use of capitals. However, friends of ED cannot guarantee the accuracy of this information.

Published by friends of ED

30-32 Lincoln Road, Olton, Birmingham,
B27 6PA, UK.
Printed in USA

ISBN 1-904344-08-9

Flash .NET

Credits

Authors
Pallav Nadhani
Gregg Wygonik
David Neal
Todd Yard
Chris Bizzell
Graeme Bull

Additional Content
Dan Squier

Technical Reviewers
Mark Grimshaw
Keran McKenzie
David Neal
Rama Ramachandran
Matt Rice

Technical Editors
Matthew Knight
Dan Squier

Commissioning Editor
Andrew Tracey

Author Agent
Chris Matterface

Project Manager
Simon Brand

Indexer
Fiona Murray

Graphic Editor
Ty Bhogal
Stuart Ibbotson

Cover Design
Katy Freer
Ty Bhogal

Managing Editor
Chris Hindley

Pallav Nadhani

"Heaven doesn't need him and Hell is afraid he might take over". That's how this chemically inbalanced Kindergarten naughty boy used to trespass around people's minds. Esoteric music pulls him, the louder the better. Gets bored without constant challenges - keeps on freaking with new technologies. Hacking, Quake III, WWE and happening movies feature among his top likes. A programmer by heart, Flash is his first love (though ever failed to draw a trapezoid). Shacks in InfoSoft with a Technology Architect board hanging outside it. He would like to thank his Mom and Dad for being the never ending source of inspiration, Monu for his continued support, and "Gadhri" for her petty mischiefs that kept him going throughout. pallav@nadhani.com

Gregg Wygonik

Gregg is a professional electronic musician who spends his days developing Flash-based software that teaches mathematics to children. When not behind a computer, in the studio, or trotting around on tour, Gregg likes to spend his "free" time with his photographer wife and their three cats. Gregg tries to keep his Flash experimentations online at www.artificialcolors.com, though keeping the site current is always easier said then done. If Gregg were a colossal death robot, he'd be Gigantor, and if he were an evil criminal, he would be Elizabeth Bathory.

David Neal

David Neal is currently the Vice-President of Web Technology and Chief Software Architect for Transcender LLC, where he is looking for every opportunity to use his .NET skills. Outside of his passion for assimilating new technology, he fancies himself a capable fingerstyle guitarist. He would like to thank his wife Tammy and four sons Caleb, Benjamin, Christian, and Drew for their unconditional love and support, and for being the best family a man could ever wish for. You can reach him at david@maxyourasp.com.

Todd Yard

After studying theatre in London, then working for several years as an actor in the US, Todd was introduced to Flash in 2000 and was quickly taken by how it allowed for both stunning creativity and programmatic logic application a truly left-brain, right brain approach to production and has not looked back. He now works as Creative Director for Daedalus Media in New York City, which specializes in the creation of Flash-based corporate presentations primarily for clients in the investment banking industry. His more frivolous work and experimentation can be found at his personal website **www.27Bobs.com**.

Chris Bizzell

As web developer for The Pinnacle Consulting Group, Chris has developed numerous dynamic web applications using ASP and ASP.NET and is excited by the endless possibilities of incorporating server-side technologies with Flash MX. After picking up a demo of Flash 4 two years ago, he became hooked on the Macromedia product line and is amazed at the steady maturation of the Flash software. When not playing with his children Cassidy and Brady Chris likes to kick around his hometown of Greenville with his wife Stacy. Thanks: I would like to thank my wife Stacy for putting up with me while this project was being completed. I would also like to thank West Goewey for getting me started, and Todd Scott and everyone at Pinnacle for giving me a chance to do something I truly enjoy for a living.

Graeme Bull

I never really had any real mind to get into web design or anything of the sort until about two years ago, though after being infected with the Flash and Photoshop virus, I can't put down my mouse, to a point where I'll just plain forget to eat and drink as I stare hard at my screen trying to get that perfect collage of pixels to come together for some fantastic creation. This is where I have got to thank my girl for coming by and bringing food to sustain me so I can continue the staring, pixel-moving and general mumbling at the screen.

Table of Contents

Introduction

So, what's this Flash.NET business all about then? Flash (aka 'Macromedia Flash MX') we all know and love: a multi-talented platform for vector graphics, animations, interactive content, and even video delivery. Thanks to scripting support in the shape of ActionScript, it's no dummy either. The rich variety of Flash content you can find on the Web testifies to its effectiveness as a medium for delivering rich, good-looking, interactive content.

Then there's .NET (aka 'Microsoft .NET Framework'), which if you believe the hype, is the latest, greatest thing to come out through the steely gates of the Microsoft Corporation. It's a massive suite of tools that's specifically designed to help developers build, deploy, and run powerful applications – on the Web, on the desktop, locally, globally, wherever, whenever.

Hmm. Even if you do believe the hype, you may be wondering what relevance .NET could possibly have to Flash designers like you and me. Surely it's a development tool aimed at hardcore developers, and it would probably take five years' study to get it going in the first place, right?

Well, it ain't necessarily so. The fact that you're currently reading a book on .NET for Flash designers should hint that this really isn't how we see things. As you're going to discover very shortly, getting started with .NET can be an absolute breeze. Once we've got going, we can hook it into our Flash movies, and begin to unleash its power.

As we've already observed, Flash MX really excels when it comes to presenting graphical, interactive content. It's a superb tool for building user interfaces and for presenting content that changes over time. While .NET has a great deal going for it, its built-in user interface support is still comparatively clunky – HTML anyone? Put them together, and you open up a whole raft of new possibilities for both: powerful logic and functionality with a rich, flexible interface on the front. Put them together, and you get Flash.NET.

> *In short, Flash and .NET are technologies that can complement each other very well indeed. By the end of this book, we hope you'll to convince you of the same.*

Power at what price?

One of the big selling points of .NET to developers is that it simplifies many of the complex tasks that normally make it such hard work to build a working application. This applies to us too – lowering the bar like this means that we can get impressive results with or without a diploma in Software Engineering. So, despite what you may be thinking, you shouldn't need an IQ test to determine whether or not to read on.

What we'll be doing throughout the book is to concentrate on simple techniques that you can use many times over. You'll see examples of Flash and .NET in tandem, and see how they can add exciting and fresh functionality to your projects.

Another big selling point of .NET is that it allows you to write your code in several different languages, without compromising on the speed and power of the finished project. One of these languages is called C#, and as luck would have it, it bears an uncanny resemblance to our old friend ActionScript.

Remember all the quantum leaps that Flash sites made when ActionScript first came on the scene? Well .NET offers us the chance to make similar leaps forward, and make them without too much pain along the way. This book is here to show you how.

How the book is structured

Chapter 1 lays some foundations, introducing the tools and technologies that we'll be using throughout the book, including Microsoft's IIS web server, the .NET Framework, and the C# programming language. By the end of this chapter, you'll have written your first ASP.NET web page, and have a simple Flash.NET application up and running.

In **Chapter 2**, we look at some specific techniques for passing information back and forth between Flash and .NET. From passing simple values, to handling structured XML data, to generating images on the server, we'll start to flex the .NET muscles and give our apps a little bite.

Chapter 3 focuses on server-side techniques for getting, setting, and manipulating data. With .NET giving us a way to control data (and even save it in files) before it even leaves the server, there's a lot we can do to reduce the load on Flash and open up brand new possibilities for storing data.

Chapter 4 then takes us on to meet the heavyweight solution for all our data storage needs: databases. We look at setting up the MSDE database engine, and see how we can write .NET code that will let our Flash movies tap right into it.

In **Chapter 5**, we tackle Flash Remoting MX, Macromedia's own technology for server-side integration with Flash movies. We see a few of the tricks we've done before made simpler, and ultimately learn how we can make use of .NET without writing any code for it at all!

Following that, we've a couple of **Case Studies**, where you'll see how some of the techniques we've learnt about have been put to use in the real world.

What you'll need

To run the examples in this book for yourself, you'll need to be running Microsoft Windows 2000/XP with Flash MX, IIS 5.0, and the following software installed:

- Microsoft .NET Framework SDK 1.0
- MSDE / SQL Server (Chapters 4 and 5 only)
- Macromedia Flash Remoting MX (Chapter 5 and Case Study 1 only)

You can find download instructions for each of these in the chapters that introduce them (1, 4, and 5 respectively).

> *IIS 5.0 is a web server that's provided with 2000/XP versions of Windows, so don't panic if it's not ringing any bells just yet – all will be explained in Chapter 1.*
>
> *If you don't already have Flash MX, then you can always download the 30-day trial edition from http://www.macromedia.com/software/flash/download/.*

Code downloads

There are lots of worked examples in this book, and while you can build most of them purely from the instructions given in the text, you may want to sneak a peek at our source files, which you can download from www.friendsofed.com.

Notably, the two case studies *don't* detail every single feature and line of code in the apps they discuss, so you will need the relevant source files to get the most out of them.

Layout conventions

We want this book to be as clear and easy to use as possible, so we've used a number of layout styles throughout.

- Practical exercises begin under a heading like this:

Build this Movie now

- Whenever we think it helps the discussion, they'll have numbered steps like this:

1. Do this first.
2. Do this second.
3. Do this third,etc...

- When referring to code in the body of the text (variables, functions, instance names, and the like), we use a fixed-width font like this to help highlight it.

- We use the same style when we're showing blocks of code:

```
if (count > 100) {
    stop();
}
```

- When we add new code to an existing block, we highlight it like this:

```
if (count > 200) {
    finished = true;
    stop();
}
```

- If a piece of code that needs to be entered as a single line is too wide to fit on the page, we'll mark it like this:

```
if (count > 200 && time > 1750 && day > 16
              ➥ && month > 10 && year > 2002) {
    finished = true;
    stop();
}
```

- The screen text style is used to emphasize text that appears on the screen.

- When we want you to navigate through a hierarchy of menus and sub-menus, we'll indicate the path like this: File > Import....

- URLs are shown like this: www.friendsofed.com

- Keyboard shortcuts are shown like this: CTRL+S.

- New or significant phrases are shown as **important words**.

> *If there's something you shouldn't miss, it will be highlighted it like this! When you see the box, pay attention!*

Support – we're here to help

All books from friends of ED should be easy to follow and error-free. However, if you do run into problems, don't hesitate to get in touch – our support is fast, friendly and free.

You can reach us at support@friendsofED.com, quoting the last for digits of the ISBN in the subject of the e-mail (that's 4089), and even if our dedicated support team are unable to solve your problem immediately, your queries will be passed onto the people who put the book together, the editors and authors, to solve. All our authors help with the support on their books, and will either directly mail people with answers, or (more usually) send their response to an editor to pass on.

We'd love to hear from you, even if it's just to request future books, ask about friends of ED, or tell us how much you got out of Flash.NET.

> *To tell us a bit about yourself and make comments about the book, why not fill out the reply card at the back and send it to us!*

If your enquiry concerns an issue not directly concerned with book content, then the best place for these types of questions is our message board lists at http://www.friendsofed.com/forums. Here, you'll find a variety of designers talking about what they do, who should be able to provide some ideas and solutions.

For news, more books, sample chapters, downloads, author interviews and more, send your browser to www.friendsofED.com. To take a look at the friends of ED Flash MX bookshelf from which this book comes, take a look at www.flashmxlibrary.com.

chapter 1: **Flash and .NET**

We're going to spend this opening chapter getting ready to work with Macromedia Flash MX and Microsoft's .NET Framework. Before we can start building applications, we need to make sure they're both installed, and that they have some way to talk to each other. If you don't have access to expensive development tools like Visual Studio.NET (and we're assuming you don't) then the simplest way to communicate with .NET is over the Web.

As luck would have it, Flash MX gives us plenty of ways to make our movies interact with the Web, with ActionScript methods for sending and receiving various types of data. We'll spend a little time looking at these in Chapter 2.

For now, the important thing is to get our foundations in place. Just so that we're all up to speed, we'll begin by looking at how the Web works, and consider the role played by servers in making web content available. We'll get a web server up and running for ourselves, and then install .NET. We'll finish things off with a Flash.NET example – a quick taster of what's in store.

So, in the course of this chapter we're going to look at the following topics:

- How the Web works.

- Dynamic content, and what it can do for a Flash site.

- Setting up the IIS web server, so that we can host dynamic web content.

- Getting to know .NET – what it is, what it does, and how we can begin to use it.

In order to see how .NET fits in with the landscape of the Web, we need to think about how the Web itself operates. The next few pages are designed to be a quick refresher on the basics of client-server systems. It might well be stuff you already know, in which case you might want to skip past it; if in doubt though, read on.

Clients and servers

The Web we all know and love is based on lots of computers, talking to each other across a massive *inter*national *network* – the Internet. Some of these machines run **web server** programs, whose job it is to stand around waiting for someone to **request something** – like an electronic waiter. They have access to a whole bunch of files and data, and can serve up copies of that data over the network in the blink of an eye. Some machines run **client** programs, and these are designed to send requests to the servers.

> *Strictly speaking, servers and clients are just programs that run on a computer. There's nothing to stop you running both on the same computer, along with any other programs you like, but to get the best performance out of a server, you need to dedicate as many of the computer's resources to it as possible. For that reason, servers are often run on dedicated machines, and you'll find that many people (rather confusingly) refer to the machine itself as 'the server'. Just remember: we're just talking about a program, not necessarily a whole machine.*

Your web browser is one familiar example of a client. Say you type an address like this into your browser:

```
http://www.friendsofed.com/support.html
```

When you hit ENTER to call up the page, the browser sends this message out onto the Internet, and the electronic equivalent of the postal service picks it up. This uses the information there to send a message to a machine called www, in a domain called friendsofed.com, asking for a file called support.html.

> *What about the first bit? Just as regular mail offers you various delivery options (express, parcel post, confirmation, and so on), requests on the Internet use different systems (called **protocols**) for sending different things around.*
>
> *HTTP is a protocol that's designed specifically for delivering web pages (and requests for web pages). Other common protocols are FTP (for file transfer) and HTTPS (for better security).*

At this point, we could go into all the details of how the Internet tracks down the exact server you're looking for: the one with access to a file called `support.html`. It basically goes to a big directory of domain names and *looks it up* – exactly as you might do if you were looking for someone's telephone number.

The important thing is that once the message does get through to the server, the server tracks down the specified file, pulls out the contents (in this case, a load of HTML) and sends them back to wherever the request came from. This is what's known in highly technical terms as the **response**.

When your client program (the browser) picks up the response, it unpacks the message (all that HTML) and uses a built-in set of rules to convert (or **render**) all the tags into a structured, visual web page. All this happens in the blink of an eye, whether the client and server programs are halfway round the world from one another, or on the self same machine.

Exactly the same process takes place when you request a SWF from the Web:

1. The client sends a request out onto the Internet, asking for a particular file from a particular server.

2. The Internet passes it on, and the server receives the request.

3. The server grabs web content from inside the requested file and sends it back to the client.

4. The client receives the copy and renders whatever's inside.

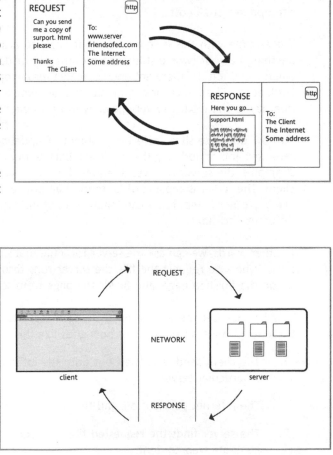

The only difference is that the browser doesn't know what rules to use for rendering SWFs; that's the job of the Flash plug-in.

Dynamic content

We can make a web page in the form of an HTML file or SWF, put it on a server, and call it up from anywhere on the Internet. But what if we want to *change* what's on the page? The server just hands over a copy of whatever it finds in the requested file, so the only way to make corrections or updates is to replace the file with a new version.

At best, that's going to be a little fiddly. The absolute minimum you need to do is open up the original file, make necessary changes, save them, connect to the server, and copy the new file over to it. Unless you're very patient (or very bored) you're not likely to want to do that more than once or twice a day. At worst, it'll become a complete nightmare, and you'll quickly learn to avoid site updates at all costs.

The trouble with this is that you're not likely to attract lots of visitors if your site never offers anything new, or (worse still) is six months out of date. No matter how good your content was when you put it up, there are only so many times people are going to look at the same stuff again. Look at any Flash news or community site, and you'll find that the content offered will vary from one day to the next, and very possibly more frequently than that.

So how do these sites solve the problem of updating? They use computers to do the dull and repetitive job of updating the site. Think back to our earlier diagram with the server and the client programs: the server receives a request for `dan.swf` or `pallav.html`, and sends the file to the client. The server is capable of far more than just serving up ready-prepared dishes, though – just like any other computer, it can follow a set of instructions and cook up some different dishes for different occasions.

In other words, we can ask the server for a file that simply contains instructions for making a web page. When we request the file, the server runs through its contents, figures out what ought to be on the finished page, and builds the page from scratch, before returning it to the client.

You'll remember there were originally four steps to the process we looked at earlier. This adds three extra ones, so the process now goes like this:

1.   The client sends a request out onto the Internet, asking for a particular file from a particular server.

2.   The Internet passes it on, and the server receives the request.

3.   The server finds the requested file and feeds its contents to a program that uses them to generate web content.

4.   The content-generating program does its stuff and generates content.

5.   It then sends the processed web content back to the server.

6.   The server takes the processed web content and sends it back to the client.

7.   The client receives the copy and renders whatever's inside.

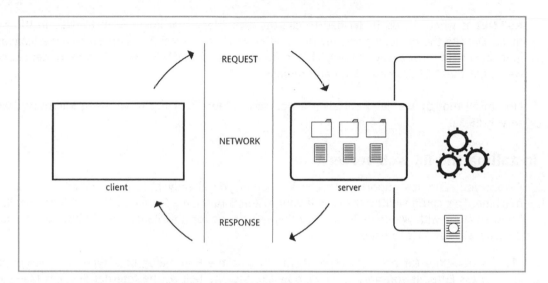

In the past, instructions on the server were all written as **server-side scripts**, very simple programs that could respond to instructions from the client – for example, "Display all news headlines added in the last seven days". Several different server-side scripting languages were (and still are) commonplace: you may well have heard of ASP, JSP, PHP, and Perl - all languages used to tell servers how to build web pages.

ASP or ASP.NET?

ASP stands for **Active Server Pages**, and is Microsoft's very own scripting language for its very own web server – **Internet Information Server** (known to friends as IIS). Whenever IIS serves up a file with the extension .asp, it knows to look for ASP scripts inside. Instead of sending the contents back to the client verbatim, the server uses a built-in ASP-reading program to follow the instructions it contains, and use them to generate the content it ultimately sends back to the client.

Early in 2002, Microsoft launched the .NET Framework, giving developers a powerhouse platform for developing and running industrial strength computer programs. What's more, Microsoft designed it to plug right into IIS, letting the web server tap straight into its central nervous system.

This means that .NET slips into the role of content-generating program: the server feeds it with instructions, and .NET duly obliges by generating web content from them.

Now, in terms of power, comparing a traditional server-side script with a .NET application is a bit like putting your dusty old N64 up against a brand new GameCube - there's really no competition.

The upshot is that anyone with IIS and .NET installed on their computer can write incredibly powerful .NET applications to generate their dynamic web content.

ASP.NET is what Microsoft decided to call the technology that links IIS up to .NET in the first place. Despite the name, it's actually quite different from 'classic' ASP, and isn't even a language in its own right - just a way of using .NET to do what we want. We'll look at it in more detail once we've got the .NET Framework up and running.

First of all though, we need ourselves a web server. More specifically, we need Microsoft's web server: IIS 5.0.

Installing the IIS web server

Before you start, it's important to check whether you already have IIS installed on your test machine. This could well be the case if your system's running a Server edition of Windows. IIS is bundled along with Windows 2000/XP so there's no need for downloads – you'll just need to have your installation CDs to hand.

1.   Start > Run (or press WINDOWS+R) to bring up the Run dialog box. Type in `inetmgr` and press ENTER. If you now see a window like the one below (the Internet Services Manager) then it looks like IIS is already installed. Make yourself a cup of tea and rejoin us in a few moments.

If not, you're probably staring at an error dialog indicating `File Not Found`. In this case, there's no IIS on your system, so let's press on, follow the instructions below, and get it running.

2. To set up IIS 5.0, go to Start > Settings > Control Panel > Add/Remove Programs, and click on the Add/Remove Windows Components icon on the left-hand side of the panel. You'll see a window like this that allows you to add optional Windows advanced components. Check the box next to Internet Information Services (IIS) and click Next. You should now see a progress bar indicating how far the installation has to go, and before long, a new message telling you that the installation is complete.

You'll be glad to hear that's all there is to it – it really was that easy!

Testing the IIS installation

Let's check that we can call up the Internet Services Manager screen:

1. Select Start > Run (or press Windows+R) to bring up the **Run** dialog box. Once again, type in `inetmgr` and press Enter.

Not only does this tell you that IIS is up and running, but the label next to each of the little computer icons tells you the name by which your machine is identified on the network. As you can see, mine is called 'goon' – make a note of your own, so you can substitute it wherever necessary.

Calling up a web page

You should now be able to call up web pages from your test machine's fully functional web server. Open up your web browser and point it at http://goon (or alternatively http://localhost, which is the standard address for accessing the web server that's running on the same machine as the browser). You should see something like this:

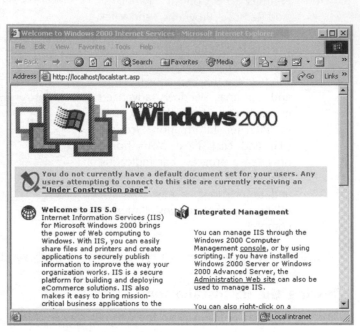

If your test machine is on a network with several others, you may want to try accessing http://goon (or rather, your own equivalent) from a browser on a different computer. As the message shown here implies, any non-local users accessing the site will receive a different page, telling them it's still under construction.

We have IIS installed, and it seems to be working. There's no sign of .NET yet though, so let's deal with that right away.

Installing .NET

.NET is available in several different forms, most of which are freely available for download from the Microsoft web site at www.microsoft.com. To be sure that all the examples in this book will work properly, you'll need to use the .NET Framework Software Development Kit (SDK), which you can download from http://msdn.microsoft.com/downloads/sample.asp?url=/msdnfiles/027/000/976/ msdncompositedoc.xml.

As you can see, it weighs in rather on the heavy side, at 131Mb. You therefore have the option to download it in ten separate pieces; along with a `setup.bat` file that you can run once they're all in place to recombine them.

Once you've completed the download, installation is nice and easy. Just double-click on the `setup.exe` file, and OK the dialog. Several minutes of whirring later, and you should find yourself with .NET installed.

A less bulky way to get hold of the .NET Framework is with the Redistributable version, which comes in at just over 20Mb. You can download this version from http://msdn.microsoft.com/downloads/sample.asp?url=/msdnfiles/027/001/829/msdncompositedoc.xml. *While it will provide you with all you need to* **run** *existing .NET applications, it doesn't support all the development features we'll be using in this book to* **create** *our own applications. Specifically, Flash Remoting for .NET (which we'll cover in Chapter 5) requires you to have the full SDK version installed.*

A new start

Now it's time to make sure everything's running properly, and start to learn about what's involved in harnessing the .NET Framework. We'll begin by seeing how to create a simple ASP.NET test page, and call it up via the server. A little later on, we'll take a closer look at the C# language that we use to write these pages.

Our first example is a simple two-line file that returns the current time as measured on the server.

1. Open up a new file in Notepad (or your text editor of choice), and add these lines:

```
<%@ Page language="c#" %>
<script runat="server">
  void Page_Load(Object sender, EventArgs e) {
    Response.Write(DateTime.Now);
  }
</script>
```

2. Save the file as now.aspx in C:/inetpub/wwwroot. This is the default folder where IIS will start looking for files. Call up http://localhost/now.aspx, and you should see something like this:

Okay, it's maybe not the most impressive display of power, but it's simple enough that we can step through the basic instructions that make up our ASP.NET page.

The first line is what's called a **page directive**. Since .NET lets us use a variety of different languages to write instructions, we need to tell it what language we're intending to use in this particular page. We can only have one language per page, and in this case, we'll be working with C#.

```
<%@ Page language="c#" %>
```

The script tags tell IIS that it should expect some code that will need to be executed on the server:

```
<script runat="server">
  ...
</script>
```

In between these script tags, we define a function called Page_Load, whose contents will automatically be run whenever the ASP.NET page is loaded up.

```
<script runat="server">
  void Page_Load(Object sender, EventArgs e) {
    // C# instructions go in here //
  }
</script>
```

Don't worry about void and the two parameters; they're part of the standard Page_Load function that ASP.NET expects to run whenever the page loads. The important thing is what we put inside this structure:

```
<script runat="server">
  void Page_Load(Object sender, EventArgs e) {
    Response.Write(DateTime.Now);
  }
</script>
```

Here's the real meat at the heard of our ASP.NET page. Using `Response.Write()` is like saying *hey... process and output whatever I give within the parentheses to the browser.* Meanwhile, `DateTime.Now` gives us the server's current date and time setting.

The end result is that when we call up the ASPX file from our web browser, IIS loads up the page, .NET executes the `Page_Load` function, and sends the current date and time back to the browser, where we can see the result for ourselves.

Careful coding

Before we go on, there's one very important thing to note about ASP.NET (particularly if you've used classic ASP in the past): the code in an ASP.NET page is *case-sensitive*. Scripting languages like VBScript and JavaScript are often very laid back about this, but .NET is very picky, especially when it's using C#. For example, you might try using `DateTime.now` in the previous example, and deliberately generating an error:

Fortunately, it seems this pickiness pays off. It may be a little frustrating, but it also helps to make .NET extremely good at tracking down errors. As you can see, it's not only homed right in on the line it doesn't like, but told us which part of it's broken.

But what does it mean by "`System.DateTime` does not contain a definition for `now`"? The error message isn't much use if we can't make sense of it. In fact, `System.DateTime` is the name of a class which contains all the functionality of working with, yes – you guessed it, dates and times. When we say `DateTime.Now`, we're accessing its static property `Now`, which contains the current date and time.

Objects, objects everywhere...

The .NET framework is almost entirely based around classes like `DateTime`, and because there are so many, it organizes them into groups called **namespaces**. `DateTime`'s defined in a namespace called `System` (hence `System.DateTime`), along with other fundamental objects we use in .NET (such as variables and arrays). All classes defined in the `System` namespace are automatically available to any ASP.NET page we write, so we know we have some basic functionality from the offset.

Note that although the `System` namespace is already included, we still need to specify that we're working with the `DateTime` class's `Now` property, and not a `Now` property in some other namespace.

More specialized objects are defined in their own namespaces. For example, `System.IO` is a namespace containing objects that pass data in and out of files, and `System.Drawing` contains objects for manipulating images.

> *You can find out more about each namespace from the local Documentation (under* Start > Programs > Microsoft .NET Framework SDK), *or the MSDN library at* http://msdn.microsoft.com/library/default.asp.

Adding a namespace to your ASP.NET page is as simple as adding a new directive – for example, if we wanted to use objects that let us draw pictures with .NET, we'd say:

```
<%@ Page Language="C#" %>
<%@ Import namespace="System.Drawing" %>

<script runat="server">
...
```

Now that we've explained that little self-induced bug, let's look at the other things we need to keep in mind while writing ASP.NET pages. We're going to be using Microsoft's C# language throughout the book, so it makes sense to start out by looking at that.

C# for the Flash coder

As I mentioned earlier, C# has a lot in common with ActionScript, making it relatively easy to move back and forth between programming for ASP.NET and Flash.

At the same time though, C# is a much deeper, more powerful language than ActionScript. It's designed to be a language that can tap right into the deepest darkest corners of .NET, and one with which you can write complex applications that squeeze every last ounce of performance from Windows itself – something that, for obvious reasons, Flash will never have access to directly.

As such, it has features that ActionScript simply doesn't need: a full-blown object-oriented programming model, exception handling, system event trapping, threading capabilities, and regular expression parsing, to name but a few.

Don't let this panic you though. Unless you intend to start programming professional, full-blown C# applications for yourself, the ins and outs of C# really don't need to get much more complex than a typical piece of ActionScript. The important thing here is that you can make sense of the code you see, and understand enough of it to spot where things might have gone wrong and tweak it to your own ends.

> *If you do want to learn how to develop your own C# applications from scratch, then we can suggest no better place to start than Wrox Press* (www.wrox.com). *Their books cover just about every conceivable aspect of C# and .NET, right from the ground up, and are aimed specifically at helping you learn development skills right up to a professional level*

Let's take a look at some of the major points of C# and how they relate to what we're used to in ActionScript.

General syntax

As we saw earlier, C# is case-sensitive, and to an even greater degree than ActionScript. If .NET says it doesn't recognize something, then the first thing to check is that 'something' is capitalized exactly as it should be.

Both C# and ActionScript use a curly brackets to group statements together, and require semi-colons at the end of statements (though again, ActionScript is rather less stringent on this point).

In both languages, comments are implemented using // and /*..*/. So, the following code snippet could work in either ActionScript or C#:

```
{
  // this line of code does nothing
  /*
     neither does this block of code
     i = i + 2;
  */
}
```

Variables and data types

ActionScript is very accommodating when it comes to variables; whatever type of data you're storing away, Flash will accept it without question, and figure out how to interpret it for itself. In programming terms, this is called **loose typing**.

```
// ActionScript variable declaration
var x = "y";
var a = 20;
var b = true;
```

These lines of ActionScript will create three new variables. Flash will automatically type the first variable as a String, the second as a Number, and the third as a Boolean. Because our variables are loosely typed variables, ActionScript will let us change their values to any other type, anywhere in our application, simply by assigning the new value.

Even though the `var` keyword is recommended for declaring "I want to use a variable called a", before you charge in and give it a value, Flash can cope if you just say `a=10;` and leave it at that.

Again, C# is a lot more fussy about this. Before we use a variable, we need to declare it, and we need to explicitly state what type of variable it will be. This is known as **strong typing**. The same example in C# would look like this:

```
// C# variable declaration
string x = "y";
int a = 20;
bool b = true;
```

Since our variables are strongly typed, C# will **not** allow us to change their type later on by simply assigning a different type value to them.

Converting data types

Just as Flash will automatically type our ActionScript variables, it will also automatically convert between different types as needed. In the following ActionScript example, we add a Number to a String, and get a result that's another String (since Flash knows that "20y" makes no sense as a number):

```
// ActionScript variable addition
var a = 20;
var x = "y";
trace(a + x);
// output: 20y
```

If we try this example in C#, we'll receive a compilation error. C# requires that *we* call the appropriate conversion methods as needed. Our example in C# would then look like this:

```
// C# string addition
int a = 20;
string x = "y";
Response.Write(a.ToString() + x);
// output: 20y
```

If we tried to convert variable `x` to an `int`, we'd have received an error, as C# has no way of converting the `String` `"y"` into a number. However, if our C# variable `x` had been storing '123' as a String, we could have done this:

```
// C# number addition
int a = 20;
string x = "123";
Response.Write(a + Convert.ToInt32(x));
// output: 143
```

The `Convert` class, as defined the `System` namespace, features several static methods like this – including `ToBoolean()` and `ToString()` – that let us force data into the type we need it in.

Operators

There's a lot of overlap between C# and ActionScript when it comes to the actual expressions and operators in the languages. Just about every ActionScript operator looks and works the exact same way in C#: arithmetic operators (+, -, /, *), assignment operators (+=, *=, %=), and so on.

In fact, there are only two ActionScript operators that aren't supported in C#: strict equality (===) and strict inequality (!==).

Once again, the following lines of code would work equally well in ActionScript or C#:

```
i = i + 2;
b += 3;
c -= (b % 5);
d++;
```

Loops and conditionals

All ActionScript loop types are also C# loop types: `while` loops, `do..while` loops, and `for` loops are identical in function and syntax. The main practical difference to note is that a C# `for` loop needs to have its counter variable declared like this:

```
for (int i=0;i<10;i++) {
    ...
}
```

The ActionScript `for..in` loop is also implemented in C#, but with one slight difference of nomenclature: it's written as `foreach..in`, though it functions the same way.

In keeping with the theme, even the conditionals are the same: `if..else` and `switch` statements are implemented identically in both languages:

```
if (i == 5) {
   j+=10;
   } else {
     j++;
   }
}
```

Of course, to go through every single function, method, and statement in both languages would be well beyond the scope of this book. By now though, you should have begun to see just how similar they are, and that you don't need to be scared by the thought of learning a brand new language.

On the other hand, it's important not let the resemblances lull you into complacency. C# and ActionScript are obviously quite distinct languages, and (as we've already seen) there *are* things that differ between the two.

That said, this brief introduction should be enough to make you feel comfortable with the C# code you'll be encountering in this book. If you decide you want to take things further, you might like to grab a book on C# programming, or peruse some of the many C# sites that pop up all over the Web – www.asp.net and www.gotdotnet.com are two that I'd particularly recommend to get started with.

Well, we've spent a good while looking at what it takes to make .NET perform tricks for us. What about the other side of the equation? Let's think about what Flash brings to the party.

Flash clients

Since version 4, Flash movies have been able to make their own decisions about what to do and show when they're played. These decisions – defined with ActionScript – can be based on whatever information the movie has access to. This is usually values set by the author and written into the movie itself, or input from the user entered while the movie was running.

We already know that a client is a program that can send out requests to a server and do something with the response it gets back from the server. Thanks to ActionScript, our Flash movies can do that as well, adding a third way to obtain information for our Flash movies to use to make decisions. For example, the home page on Macromedia's web site features a Flash movie called `home_main.swf`, shown on next page.

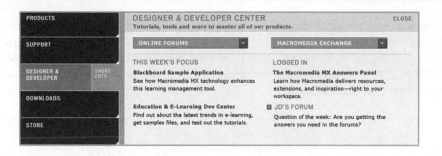

The Flash movie is normally embedded in the default page under www.macromedia.com, and if you visit the site regularly, you'll know that the information shown changes from day to day. It's the same SWF, but the information you're seeing – the actual content – is being pulled in from external files.

The presentation (layout and interface) is always the same, so this has been coded into the SWF. On the other hand, the content (text, links, list items) will change from week to week, so it's stored in a separate file, which is easier to update.

For example, the Designer & Developer Center page shown is based on a text file at: http://www.macromedia.com/home_movies/home_desdev.txt:

Hmm. It's not terribly easy to read, unless you happen to be a Flash movie. All the % signs and numbers are actually a way to represent characters like spaces and slashes – it's a system called **URL-encoding** – so it actually reads a little more like this:

```
c3_featureIntro=
c3_feature=Blackboard Sample Application
c3_featureUrl=/go/081502_blackboard
c3_featureTxt=See how Macromedia MX technology enhances this learning management tool.
c3_feature2=<b>Education & E-Learning Dev Center</b>
c3_featureUrl2=/go/081502_edudevcntr
c3_featureTxt2=Find out about the latest trends in e-learning, get samples files, and test out the tutorials.
c3_feature3=
c3_featureUrl3=
c3_featureTxt3=
c3_trainingTxt=Question of the week: Are you getting the answers you need in the forums?
c3_trainingUrl=/go/jdforum/
c3_tip=The Macromedia MX Answers Panel
c3_tipUrl=/go/loggedin/
c3_tipTxt=Learn how Macromedia delivers resources, extensions, and inspiration-right to your workspace.
c3_forum_header=ONLINE FORUMS
```

Just imagine a few added quote marks and semi-colons, and this could easily be a page of ActionScript, with variables called `c3_feature` and the like being given values such as `Blackboard Sample Application`. In fact, that's precisely what *does* happen. When a Flash movie pulls in the URL-encoded text file, it just sees a great long string of variable assignments, and creates them all automatically.

> *It's important to note that Flash movies can only request files from their **own domain**. In this case, the movie and the text file are from* macromedia.com. *If we copied the movie to the friends of ED server, ran it, and asked for the text file, it wouldn't work. The text file would still be on* macromedia.com *– a different domain – and the movie can't access it.*

Once we've stored all these imported values in ActionScript variables, we can use the information in all kinds of ways to control what the movie does and what it looks like. The useful aspect of this comes when we don't just ask Flash to load static values in, but ask for some dynamic data.

So, instead of asking Flash to upload some information that we've changed by adding a new file to the server, we ask it to go and obtain some values that change. For example, you could ask Flash to report back on the weather from a place where weather reports are kept. In the following example, we're going to check on the time.

Making a clock in Flash

For our first example, we're going to use the output of a C# ASP.NET page to set the time on a Flash clock-face. It's not exactly revolutionary, since we can already tell the time in ActionScript, but it does serve to demonstrate just how easily Flash can enhance the raw data we get back from the web server.

Let's start by building the ASP.NET page that's going to send us the time on the server. It's not so different from our original `now.aspx` page, except that the data it sends us needs to be in URL-encoded form.

1. Create a text file, and enter the following script:

```
<%@ Page language="c#" %>

<script runat="server">
  void Page_Load(Object sender, EventArgs e) {
DateTime currentTime = DateTime.Now;
Response.Write("&Hour=" + currentTime.Hour);
Response.Write("&Minute=" + currentTime.Minute);
```

continues overleaf

```
     Response.Write("&Second=" + currentTime.Second);
   }
</script>
```

2. Save the text file in your wwwroot folder, calling it time.aspx. Test it by pointing your browser to http://localhost/time.aspx, and you should see something like this:

This may look odd, but don't worry; it's precisely what we need. Each & character separates a new variable, so that when we pull this data into Flash, we'll create three variables called Hour, Minute, and Second, with values of 12, 51, and 39.

Before we move on to look at the Flash movie, let's just take a quick look at the code we're using here.

We start with the standard page directive, specifying the programming language we'll be using. We follow this up with the main script, and the equally standard Page_Load function.

```
<%@ Page language="c#" %>

<script runat="server">
  void Page_Load(Object sender, EventArgs e) {
  // C# code in here //
  }
</script>
```

Okay, that's our standard template for ASP.NET pages – nothing new there. Now we plug in the C# that's going to run when the page is called up.

```
  void Page_Load(Object sender, EventArgs e) {
    DateTime currentTime = DateTime.Now;
    Response.Write("&Hour=" + currentTime.Hour);
    Response.Write("&Minute=" + currentTime.Minute);
    Response.Write("&Second=" + currentTime.Second);
  }
```

Once again, we use the `System.DateTime` class (and its `Now` property) to tell us the time. This time however, we store it in a `DateTime` object called `currentTime`. Note that we declare the object in just the same way as we'd declare a variable: first state the type, then the name; after that, we can store any `DateTime` object we like in there.

Now that we have a reference to the current time, we can use its Hour, Minute,and Second properties to pull out the specific numbers we're interested in. Just as in ActionScript, we using the '+' operator to concatenate (or string together) the output strings.

Okay, hopefully that wasn't too painful, and you've made sense of what we're doing on the server. Now let's jump across to the client, and see about using this information in Flash.

3.   Open up Flash MX and create a new movie. Save it as `clock.fla`.

4.   You now need to create the six graphical elements shown below, and turn them each into movie clips. It doesn't matter whether or not they look identical to mine, though if you do want to recreate it exactly as shown, you can always import my graphics from the relevant file in the download bundle.

Either way, you need six movie clips, representing the clock-face, the three hands, and the two circular elements that fasten the hands onto the clock.

5.   Now make sure the registration point for each of the hands is set to the bottom point ,around which we want them to rotate.

6. With one instance of each hand on the stage, use the Property inspector to give them instance names of `minuteHand_mc`, `hourHand_mc`, and `secondHand_mc` respectively.

7. Create a new movie clip called `clockHands` (instance name `clockHands_mc`) and put the hands and the center circles inside it. Arrange them over the clock-face as shown below.

8. You should now have just two movie clips (`clockFace` and `clockHands`) in the first frame of the main timeline.

9. Select that frame, open up the Actions panel, and attach the following ActionScript to it:

```
clockHands_mc._visible = false;
frame = 0;
myTime = new LoadVars();

myDate = new Date().getTime();
myURL = "page.aspx";
myUrl += "?nocache=" + myDate;
myTime.Load(myURL);

myTime.onLoad = function() {
    with (myTime) {
        clockHands_mc.hourHand_mc._rotation = our*30+(Minute/2);
        clockHands_mc.minuteHand_mc._rotation =
Minute*6+(Second/10);
        clockHands_mc.secondHand_mc._rotation = Second*6;
    }
    clockHands_mc._visible = true;
};

onEnterFrame = function() {
```

29

continues overleaf

```
                    if (frame % 11 == 0) {
                            clockHands_mc.hourHand_mc._rotation += 1/240;
                            clockHands_mc.minuteHand_mc._rotation += 1/10;
                            clockHands_mc.secondHand_mc._rotation += 6;
                    }
                    if (frame % 120 == 0) {
                            myURL = "page.aspx"
                            myURL += "?nocache=" + (myDate + getTimer())
                            myTime.Load(myURL);
                    }
                    frame++
            };
```

10. All that's left now is to publish the movie. Remember though, we're pulling data out of an ASP.NET page, so we need to call up the movie via the web server – it won't work if we run it in the standalone Flash player. No problem though. Just press SHIFT+CTRL+ALT+S to publish the movie (called `clock.swf`) to the wwwroot folder that we used before. Now you can point your browser at http://localhost/clock.swf, and you'll see the clock in action.

The key ActionScript in this example is the lines responsible for calling up the ASP.NET page we made earlier:

`myTime.Load(myURL)`

This loads the server's response into an object called `myTime`, and interprets it as variables to be stored inside that object. `myTime` is a `LoadVars` object, which we'll look at in more detail in Chapter 2.

Let's imagine running the movie at exactly a quarter past ten in the morning. The movie would call up the ASP.NET page, and the web server would send back `Hour= 10&Minute =15&Second=0`. Back in the movie, the ActionScript object `myTime` would now get three new properties: `myTime.Hour` (with a value of 10), `myTime.Minute` (with a value of 15), and `myTime.Second` (with a value of 0).

Once that's all been dealt with, we set the clock hands to show the right time and make them visible.

The rest of the code deals with updating the time shown: every 12 frames (roughly a second, with the movie playing at 12fps) we add a second to the display, while every 120 frames (roughly 10 seconds) we update the time from the server again, so that any variations in the Flash player's frame rate don't get the chance to take us too far out of sync.

Avoiding cached data

Whenever we're working with dynamic content there's a very important factor we need to keep in mind. When a movie imports data from the server, it actually gets pulled in through the browser. The browser will normally **cache** data received from the server-side script and won't bother to reload it unless we specifically ask it to.

We therefore need to make sure that the data requested from the server-side script is fresh and not the **cached** one. The easiest way to do this is to add a query string to the end of the URL, specifying a value that's guaranteed to change between requests.

You may have noticed in the above code the addition of this query string to the end of our myURL variable. As time is constantly changing, we took the simplest route, and used the current time to create our query string:

```
myURL += "?noCache="+myDate
```

We initially created a new time using ActionScript's Date object and its getTime() method. The getTime() method returns the number of milliseconds since January 1st 1970.

```
myDate = new Date().getTime();
```

We then build the URL to our ASPX page by first initializing a variable to hold the name of our ASPX page. Then we add a query string "?nocache=" to the URL (this can be any name you want), and finally our time variable:

```
myURL = "page.aspx"
myURL += "?nocache=" + myDate;
```

If you were to trace out the contents of myURL at this point, you would see a result that looks like this:

```
page.aspx?nocache=1031352545742
```

Because of the nocache query string variable, whenever we invoke myVars.load() the browser spots that the specified URL is new, so it always reloads the document. This works well the first time we load the variables, but we need to make sure we use a unique query string for each subsequent call to the server.

When you create a Date object in ActionScript, that object becomes a static capture of the exact moment in time when it was created. Every call to the getTime() method of that specific date object would always return the same value. To continually update the time, we would need to create a new date object for each request.

However, Flash has another method that allows us to avoid the need of constant new object creation. The ActionScript getTimer() method returns the number of milliseconds that have elapsed since the player loaded and the current movie started.

Since our original date object was unique, and getTimer() returns a constantly changing value, we can simply add the two values together to get as many unique numbers as we need (well, at least 1000 per second). Putting this into practice, our code to update the clock looks like this:

```
myURL = "page.aspx"
myURL += "?nocache=" + (myDate + getTimer());
myTime.load(myURL);
```

Note that this no-caching technique will only work if you call up the movie from a web server. Since we've used a relative URL (with no domain or machine name specified), the standalone player will just assume you want to open up a local file, just as if you'd double-clicked on it.

Unfortunately, Windows itself won't know what to do with the query string, so you'll get an error message. If you need to work with a standalone movie or projector, you can fix this by specifying an absolute URL – for example:

```
myURL = "http://goon/page.aspx"
myURL += "?nocache=" + (myDate + getTimer());
myTime.load(myURL);
```

Summary

Well, here ends the first part of our crash course. We've covered a lot of ground in this chapter, and hopefully got you up to speed with the fundamental hows and whys of Flash and .NET.

We started off by looking at the client-server relationship, and considered how the server can enrich otherwise static web content by serving up dynamically generated pages. Then we got down to business and installed the IIS web server along with the .NET Framework SDK. Once we'd made sure they were up and running, we took a brief look at what makes .NET tick, considering the objects defined in its various class libraries (or namespaces) and the C# syntax that lets us do useful things with them.

We finished things off with a quick Flash.NET example, which demonstrated how we can use Flash to present our server data in a more intuitive, graphical fashion. Okay, we're hardly breaking new ground yet, but we now have the basic tools and skills in place. We're all set to start building applications that can really capitalize on the flow of data and content back and forth across the network. Bring on Chapter 2!

chapter 2: **Talking to the server**

Now we have an overview of what goes on when Flash starts talking to the web server, it's time to start thinking about the mechanics involved in producing this conversation between Flash and the server. There are several different ways to hook them up, which correspond to the *type* of information you want to pass and the technical resources you have available.

Macromedia Flash Remoting MX for .NET is one technology that's very specifically aimed at making this process easy and flexible, and we'll be devoting a whole chapter to it later in the book. For now though, we're going to concentrate on what's possible using Flash MX's built-in functionality.

We'll focus on three main areas:

- Sending simple values (flat data) to and from the server.

- Sending more complex information (structured data) to and from the server.

- Generating rich content on the server, and sending it back to Flash.

By the end of the chapter, you'll be all set to send your data to wherever you need it.

Flat data

The simplest sort of information we're likely to want to work with is a plain old ActionScript variable. Each one consists of a name (which we use to refer to it in our code) and a value (which is what we store inside it, and pull out when we need it). Whatever we store inside a variable, we can describe it completely in terms of this name/value pair.

As far as we're concerned, every variable exists independently, unrelated to any other variable. This is unordered, unstructured, **flat** data – each variable is just as important as the next, and there's no kind of link between any of them.

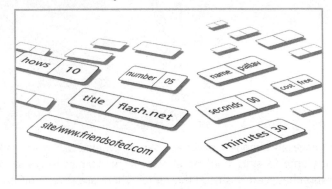

We used flat data in the last chapter, when we used a URL-encoded string to pass server data (telling us the time) to variables in our Flash movie. In that case, we had three pieces of information to convey: the hours, minutes, and seconds that described the current time.

You might think these were related, but the movie didn't know that. We told it exactly how to use the variables `hours`, `minutes`, and `seconds`. We knew in advance what data the web server would send us each time, and knew exactly how the Flash movie needed to use it.

Sharing flat data with the server

ActionScript gives us several different ways to pass flat data to and from the server:

- `getURL()` is an action that lets you call up web pages in a specified browser window (or a particular HTML frame in the current window).

- `loadVariables()` and `loadVariablesNum()` are actions that let you load URL-encoded variables into a specified clip or level within your movie.

- `LoadVars` is a type of object that you can use to send and receive URL-encoded variable.

The first three of these have now been around for several generations of Flash, and while they're still supported in Flash MX, they aren't nearly so flexible as their younger cousin. `LoadVars` was introduced with Flash MX, and because it's a bona fide ActionScript object, it fits right in with MX's object-centric coding style.

There's a great deal we can do with it, and unless you're specifically trying for backwards-compatibility, LoadVars is almost always the best choice for sharing flat data. We've already seen how easy it is to pull simple variables into a Flash movie using the `LoadVars` object and its `load()` method. As we're about to see, there are plenty more were that came from.

Using LoadVars to pull in data from the server

The ActionScript LoadVars object is specially designed to help us transfer name-value pairs between our movie and the server. So how do we actually use it? Our first step is to create an instance:

```
myVars = new LoadVars();
```

Now that we have a real object called myVars to play with, we can take a good look at what it's capable of. As we saw in Chapter 1, loading information is fairly simple. We can just say:

```
myVars.load("data.txt");
```

Let's assume we've created a file called data.txt, and placed it in the same folder as the compiled SWF (somewhere under that ubiquitous wwwroot folder). We know that Flash expects to find data in the form of name-value pairs, so we've filled the text file with some lovely URL-encoded data like this:

```
title=Main+Page&color=blue
```

When our movie runs, it will call up this text file from the web server. It then takes whatever the server sends back, and stores it inside the myVars object. In theory, we can now use some of the object's other methods and properties to take a look at the data. For example, myVars.title should now have the value "Main Page", while myVars.color should hold "blue". But do they?

Say you attach these two lines of ActionScript to the first frame in an empty Flash movie, and add a third line to trace out the values:

```
myVars = new LoadVars();
myVars.load("data.txt");
trace("Title: " + myVars.title);
```

Test run this movie, and you'll find that nothing shows. All the same, if you hit CTRL+ALT+V to summon up the Debug Variables in the Output window, you'll see a different story. Sure enough, we see a LoadVars object called myVars that has properties title and color, whose values are just as we expected:

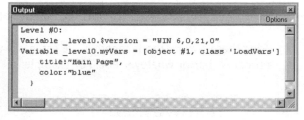

```
Output                                    [x]
                                    Options
Level #0:
Variable _level0.$version = "WIN 6,0,21,0"
Variable _level0.myVars = [object #1, class 'LoadVars']
    title:"Main Page",
    color:"blue"
 }
```

So what's the problem? Simple. Flash runs through all its lines of ActionScript as quickly as possible. Trouble is, the server takes a few moments to send back the data, so when Flash traces out the title property, it's showing a value that hasn't been set.

Once the properties are set, we'll be ready to use them. What we really need is a way to hold off using the myVars properties until we're sure the data's been received. Fortunately, this is something that's quite easy to do.

Monitoring the downloaded data

The LoadVars object features an onLoad event, which is triggered whenever the object finishes loading in data. If we write a callback handler for this event, we can be sure that any actions inside it won't run until the loading is complete:

```
myVars = new LoadVars();
myVars.load("data.txt");
myVars.onLoad = function() {
  trace("Title: " + myVars.title);
};
```

Try the movie again, and you should see the expected value traced out:

There are several other ways to keep an eye on whether the data's loaded or not, one of which is the loaded property. This gives us a Boolean value: true if the data's loaded, false if not.

```
Output                              [x]
                          Options
Title: Main Page
```

If we're downloading large amounts of data, it may take a while. We may therefore want to keep an eye on how much we've received so far, and how much more there is to go. The most obvious thing we might do with this information is to build a progress bar, showing us what percentage of the total file we've downloaded.

LoadVars has another couple of methods that we can use to help us do just that:

- getBytesTotal() returns the total number of bytes to be downloaded.

- getBytesLoaded() returns the number of bytes already downloaded.

Using these two methods together, we can easily work out a 'percent downloaded' value to drive a progress bar or whatever else. For example:

```
onEnterFrame = function() {
  if (!myVars.loaded) {
    percentProgress = myVars.getBytesLoaded();
    percentProgress /= myVars.getBytesTotal();
    percentProgress *= 100;
  }
};
```

This isn't the limit of what we can do with `LoadVars`, but it's as far as we need to go just now. The next step is to get rid of the text file, and think about calling up our data from an ASP.NET web page.

Generating dynamic data on the server

Of course, we've already done this back in Chapter 1. The whole idea of the clock example was to show a simple ASP.NET page that generates URL-encoded data for us on the fly. Writing the page itself isn't really too hard:

```
<%@ Page language="c#" %>

<script runat="server">
   void Page_Load(Object sender, EventArgs e) {
DateTime currentTime = DateTime.Now;
Response.Write("&Hour=" + currentTime.Hour);
Response.Write("&Minute=" + currentTime.Minute);
Response.Write("&Second=" + currentTime.Second);
      }
   </script>
```

We have a standard template for the page (in normal type) and some page-specific C# code that generates the data for us. We could just as easily write a page that sent us back a random entry in a list of jokes:

```
<%@ Page language="c#" debug="true" %>

<script runat="server">
   void Page_Load(Object sender, EventArgs e) {
      string[] jokes = new String[5];
      jokes[0] = "gag=spade&punchline=Doug";
      jokes[1] = "gag=car&punchline=Jack";
      jokes[2] = "gag=seagull&punchline=Cliff";
      jokes[3] = "gag=paper+bag&punchline=Russell";
      jokes[4] = "gag=elephant&punchline=an+ambulance";

      Random rnd = new Random();
      Response.Write(jokes[rnd.Next(5)]);
   }
</script>
```

Here, we create an array of five strings, and used each one to store a pair of URL-encoded variables. Then we make a `Random` object (another one from the `System` namespace) and call its `Next()` method to generate a random number between 0 and 4. Then, we just spit out the randomly selected data.

Try putting this code in a file under `wwwroot`, and call it up from your browser in the usual way:

Hit Refresh a few times, and you'll see the different 'jokes' appearing. So what about a bit of presentation? We're hardly looking at the funniest gag known to man...

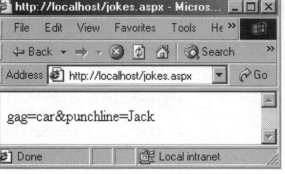

Here's a bit of ActionScript code that pulls our would-be gag into a movie, so that we can see the joke in all its glory:

```
myJoke = new LoadVars();

myJoke.onLoad = function() {
  joke_txt.text = "What do you call a man with a ";
  joke_txt.text += myJoke.gag + " on his head...?";
  punchline_txt.text = "???";
}

answer_btn.onRelease = function() {
  myJoke.Load("jokes.aspx");
  punchline_txt.text = myJoke.punchline;
}
```

And here's the end result:

Okay, so the joke still isn't that hilarious, but you can get the idea all the same...

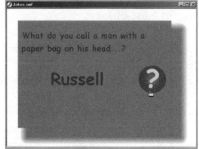

Where does Flash look for the data?

Every time we use `LoadVars.load`, we need to point it at a specific data source. In our first example, that was a text file in the same directory as the compiled SWF, so we didn't need to qualify the filename in any way:

```
myVars.load("data.txt");
```

When we run the SWF in the Flash projector (as happens when we do a test run), Flash will assume it needs to look for `data.txt` in the same physical location as itself – that is, it interprets `data.txt` as `C:/inetpub/wwwroot/data.txt`, and uses Windows to open it up. In that case, the file didn't need any special processing, so we let Windows get on with opening up (as if we'd double-clicked on it) and pulling out the raw text for us.

Now we're dealing with an ASPX file, we can't rely on Windows any more – the contents of the file only make sense if we call them up via the web server. There are two ways we can get Flash to do this:

- Call up the SWF from the web server, and view it via the browser plug-in. This way, Flash will interpret `jokes.aspx` as `http://goon/jokes.aspx` (remember that `goon` is the name of my machine – yours will probably be different).

- Explicitly call up the ASPX file from the web server using an **absolute URL**. This way, we specifically say `myVars.load("http://goon/data.txt")`, so there's no room for confusion. Now we can call up the SWF via the browser plug-in or via the projector, and it shouldn't make any difference.

There's one slight problem with the second approach as it stands. For security reasons, the Flash player is designed to strictly limit how much access movies have to the Web. This means the `http://goon/` path will *only* work for a movie that's been called up from my machine. Likewise, if we published our movie on friendsofed.com, we'd *only* be allowed to request files from friendsofed.com, and not from any other domain.

If you're using the first technique (in technical terms, using a **relative URL**) this isn't a problem; Flash assumes you're asking for a document in the same place as the movie came from, and that's always allowed. It's only when you specifically start trying to load documents from a different domain that you'll find it doesn't work.

Now that we've figured out how to pull dynamic data off the server, let's think about the opposite challenge: sending data *from* the movie *to* the server.

Using LoadVars to send data to the server

Sending Flash data off to the server is really just as simple as loading it up. Once again, we have the `LoadVars` object to thank, and two more methods to think about:

- `Send` takes variables from the `LoadVars` object and sends them to a specified file on the server.

- `SendAndLoad` takes variables from the `LoadVars` object, sends them to a specified file, and then imports whatever variables the server sends back.

Unlike the `Load` method, we don't have the option to point to a static file here. Sending data to a text file, for example, wouldn't have any effect at all on it. It's only useful to send it to a server-side script, which we can program to make use of the information it's receiving.

The information gets formatted in the same way as before: using a URL-encoded string to represent name-value pairs. However, we have a choice as to how it's sent to the server. One way is called the GET method, which involves attaching it to the end of the URL. We can recreate this from a browser, which makes it useful for testing purposes. For example:

```
http://localhost/page.aspx?name=dan&city=birmingham
```

This will send the two variables `name` and `city` to the server along with the page request. In a moment, we'll see how to grab these values and make use of them once they arrive at the server.

The main drawback to this method is that you're limited to 255 characters in the attached string (known as a **query string**). The other option is to use POST, which tucks the same data away in the body of the HTTP server request.

Handling flat data on the server

Now we just need to think about how to access the data in our ASP.NET page. Fortunately it's not much more complicated than the equivalent technique in ActionScript. There's an object called `Request` (based on a class called `HttpRequest`, defined in the `System.Web` namespace, just in case you're interested) that ASP.NET generates automatically when a page gets executed. Inside this object, you can find all kinds of information sent over along with the client request.

Try out this little script, and you'll see just how much information gets sent across with a typical page request:

```
<%@ Page language="C#" debug="true" %>

<script runat=server>
  void Page_Load(Object sender, EventArgs e){

    string Query = Request.ServerVariables.ToString();
    foreach (string pair in Query.Split('&')) {
      Response.Write(pair+"<br/><br/>");
    }
  }
</script>
```

Save it in `wwwroot` as `requestInfo.aspx`, and call up your browser. Point it at, http://localhost/requestInfo.aspx?trash=DUMMY and scroll down the resulting page until you find an entry called `QUERY_STRING`. This is where ASP.NET has picked up our URL-encoded trash value.

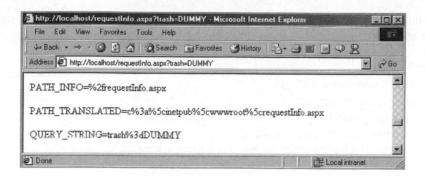

Fortunately, there's a simpler way to access it than looping through all the server variables. The `Request` object lets us do this:

```
<%@ Page language="C#" debug-"true" %>

<script runat=server>
  void Page_Load(Object sender, EventArgs e){
    string queryVar = Request["trash"];
    Response.Write(queryVar);
  }
</script>
```

Lo and behold, we've stored the value of our `trash` query variable in a C# string called `queryVar`. Now we can do whatever we like with it in our server-side code.

Theme chooser

In this example, we're going to create a movie that can send a message to the server and import its response. We're going to create a theme chooser. We'll show a list of styles in the Flash movie, and when the user selects one, we'll ask the server to send us the preset properties corresponding to that theme – in this case, simply background color plus color, face, and size of the font to use.

> *In this case, we're going to have our style properties hardwired into the ASPX. If you were doing this for real, you'd probably have them stored elsewhere in a file, and possibly even allow users to add their own customized themes to the list. In the next chapter, we'll look at some techniques that could help you to make that sort of thing a reality.*

1.   As usual, we'll start at the bottom and work our way up. Here's the ASP.NET page that's going to feed us with information for each theme. Create a text document and add this code:

```
<%@ Page language="c#" %>
<script runat="server">
  void Page_Load(Object sender, EventArgs e) {
     // initialize our variables
     string bgcolor, fontface, fontsize, fontcolor = "";

     switch (Request["Theme"]) {
       case "1":
          // Green theme
          bgcolor = "DFFFDF";
          fontface = "Verdana";
          fontsize = "10";
          fontcolor = "#889E6D";
          break;
       case "2":
          // Blue theme
          bgcolor = "E1F5FF";
          fontface = "Arial";
          fontsize = "11";
          fontcolor = "#0372AB";
          break;
       default:
          bgcolor = "333333";
          fontface = "Courier";
          fontsize = "12";
          fontcolor = "#DDDDDD";
     break;
     }
     Response.Write("&bgcolor=" + bgcolor);
     Response.Write("&fontface=" + fontface);
     Response.Write("&fontsize=" + fontsize);
     Response.Write("&fontcolor=" + fontcolor);
   }
</script>
```

This page is responsible for requesting the theme code (sent by the Flash client) and serving the properties of this theme in URL-encoded format.

2. Save it in `wwwroot` as `themeChooser.aspx`, and test it's working okay by pointing your browser at `http://localhost/themeChooser.aspx`:

```
http://localhost/themeChooser.aspx - Microsoft Internet Explorer
File  Edit  View  Favorites  Tools  Help
← Back ▾ → ▾ ◯ ▤ ⚅ | ◻Search ▨Favorites ◉History | ▨▾ ▨ ◼ ▤ ◯ »
Address ▤ http://localhost/themeChooser.aspx                    ▾  ⟳Go

&bgcolor=#333333&fontface=Courier&fontsize=12&fontcolor=#DDDDDD

▤ Done                                          ▦ Local intranet
```

Sure enough, we get some URL-encoded data describing the default style (which look like it'll be rather dull).

3. Now try sticking a query string on the end of the URL, as shown here:

Great! It's spotted that we want a different theme, so it sends back different data. Now it's time to put that data to use, and build our Flash front-end.

```
http://localhost/themeChooser.aspx?Theme=1 - Microsoft Internet Explorer
File  Edit  View  Favorites  Tools  Help
← Back ▾ → ▾ ◯ ▤ ⚅ | ◯Search ▨Favorites ◉History | ▨▾ ◯ ◼ ▤ »
Address ▤ http://localhost/themeChooser.aspx?Theme=1              ▾  ⟳Go

&bgcolor=DFFFDF&fontface=Verdana&fontsize=10&fontcolor=#889E6D

▤ Done                                          ▦ Local intranet
```

4. Create a new Flash movie and save it as `themeChooser.fla`.

5. We need a movie clip to serve as the background. Create a square with a solid fill and no stroke. Convert this to a movie clip and give it an instance name of `MovBg`. Rename the layer with your clip on as `Background`, and resize the movie clip until it covers the entire stage.

6. Add two additional layers to your movie called `Content` and `Actions`. Make sure that your Background layer is at the bottom, so that it stays in the background.

```
                              👁 🔒 ☐ | 1    5    10
🗋 Actions        • • ☐ |
🗋 Content        • • ■ |
🗋 Background  ✏ • • ■ |
```

7. Drag a combo box from the Components panel and assign the properties in the screenshot to the combo box. As you can see, this will be our list of themes.

8. Create a dynamic multi-line textbox on the Content layer. Down in the Property inspector, set Var to `txtContents` and make sure that the Render Text as HTML option is selected.

```
▾ Properties
┌─────────────┐   Editable       false
│  Component  │   Labels         [Please select one..,Classy Green,Trendy Blue]
│  cbThemes   │   Data           [0,1,2]
│             │   Row Count      8
│ W: 200.0  X: 8.3 │  Change Handler   fnChangeTheme
│ H: 17.0   Y: 54.9 │
```

9. Let's now create a dynamic textbox for relaying messages, so we can let users know what's happening once they've selected a theme. Set Var to txtMessage. The stage should now look something like this:

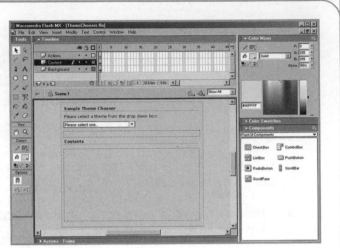

10. Finally, select frame 1 on the Actions layer and call up the Actions panel. Add the following code:

```
var contents = "We all..."; // add your own text here
txtContents = contents;

function fnChangeTheme() {
  myVars = new LoadVars();
  myVars.theme = cbThemes.getSelectedItem().data;
  if (myVars.theme != "0") {
    myVars.sendAndLoad("themeChooser.aspx", myVars, "POST");
    txtMessage = "Please wait...Loading Theme...";

    myVars.onLoad = function(success) {
      if (success == true) {
        // Set background color
        clrbg = new Color("MovBg");
        clrbg.setRGB(parseInt(myVars.bgcolor, 16));
        // Set font properties
        txtContents = "<font face='"
                          ➥ + myVars.fontface
                          ➥ + "'size='"
                          ➥ + myVars.fontsize
                          ➥ + "' color='"
                          ➥ + myVars.fontcolor+"'>"
                          ➥ + contents
                          ➥ + "</font>";
        //Remove the loading message
        txtMessage = "";
      } else {
```

continues overleaf

```
            txtMessage = "An unknown error occurred!!!";
        }
    };
}
}
```

In the above code, we first set our `Content` textbox to display some text. Thereafter, in the change event handler function of our Combo Box `cbThemes`, we send the theme code to the ASP.NET page `themeChooser.aspx` using the `LoadVars` object and wait for the response. When the response is received, we change the color of the background and the font properties.

11. Export the movie from Flash, make sure your SWF and ASP file are in the `wwwroot` directory, and call up the SWF in your browser:

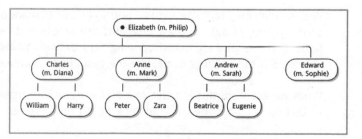

Now that we know how to send variables back and forth across the nebulous sea of interconnected clients and servers, let's set our sights a little higher. Flat data is all well and good in situations like this, where we're just interested in isolated values. Sooner or later though, we're going to need more – we'll want data in a form that can describe how different values are related to each other.

Structured data

So, how do we pass data between Flash and .NET if it contains more subtleties than our name-value pairs can describe? If we were dealing purely with ActionScript (or purely with C#), the answer would be obvious: use an array, or even an object. Arrays and objects are both designed to hold several pieces of data under one roof, which means that we can group together several values in one place. We can also group together groups, and even group groups of groups. In fact, there's virtually no limit to how far we can take this – ultimately this means that we can store lots of values in very well-defined relationships.

For example, we might want to send information about the different members of a family. Whatever information we choose to record for each individual, we still need a way to keep track of how they're all related to one another:

In this case, we're looking at the descendants of a woman called Elizabeth, who has four children, three of whom have a couple of kids of their own. From the tree structure you can instantly see that Anne and Edward are siblings, as are William and Harry, and that Andrew is Eugenie's parent.

Elizabeth's family group consists of herself (and her husband Philip) plus four smaller family groups. Each group can be treated in its own right or as part of the bigger picture, and there's no limit to how many subgroups you can have.

But once we've got these groups of groups of groups of groups, how can we send them over the network? URL-encoded query strings are designed for simple name-value pairs, so that's probably a dead end. We have to look for something else.

As we're dealing with a different kind of data, it makes sense to arrange it in a different format. Fortunately, there's a format that's designed precisely for this sort of thing: **XML**.

Understanding XML

XML is a text-based language that's specifically designed to represent structured data. One quite familiar example of structured data is a list of personal contact details. For each person, you're likely to want to store information like address and telephone numbers, and each address will most likely break down in the same way, with separate values for house number (or name), street, city, state, and zip code.

Here's how we might represent one such contact using XML:

```
<contact name="Bob Smith">
  <phone id="home">555-555-1212</phone>
  <phone id="mobile">555-555-8640</phone>
  <address id="home">
    <house>123</house>
    <street>Norham Gardens</street>
    <city>Muncie</city>
    <state>IN</state>
    <zip>47302</zip>
  </address>
</contact>
```

We use matching tags like `<this>` and `</this>` to mark out data groups called **elements**. Some of the pieces of data in these elements are simple text, while others are elements in their own right. Some of the elements' opening tags define **attributes**, and these help us to distinguish elements with the same name, like the two phone numbers.

What we get from this is a tree-like hierarchy of information, with each element and each piece of text forming a **node** (or branching point) on the tree.

From the information we have here, we can see that there are three ways to contact Bob Smith:

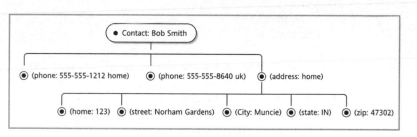

- On his home phone (555-555-1212)

- On his mobile phone (555-555-8640)

- By mail, at his home address (123 Norham Gardens, Muncie, IN 47302)

Despite being in a machine-readable format, the data's actually structured in the same way it would be in the real world. What's more, we don't need specialized software to read or write it – you can do both straight from Notepad. So how about getting Flash to do the same?

Working with XML in Flash

ActionScript in Flash MX has built-in features for interpreting XML, so we don't even need to get our hands too dirty figuring out how the data we import actually fits together. To help understand how XML works inside Flash, let's put together a small application that loads up an XML document from a file on the server. Once Flash has parsed the data (that is, run through all the XML-formatted text and figure out what it means), we'll display it in a useful way.

Address book

1. Let's start out by creating an XML file. If you want to do it yourself, just call up Notepad and type in the XML document we looked at earlier. Add a few more contacts along the same lines, and finish off by adding a couple of `address_book` tags to the beginning and end. You end up with something like this:

    ```
    <address_book>

       <contact name="Bob Smith">
          <phone id="home">555-555-1212</phone>
          <phone id="mobile">555-555-8640</phone>
          <address id="home">
             <house>123</house>
             <street>Norham Gardens</street>
             <city>Muncie</city>
             <state>IN</state>
             <zip>47302</zip>
    ```

49

continues overleaf

```
        </address>
     </contact>

     ... add some more contacts here if you like...

     <contact name="Jane Doe">
        <phone id="home">555-555-3789</phone>
        <address id="home">
           <house>1829</house>
           <street>Woodstock Road</street>
           <city>Dallas</city>
           <state>TX</state>
           <zip>13749</zip>
        </address>
        <email id="home">jdoe@hotmail.com</email>
     </contact>

  </address_book>
```

Save this file as `addresses.xml` under your `wwwroot` folder. Now let's see about reading this information into Flash, and we can do something about presenting it properly.

2. Create a new Flash document and save it as `addressBook.fla` in the same place as the XML file.

3. Place a ListBox component on the stage, along with seven dynamic text fields. Arrange them so that they look something like this:

4. Use the Property inspector to give the ListBox component an instance name of `address_list`. We'll set the change handler in our code later on, so you can leave all the other parameters alone.

5. Now give each text field an instance name based on its purpose (indicated here by the default text in each field). For example, the Phone text field should be called `phone_txt`, while the Address field should be `address_txt`, and so on.

6. Now it's time to start adding in the ActionScript that'll make our example work. Open up the Actions panel and select frame 1 on the main timeline. Add in the following code:

```
myXML = new XML();
myXML.ignoreWhite = true;
myXML.load("addresses.xml");
status_txt.text = "Loading XML";
```

We begin by creating an XML object to hold the raw data, and tell it to ignore whitespace in the XML document. Otherwise, Flash will interpret every space, tab, and new line in the document as a node in its own right, and cause us a lot of confusion in the process! Finally, we load in the XML and set the status text accordingly.

7. Next, we have to specify what happens once the XML has loaded:

```
myXML.onLoad = function(success) {
  if (success) {
    status_txt.text = "Parsing XML";
    setupContactList(this.firstChild);
  } else {
    status_txt.text = "Error Loading XML";
  }
}
```

Here, we use a parameter called `success` to tell us whether the XML's loaded in okay. If so, we call a function called `setupContactList`, which will do exactly what it says: set up our list box, and fill it with information about each of the contacts. We send it `this.firstChild`, which is the root node of the `myXml` object – in other words, the `address_book` element.

8. Our next job is to define that function. It needs to loop through each of the nodes directly under the input XML (our `address_book` element once again):

```
function setupContactList(inputXml) {
  contact = inputXml.firstChild;

  do {
    address_list.addItem(contact.attributes["name"]);
  } while (contact = contact.nextSibling)

  status_txt.text = "Ready.";
}
```

Each node corresponds to an individual contact. We therefore loop through all the sibling contacts, pulling out the name attribute for each one and adding it to the address list as a new item.

Try test running the FLA now:

Well, we've managed to add our contacts to the address list, but we still need to find a way to show their details in the dynamic text fields. Don't worry – not too much further to go!

> Macromedia Flash MX - [AddressBook.swf]
> File Edit View Control Debug Window Help
>
> Bob Smith
> Jane Doe
>
> Phone
> Address
> City   State
> Zip
> Email
>
> Ready.

9. We need to specify what will happen when we select a contact from the address list. We know that the selected item's label corresponds to one of the contact names in our XML document (since that's how it got there in the first place!) so we loop through all the contact elements in myXML until we find a match:

```
function showAddress() {
  contactName = address_list.getSelectedItem().label;
    rootNode = myXML.firstChild;
    contact =.rootNode.firstChild;
    do {
    if (contactName == contact.attributes["name"]) {
      break;
    }
  } while (contact = contact.nextSibling)

  resetFields();
  drillDown(contact.firstChild);
};
```

At that point, we break out of the loop, and call our final pair of functions. The first, resetFields(), will need to blank all the dynamic text fields, while the second, drillDown(), will take a look at what's inside the matching contact element and use whatever it finds to give the text fields appropriate values.

Of course, we mustn't forget to set showAddress() as the handler function for changes to the list selection:

```
address_list.setChangeHandler("showAddress");
```

10. Okay then, now onto the resetFields() function:

```
resetFields = function() {
    phone_txt.text = "";
    address_txt.text = "";
    city_txt.text = "";
    state_txt.text = "";
    zip_txt.text = "";
    email_txt.text = "";
};
```

11. Nothing too complex here – we just blank all the relevant text fields.

This one's a little more interesting, though you'll be glad to hear it's the very last part of our code:

```
function drillDown(xmlNode) {
  var xmlNode;
  do {
    // new code will go in here
  } while (xmlNode = xmlNode.nextSibling)
}
```

This part's fairly easy, and just repeats what we've seen before. We take an XML node and loop through all its siblings until we run out of siblings. When we called it earlier, we gave it the contact's first child node as a starting point, and which will be either a phone, address, or email element.

12. Now we have to tell Flash what to do when it finds one of those siblings:

```
function drillDown(xmlNode) {
  var xmlNode;
  do {
    att = xmlNode.attributes["id"]
    switch (xmlNode.nodeName) {
      case "phone":
        if (att == "home") {
          phone_txt.text = xmlNode.firstChild.nodeValue;
        }
        break;
      case "address":
        if (att == "home") {
          drillDown(xmlNode.firstChild);
        }
        break;
```

```
        case "email":
          if (att == "home") {
            email_txt.text = xmlNode.firstChild.nodeValue;
          }
          break;
    }
  } while (xmlNode = xmlNode.nextSibling)
}
```

We do that by switching on the nodeName. If we're looking at a phone element, we get its contents (that is, the value of its child node) and assign them to the phone text field. We do likewise if we're dealing with an email element.

If we're looking at an address element though, we need to dig a little deeper, so we call the drilldown() function again, setting it off from the first element inside the address.

Note that since we only have one text field for each form of contact, we only want one of each. We therefore make sure that we're only considering elements that have an id attribute of "home".

13. Since we're now digging into the address element too, it looks like our switch statement will need to deal with a few extra cases:

```
        case "email":
          if (att == "home") {
            email_txt.text = xmlNode.firstChild.nodeValue;
          }
          break;
        case "house":
          address_txt.text = xmlNode.firstChild.nodeValue;
          break;
        case "street":
          address_txt.text += " "
          address_txt.text += xmlNode.firstChild.nodeValue;
          break;
        case "city":
          city_txt.text = xmlNode.firstChild.nodeValue;
          break;
        case "state":
          state_txt.text = xmlNode.firstChild.nodeValue;
          break;
        case "zip":
          zip_txt.text = xmlNode.firstChild.nodeValue;
          break;
    }
```

continues overleaf

```
        } while (xmlNode = xmlNode.nextSibling)
    }
```

Whew! After all that, it's time to save the finished FLA, then compile and run it by pressing CTRL+ENTER. Your final application, after loading the XML and selecting a record should look like this:

That's it! Try going back and adding records to your XML document, or removing fields from certain records to see how they are handled. Of course, in our example, any extra fields you create will be ignored, as we only display a few specific fields.

Writing ASP.NET pages that generate XML

We have seen how to load XML into Flash and traverse through it. Up until this point we have been using static XML documents – XML documents that are physically present on the disk. In real-world applications, however, this might not be the case. An ASP.NET page can dynamically generate XML documents with new data, which can then be accessed by Flash.

There are several ways we can use .NET to generate XML documents from structured data. The first one we're going to look at involves working with .NET's XmlDocument object (defined in System.Xml for all you namespace junkies...).

This is the main object that .NET uses to handle complete XML documents, and there are two ways to feed it with structured data:

- LoadXml() is a method that lets us pass XML-formatted text directly into the object, creating all the elements, attributes, and values we could possibly want.

- CreateNode(), CreateAttribute(), and CreateElement() are just a few of the builder methods that let us build XML documents programmatically.

LoadXml

Consider the following ASP.NET code:

```
<%@ Page Language="c#" ContentType="text/xml" %>
<%@ Import namespace="System.Xml" %>

<script runat="server">
```

55

continues overleaf

```
void Page_Load(Object sender, EventArgs e) {
    string xmlString = "<root><element>";
    myXml += "text</element></root>";

    XmlDocument xmlDoc = new XmlDocument();
    xmlDoc.LoadXml(xmlString);
    xmlDoc.Save(Response.Output);
}
</script>
```

We first render the Page directive and use `ContentType` to specify that we're going to be sending back XML data rather than plain text or HTML. Next we import the `System.Xml` namespace, so that we can use `XmlDocument` objects in our code.

Inside the main body of the page, we set up a string called `xmlString` to contain our raw XML. Then we just call `LoadXml()`, using `xmlString` as an argument. Now we use the `Save` method to send the object's contents off to the output stream `Response.Output`.

Run the script and you'll see an output as here:

Here, notice that the ASP.NET page has added an extra first line to our document. This line is known as the **XML declaration,** and indicates the version of the XML document and the character encoding used. Although our XML object in ActionScript will parse this line into its own property, it isn't of use to us, so we can ignore it for the moment.

```
<?xml version="1.0" encoding="utf-8" ?>
- <myxmldoc>
    <myelement>mytext</myelement>
  </myxmldoc>
```

Builder methods

Let's look at a slightly different technique for building XML documents in ASP.NET, utilizing the builder methods of `XmlDocument` object. We'll build a simple XML document like the one below:

```
<tips>
  <tip id='1'>
    Look before you leap.
  </tip>
</tips>
```

Put the following code in a file called `BuilderMethods.aspx`:

```
<%@ Page Language="C#" ContentType = "text/xml" %>
<%@ Import Namespace="System.Xml" %>
```

```
<script runat="server">
  void Page_Load(Object sender, EventArgs e) {

    XmlDocument xmlDoc = new XmlDocument();

    XmlElement rootElement = xmlDoc.CreateElement("tips");
    XmlElement msgElement = xmlDoc.CreateElement("tip");
    msgElement.SetAttribute("id","1");
    msgElement.InnerText = "Look before you leap.";

    rootelement.AppendChild(msgElement);
    xmlDoc.AppendChild(rootElement);

    xmlDoc.Save(Response.Output);
  }
</script>
```

Once again, we start off by rendering the `Page` directive and importing the `System.Xml` namespace. Then we open the main code block and set about creating some objects.

Note the types of object we create: one `XmlDocument` and two `XmlElements`. Once we've created the separate elements (and set up text and attributes for `msgElement`), we use the `AppendChild()` method to arrange them. First, we put `msgElement` inside `rootElement`, and then put `rootElement` inside `xmlDoc`.

Finally, we save `xmlDoc` to the `Response.Output` stream again, giving us the result we're hoping for:

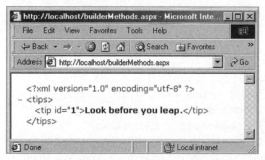

Before we finish looking at XML on the server, there's one more option to introduce, which doesn't involve the `XmlDocument` object at all. It's a special type of ASP.NET page called a **web service**.

Web services

At a very basic level, a web service is just like any other web page, except that it sends out all its content in the form of an XML document. This can be very useful when it comes to sharing information around on the Web. For example, you might want to keep an eye on how your favorite book's doing on Amazon.com.

If you've only got the web page on Amazon.com to work with, you'd need to go and look at it every day to keep track of the book's ranking. With a web service, you could write a little application that calls up the XML describing that particular book, pull out the rank element, and look at its value. Then you could store it away somewhere and even plot the book's progress from one day to the next.

Because web services are such a useful mechanism, Microsoft decided to build them right into ASP.NET, which makes life nice and easy for us now that we're trying to summon up XML on demand.

Take, for example, the random joke generator we looked at earlier. We built an array of strings, each of which contained gag and punchline information for making up a joke. If we rewrote it as a web service, we could send back the whole array as an XML document, and leave Flash to pick out the jokes.
Here's the code we'd need to send back that array:

```
<%@ WebService Language="c#" class="JokeList" %>

using System.IO;
using System.Web.Services;

[WebService(Namespace="flashDotNet")]
public class JokeList: System.Web.Services.WebService {

  [WebMethod]
  public string[] getJokes() {
    string[] jokes = new String[5];
    jokes[0] = "gag=spade&punchline=Doug";
    jokes[1] = "gag=car&punchline=Jack";
    jokes[2] = "gag=seagull&punchline=Cliff";
    jokes[3] = "gag=paper+bag&punchline=Russell";
    jokes[4] = "gag=elephant&punchline=an+ambulance";
    return jokes;
  }
}
```

It's a bit different to the ASP.NET pages we're used to, but it's really just another template we can use and re-use wherever we need to.

The important thing to notice is that we're actually defining a **class**. In this case, it's called `JokeList`, and features one method called `getJokes()`, whose sole job it is to return our list of jokes. However, because we've specified that it's a web method, we don't need all sorts of fancy C# code to instantiate a `JokeList` object before we use it – the whole thing can be accessed over the Web. Let's see how.

Throw this in a text file, and save it in `wwwroot` as `JokeList.asmx`. Make sure you get the extension right – ASMX – since ASP.NET will need this to spot that it's dealing with a web service. Now use your browser to call up the file from `localhost`:

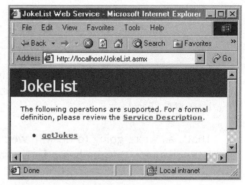

The screen you should now be seeing is a handy little test system that's built into all ASP.NET web services. It tells us what the service is called, and gives us links to the Service Description (an XML document describing `JokeList` in minute detail) and each of its available **web methods**. We've only defined one – `getJokes` – so click on that entry to call it up:

Now we get another test screen, with a button labeled Invoke. If we'd designed our web getJokes method to take parameters, we'd see some input boxes here where we could type in test values. As it is, we haven't, so click on the button, and you should see the finished result:

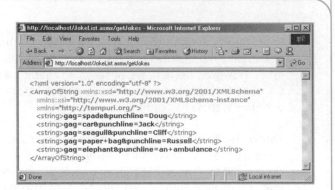

It's an XML document that completely describes the array of strings we built earlier. No fussing around with children, parents, and siblings; just an automatic translation of the C# jokes array into XML. Easy!

That's all we're going to do with web services for now, but we'll be seeing lots more on them in later chapters. Despite being fairly simple to build, they can be *incredibly* useful.

Rich content

Flash MX's dynamic loading options aren't limited to variables (using LoadVars as we saw in the last chapter) and XML (some more on this shortly). We can just as easily call up images, sounds, and Flash movies from the server:

- loadMovie() and loadMovieNum() are actions that let you load JPEGs and SWFs into a specified clip or level within your movie.

- The Sound object can be used to load and play audio files.

You might use dynamically generated data to control which audio files your movie imports, or maybe even get the server to generate an image for you, based on data you've sent it. Let's finish off the chapter with an example that does just that.

Fractal explorer

Wonderful as it is, there are still certain areas where Flash MX is lacking. Two particular gaps are in the realms of bitmap manipulations and speedy hard-core math. Fortunately, these are two gaps C# can fill perfectly.

Seeing as we can easily send data back and forth between Flash and an ASP.NET page, we can now put together applications that make use of the strengths of both languages, and do stuff Flash hasn't been able to do before. Let's look at an example that makes use of these newfound client-server communication skills: a fractal navigator, that gives us a Flash interface for exploring an infinitely complex mathematical image called the Mandelbrot set.

We need to start by writing the ASP.NET page that's going to generate our graphics.

1. Create a new text file in Notepad and save it as `mandelGen.aspx`. As before, we start our new ASPX file with the page directive specifying C# as our default language:

    ```
    <%@ Page Language="C#" ContentType="image/jpeg" %>
    ```

    This time, we have a `ContentType` attribute to let the calling application (in this case our Flash movie) know that the content coming back is a JPEG-formatted image. If we hadn't done this, Flash wouldn't know we were sending back a JPEG, and would probably try to load in the data as a movie clip.

    > In fact, this setting will allow us to send our generated image to any client application that's capable of handling JPEG images, even if it's just the `src` attribute of an HTML image element. Cool!

2. Next, we import the all namespaces we're going to need. The classes contained in these namespaces are responsible for image creation and manipulation, and for general data I/O:

    ```
    <%@ Import namespace="System.IO" %>
    <%@ Import namespace="System.Drawing" %>
    <%@ Import namespace="System.Drawing.Imaging" %>
    <%@ Import namespace="System.Drawing.Drawing2D" %>
    ```

3. Now we're ready to start building our main page functionality. The `Page_Load` function can be broken down into three relatively small, separate sections. First, we deal with the query string variables coming from Flash:

    ```
    int xSize = Convert.ToInt32(Request["xSize"]);
    int ySize = Convert.ToInt32(Request["ySize"]);
    double x0 = Convert.ToDouble(Request["x"]);
    double y0 = Convert.ToDouble(Request["y"]);
    double scale = Convert.ToDouble(Request["scale"]);
    int limit = Convert.ToInt32(Request["limit"]);
    ```

    These values tell .NET how big the final image should be (in pixels), where on the fractal we want to look, how much of it we'd like to see, and how much work we'd like it to do figuring out what the fractal looks like. We'll see shortly how each of these affects the final image. Note that we have to explicitly convert all the query variables from strings into appropriate C# data types.

4. Now we have our working variables defined, we create a blank `Bitmap` object (called `outputBmp`) in the server's memory, and cycle through x and y values looking at every pixel on it:

```
Bitmap outputBmp = new Bitmap(xSize, ySize,
                           ➥ PixelFormat.Format24bppRgb);

for(int x=-xSize/2; x<xSize/2; x++) {
  for(int y=-ySize/2; y<ySize/2; y++) {
     // Set color values for each point on the image
     double scaleFactor = 4/scale;
     int level = mandel(x0+(scaleFactor*x/xSize),
                      ➥ y0+(scaleFactor*y/ySize),limit);

     int R = (level)*16;
     int G = (level/4)*16;
     int B = (level/16)*16;

     // Set pixel output color based on color components
     Color outputCol = Color.FromArgb(R%255,G%255,B%255);

     outputBmp.SetPixel(x+xSize/2,y+ySize/2,outputCol);
  }
}
```

For each pixel, we calculate the point it corresponds to on the fractal, and plug that point's coordinates into a function called `mandel()`, which is going to do all the hard work for us – we'll get onto it in a moment.

5. Finally, we output the image to the client:

```
outputBmp.Save(Response.OutputStream, ImageFormat.Jpeg);
outputBmp.Dispose();
```

Now, for the science bit – hold tight! The function we need to create a fractal image is a wonderful piece of recursive mathematics that's a lot easier to show than it is to explain. So here it is:

```
public int mandel(double i0, double j0, int limit) {
  int n=0;
  double i=0,j=0,iTemp=0;

  while ((i*i)+(j*j)<4 && n++<limit) {
     iTemp = (i*i)-(j*j)+i0;
     j = (2*i*j)+j0;
```

```
        i = iTemp;
    }

    if (n==limit+1){
        n=0;
    }

    return n;
}
```

So what's going on here? Well, we stick our coordinates into an equation, pull them out the other end, and see if they've got too large along the way. If not, we put them through again and test them again, over and over, until they do go over a certain value (in this case 4). Once we've finished looping (or got bored waiting), we send back the number of completed loops, and that's what the previous code uses to work out what color to plot.

> *I won't try and explain exactly why it works here – that's just a little beyond the scope of this book! If you're interested in finding out more, then you can always search the Web for information on Benoit Mandelbrot, who first discovered this strange and beautiful mathematical pattern.*

Once the ASP.NET page is saved, you can test it in a browser, and watch as it generates images from nothing more than a few numbers. Don't forget to include a query string, or .NET won't have a clue what to do! Here are some you might like to try out:

```
?xSize=400&ySize=400&x=-1.49&y=0&scale=100&limit=25
?xSize=400&ySize=400&x=-1.49&y=0&scale=100&limit=200
?xSize=400&ySize=400&x=-1.25&y=0.019&scale=5000&limit=200
?xSize=400&ySize=400&x=-1.25&y=0.019&scale=5000&limit=1000
?xSize=400&ySize=400&x=-1.25&y=0.019&scale=10000&limit=1000
?xSize=400&ySize=400&x=-1.25&y=0.019&scale=100000&limit=5000
```

Now we're ready to build our nice Flash interface, so that it's a little easier for us to find our way around it. Create a new Flash document, and save it as `mandelbrotBrowser.fla`. You'll need to start by adding the following objects to the stage:

- One dynamic text field, instance name `scale_txt`.

- Two dynamic text fields, with `Var` set to `xCoord` and `yCoord` respectively.

- One dynamic text field, with `Var` set to `limit`.

- One button of whatever shape or style you like, which we'll use to use to refresh our image after zooming in or out.

- One ScrollPane component, instance name `pane`, scroll content set to `canvas` and all properties set to `true`.

- One ScrollBar component, instance name `scrollBar`, horizontal set to `true`;

- Two IconButton components, instance names `zoomIn_btn` and `zoomOut_btn`. The icon property for each should be set to `zoom`, referring to a movie clip that we'll create in a moment. All other properties can be left at their default values.

> *You can find the IconButton component in the "Flash UI Component Set #2", which you can download free from the Macromedia Flash Extension Exchange area at www.macromedia .com.*

- One off-stage movie clip to act as a placeholder when we zoom in and out. This movie only resides in the Library, as we will generate instances of it on the stage with ActionScript. This is given a linkage name of `placeHolder` via the Linkage properties. The graphics can be anything you want, but we used a solid rectangle the same color as our background, so the scrolling area appears blank.

- Several static text fields to act as captions for the data we're displaying.

Obviously you can spice up the display as much as you want. However, once all the components, buttons, and text fields are on stage, you should be looking at something similar to this:

Now that we have all the items we need on the stage, change its background color to a nice mid-gray.

Next, create another movie clip, which we'll going to use as the icon for our zoom buttons. It should consist of a graphical representation of a magnifying glass with a little plus sign ("+") next to it. We'll make the plus sign out of two separate movie clips, so that we can turn the vertical line off to make our zoom out icon. To do this, we will need to give both lines an instance name. The horizontal line will be named `barH_mx` and the vertical one will be `barV_mc`. It should look like this:

Note that this image is zoomed in to 800% to show the selected vertical bar movie clip. After the graphic's created, we need to give this movie clip linkage properties so that our two IconButton components can import it.

Open the Library panel and right-click on the magnifying glass clip. Select **Linkage** from the pop-up menu, check the **Export for ActionScript** box, and give the clip a linkage name of **zoom**.

We're now ready to write the code that'll pull all this together. Once again, there's quite a lot to wade through, so let's break it down a little.

Setting up

We begin by setting up all the variables our movie will use, and configure the various controls on the stage. The first two variables are simple enough:

```
// variable to hold the name of our ASPX page
aspx = "mandelGen.aspx";

// trash variable to avoid data caching
myTrash = new Date().getTime();
```

Limit scrollbar

The `limit` variable will control how intricate the fractal will be. Higher values will produce more complex details in the images, but they'll also cause .NET to take longer generating those images. We'll control it using the `scrollBar` component:

```
limit = 200;

// limit scrollbar values to between 0 and 1000 with
// 100 step increments if clicked in the slider area
scrollBar.setScrollProperties(100, 0, 1000);

// initial scrollbar "thumb" position
scrollBar.setScrollPosition(limit);

// set change handler for scrollbar controlling 'limit'
scrollBar.setChangeHandler("limitUpdate");

// update value of limit with scrollbar position
function limitUpdate() {
   limit=scrollBar.getScrollPosition();
}
```

Scale and the zoom buttons

The `scale` variable controls how much of the fractal image we'll see within the scroll pane. It's initially set to 1, showing us the whole fractal, but higher values will show us smaller and smaller sections of the image.

```
// initial scale factor
scale = 1;
```

The zoom buttons will put us in control the scale factor, letting us zoom in and out of the fractal image:

```
// get reference to mc used as icon in 'zoom out' button
icon = zoomOut_btn.getIcon();

// turn vertical bar off to make 'plus' into 'minus'
icon.barV_mc._visible = false;

// determine how far to zoom in and out (in percent)
zoomIn_percent = 110;
zoomOut_percent = 90;

// set change handlers for our zoom buttons
```

continues overleaf

```
zoomIn_btn.setChangeHandler("zoomIn")
zoomOut_btn.setChangeHandler("zoomOut")

// define change handlers for our zoom buttons
function zoomIn() { zoom(zoomIn_percent); }
function zoomOut() { zoom(zoomOut_percent); }
```

We'll look at the `zoom()` function itself in a moment.

Scroll pane and the refresh button

Finally, we get a reference to the content area of our scroll pane, and wire up the refresh button so that it will update the image being shown:

```
content = pane.getScrollContent();

refresh_btn.onRelease = function() {
   imageUpdate("true");
}
```

Now it's time to get serious about controlling the scroll pane and what's inside it.

Zooming

Whenever we zoom in or out of the image, we need to do several things: update the value of `scale`, resize the scroll pane's content (and refresh the pane so that the scroll bars take account of the content's new dimensions), reposition the pane's content (so that the center of the image always stays in the same place), and update the scale value being displayed.

```
// ZOOM FUNCTION
function zoom(zoom_percent) {
   // update scale value
   factor = zoom_percent/100;
   scale *= factor;
   // scale cannot be less than 1
   if (scale<1) {scale=1;}

   // update image dimensions and refresh pane
   content._width = 300 * scale;
   content._height = 300 * scale;
   pane.refreshPane();

   // maintain position of image center
   pos = pane.getScrollPosition();
   pane.setScrollPosition(((150+pos.x)*factor)-
```

continues overleaf

```
➡ 150,(((150+pos.y)*factor)-150);
// update displayed scale value
  scale_txt.text = int(scale*100)+"%";
}
```

The values of 300 and 150 are the visible dimensions of the scroll pane's contents. They also happen to be the size of the images we're going to create in the next function...

Updating the image

Here's the real meat of this particular application, so hold your breath – we're going in!

```
// IMAGE UPDATE FUNCTION
function imageUpdate(refresh) {

  // get latest coords from scroll pane position
  pos = pane.getScrollPosition();
  // calculate our location depending upon zoom level
  xCoord = (4*(pos.x+150)/(300*scale))-2;
  yCoord = (4*(pos.y+150)/(300*scale))-2;

  // set up image query string from coords/scale/limit
  query = "?xSize=300&ysize=300&x="+xCoord;
  query += "&y="+yCoord;
  query += "&scale="+scale;
  query += "&limit="+limit;
  query += "&nocache=" + (myDate + getTimer());
```

We now have three different plans of attack. If scale equals 1, then we simply load the complete Mandelbrot set into level 0, giving us a fixed backdrop for all our other bits and pieces:

```
if (scale == 1) {
  // load the base image into level 0
  frame=content.placeHolder_mc;
  with(frame){
    loadMovie(aspx+query,0);
  }
}
```

Otherwise, if scale is still less than 10, we load in the close-up image and scale it down so that it can fit seamlessly onto the (now scaled up) contents of the scroll pane:

```
} else if (scale<=10){
  // attach a placeholder over base image for close-up
  level = random(10);
  frame=content.attachMovie("placeHolder","frame"+level,level);
```

continues overleaf

```
        // load in scaled down close-up
        with(frame){
          _width = 300/scale;
          _height = 300/scale;
          _x = pos.x/scale;
          _y = pos.y/scale;
          loadMovie(aspx+query,level);
        }
```

Going further, once `scale` is greater than 10, we place our scaled down image inside another scaled down movie clip to maintain accuracy as we zoom further into the pane contents:

```
      } else {
        // attach 1/10 size placeholder to frame small movie
        level = 10+random(100);
        frame=content.attachMovie("placeHolder","frame"+level,level);
        with(frame){
          _width = 30;
          _height = 30;
          _x = int(pos.x/scale);
          _y = int(pos.y/scale);
          // attach a placeholder over inside frame
          place = attachMovie("placeHolder", "place"+level,level);
        }
        level = random(10);
        // load in scaled down close-up
        with(place){
          _width = 3000/scale;
          _height = 3000/scale;
          _x = (10*pos.x/scale)%10;
          _y = (10*pos.y/scale)%10;
          loadMovie(aspx+query,level);
        }
      }
    pane.setScrollPosition(pos.x,pos.y);
  }
```

Finally, we call up the main function to get us rolling when the movie starts up:

```
    imageUpdate();
```

If you were now to run this movie inside the Flash IDE, you'll get an error telling you why it doesn't work – the movie can't find the ASPX page. Of course, we need to make sure the SWF is generated in the same folder under `wwwroot` as our `mandelGen.aspx` file, and call it up via the server. Here's a shot of the finished application in action:

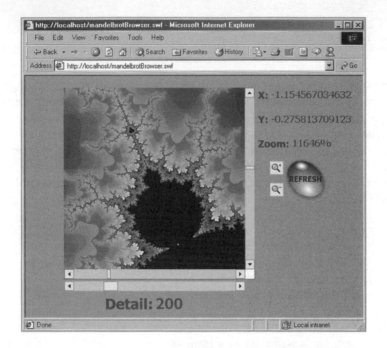

What you're looking at is a Flash application that allows a user to zoom in and out of, and pan around our mathematically generated fractal image. The image is generated on the fly on the server through an ASP.NET page written in C#. Since Flash MX can dynamically load JPEG images via the `loadMovie()` method, the page returns the image as it generates it, just as if the image were static on the server. Way cool!

Summary

Well, here ends the second chapter. We've seen how to handle flat and structured data on both the client and the server, and learnt some important techniques for passing them both back and forth. We've also seen how to use ASP.NET to write web services and generate images from scratch.

Along the way, we've seen a few simple Flash-fronted examples that could easily be expanded on after we learn how to read and write file data on the server – and that's precisely what we're going to focus on in Chapter 3.

chapter 3: **Storing and sourcing data**

So far, we've managed to set up some lines of communication between our Flash movies and server-side scripts. We've seen how to make the server process information we send to it, whether that's in the form of flat or structured data, and send back the results as query strings, XML, or even JPEG images. In this chapter, we're going to start looking at what happens when we tell ASP.NET to go get some information from elsewhere.

The theme of this chapter is really data *storage*. Whatever data we use in a Flash.NET application, it'll need to come from somewhere – so far, it's always been a choice between data from the user (input when the application runs), data from the SWF (hardwired when we compile it), or data from the ASPX (again, hardwired when we write it).

The only thing that's ever going to affect what these applications do is the user input. All the other data is hardwired into the application itself, so it can never change (unless you rebuild the files, which doesn't really count!) So, what can we do to change things?

Different sources of data

In every example we've seen up until this point, we've used ASP.NET as a data source in its own right, hardwiring options and information into the ASPX files wherever needed. In fact, most of the examples could easily have used the SWFs themselves to store the same data and processing code, though it would have made them a great deal larger and slower.

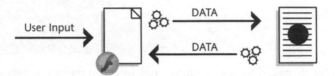

Things get a lot more exciting when we start sourcing data from other places. So, instead of thinking in terms of the diagram above (which is what we were doing in the last chapter), we can start to think in terms of the one below:

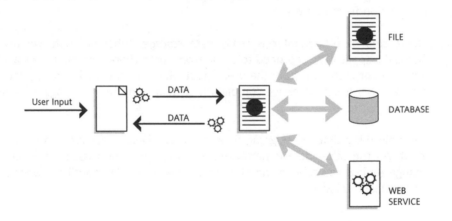

Files don't just disappear when we shut down the application, so whatever data we store in them will survive from one use to the next. But we've seen how easy it is to load file data into SWFs – why don't we cut out the middleman and just load the data straight into Flash? Well, there are several very good reasons:

- **Bandwidth.** The Flash client may not need all the data that's stored in the file. If we can get the server to whittle down our raw data, there's less to be sent across the network, and less of a bottleneck while the user waits for their SWF.

- **Processing.** Assuming we need to process the raw data, it'll be quicker to do it on the server. Flash is fairly well equipped with data processing tools, but it's still far more of a presentation tool than it is a data junkie. It's not the fastest thing in the world for number crunching, whereas that's just what .NET excels at.

- **Security.** Flash movies can only view files that are exposed by the web server, so the same files can be seen by anyone with a web browser and the right URL. By contrast, an ASP.NET page can access any file on the server machine, so it can expose (or hide) whatever information it wants to from the outside world.

- **Write access.** Flash movies are only able to read data from files that already exist, whereas server-side scripts can modify and add data to existing files, and even create brand new ones. This opens up a great many new possibilities, as we're about to see.

We're going to use the following examples to illustrate all these issues, and show you what it takes to write ASP.NET pages that can read and write file data.

Setting up read/write access

Before we move onto the exercises, we need to sort out a few settings. Your machine will understandably be a little reluctant to give ASP.NET full, unfettered access to any file on its hard drive. This means that your scripts won't be allowed to read or write to files unless you've specifically given them permission to.

Fortunately, it doesn't take long to set up all the permissions you need. The simplest way to do this is to create a new folder (*outside* the wwwroot directory, so that no-one can see it over the Web) – I suggest you put it in the C:/ drive root directory, and call it MyData.

	Name △	Size	Type
Local Disk (C:)	Documents and Settings		File Folder
	Flash Toolbox		File Folder
	Flash.NET		File Folder
MyData	Inetpub		File Folder
File Folder	My Documents		File Folder
	My Music		File Folder
Modified: 07/10/2002 11:24	MyData		File Folder
	PHP		File Folder
Attributes: (normal)	Program Files		File Folder
	Shockwave		File Folder
	TEMP		File Folder
	Windows Update Setup Files		File Folder
	WINNT		File Folder

Right-click on the new folder, select Properties, and take a look at the Security tab on the dialog that appears.

Now hit the Add button, so that we can add a new entry to the list of names up top. Here's the dialog that should appear; all you need do here is type in goon\aspnet (remembering of course to replace 'goon' with the name of your own machine).

Hit OK to confirm, and you'll find yourself back at the Properties dialog, with one new entry shown in the list of names.

Make sure the new entry – shown here as aspnet_wp account (GOON\ASPNET) – is selected, and check the bottom left checkbox to allow ASP.NET write permissions on the files in this folder.

If you try out the following examples without setting up the relevant permissions, you'll probably get an UnauthorizedAccessException error for your troubles. It's an easy step to forget, so if you do see this error message, in your browser the first thing to do is check the permission settings on the files you're trying to access.

We now have a folder that ASP.NET can freely use to read and write files in. What's more, its contents are safely hidden away from the Web, so whatever data we keep in those files can only be seen if we want it to be seen.

Let's start putting it to use!

Building a login system

Let's say you have some content that you'd like to make available on the Web, but don't want the whole world looking at it. Maybe it's a confidential business report, a beta for your latest experiment in Flash, or a gallery of family snaps from last Thanksgiving. Whatever your reasons are, you want to keep it private, and be sure it's only accessible by a select few individuals.

This is where a bit of dynamic content can make a big difference. If you make sure the content's only ever exposed through an ASP.NET page, you can tell that page to limit access to authorized visitors.

But how will it know which visitors are authorized? Simple: you build a login screen and have your trusted users enter a username and password whenever they want to access the secure content. The server checks submitted values against a pre-defined list, and only authorizes the current user when it finds a match. No match, no content. This is a process known technically as **authentication**.

A very simple authentication process might work like this:

1. An anonymous site user requests some content that's meant for privileged eyes only.

2. The **server** checks to see whether they've sent a valid username-password pair along with their request. Assuming they haven't, it sends back a message saying that they're not permitted to view it, and the client displays a login interface.

3. The user can now either cancel the original request or type in their name and password to resubmit. Assuming they do the latter (since the former isn't very interesting), a new request is sent to the server.

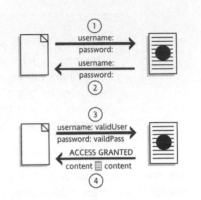

4. Once again, the **server** checks to see if the request includes a valid username-password pair. We already know what happens if it doesn't, so this time we'll assume that it does: the server now just sends back the content, which the client displays.

Okay, this isn't exactly a top-grade security system, and we certainly wouldn't advise you to keep your black-op secret documents hidden behind it. Anyone who *really* wants to break in probably won't take too long to find a way. However, it's a good start, and a great deal more secure than the Flash-only alternative. Without the server script, you'd need to include every valid password in the SWF itself, from where any curious SWF-sniffer could dig them out in seconds.

> In fact, .NET itself offers up an incredible array of powerful, dedicated security features in the `System.Security` namespace. They're well beyond the scope of this book, but it's well worth knowing they're there all the same.

Our login system's going to consist of four files: a Flash movie, an ASP.NET page, and a couple of text files, one containing the secure content, the other a list of valid usernames and corresponding passwords. We'll use the ActionScript object `loadVars` to pass data to and from the server-side script, and a brand new ASP.NET technique to pull in the password list and take care of validating the user input.

Setting up the passwords

5. Fire up Notepad and enter a few username/password pairs as shown here. Make sure you put the word END at the end of the list, so that the ASP.NET page will know when it's reached the end of the list.

```
pallav:nadhani
gregg:wygonik
david:neal
todd:yard
END
```

6. Save the file as `passwords.txt` in the `C:/MyData` folder.

Defining the secure content

7. Now create another text file, and add in a little test content.

```
content.txt - Notepad
File Edit Format Help
This information is secure, and cannot be accessed via the web
without a valid login name and password combination.
The list of valid combinations is stored in a file called
<font face='courier'>passwords.txt</font>, while the text
you're now reading comes from a file called <font
face='courier'>content.txt</font>.
```

8. Save it in `C:/MyData` as `content.txt`.

Building the ASP.NET page

This part of the application has to pick up the username and password combination sent by the Flash movie, open `passwords.txt` and read each line in turn, check if the sent combination matches any of the lines in the text file, and send back a validation response and (if the user's been authenticated) some secure content as well. Let's see how we can put it together:

9. Create a new file in `wwwroot`, save it as `Login.aspx`, and add in the following code.

```
<%@ Page Language="c#" debug="true" %>
<%@ Import NameSpace="System.IO" %>

<script runat=server>
  void page_load(Object sender , EventArgs e) {
    // main page code goes in here
  }
</script>
```

As usual, we begin with the standard ASP.NET template. Note that just after the C# `Page` directive, we include the namespace `System.IO` – we'll need objects from `System.IO` in order to work with files on the server.

10. Next, we call up whatever username and password values were sent over with the page request, and store them in local string variables:

```
...
  void page_load(Object sender , EventArgs e) {
    String myName = Request["username"];
    String myPass = Request["password"];
  }
</script>
```

11. Next, we declare the local variables we'll be using in this page:

```
...
  void page_load(Object sender , EventArgs e) {
```

continues overleaf

```
            String myName = Request["username"];
            String myPass = Request["password"];


        Boolean authorized = false;
            String myLine;
            String[] myValues;
        }
    </script>
```

The first new variable authorized will indicate whether the username/password combination supplied by the user is correct or not. It's safest to assume not, so we set it to false for now.

We'll use the myLine string variable to store each of the lines pulled out of the passwords.txt file, and the myValues string array to grab separate values for the username and password.

12. We're now ready to compare the user-submitted values for myName and myPass against each of the combinations we stored in the passwords.txt file just a few moments ago:

```
        ...
        Boolean authorized = false;
        String myLine;
        String[] myValues;

        String passFile = "C:/MyData/passwords.txt";
        FileStream fs = new FileStream(passFile, FileMode.Open);
        StreamReader sr = new StreamReader(myStream);

        do {
          myLine = sr.ReadLine();
          myValues = myLine.Split(':');
          if (myValues[0]==myName && myValues[1]==myPass) {
            authorized = true;
          }
        } while (myLine != "END");

        fs.Close();
    }
    </script>
```

First of all, we need to open the file. To do this, we create a FileStream object called fs, using two arguments: the first is a string called passFile, which specifies the file we want to access; the second specifies how this file should be accessed. In this case, we just want to open an existing file (rather than create a new one) so we use FileMode.Open.

The next step is to make a `StreamReader` object called `sr`. We'll use this to read data from `fs`, and find out what's inside the `passwords.txt` file.

Now we read each line in the file: for each line, we pull it into `myLine`, split each colon-separated pair into separate string elements in the `myValues` array, and check if they match the submitted values. If (and *only if*) we do find a match, we set authorized to `true`.

Once we spot the word `END`, we know we've hit the end of the file, so the `do` loop ends and we close the file stream (so that other people can access the file).

13. Now we need to load in our secure content, which is also stored in the `MyData` folder, inside a file called `content.txt`.

```
...
} while (myLine != "END");

fs.Close();

String contentFile = "C:/MyData/content.txt";
fs = new FileStream(contentFile,FileMode.Open);
sr = new StreamReader(fs);

String content = sr.ReadToEnd();
fs.Close();
}
</script>
```

This is almost identical to the technique we used before to load up our password list. The only difference is that we use the StreamReader method `ReadToEnd()` to pull the *entire* file into the string variable content in one go, rather than looping through individual lines.

14. Now, if we've found a valid username/password combination, we need to send back the secure content. If not, we just send back 'access denied':

```
String content = sr.ReadToEnd();
fs.Close();

if (authorized) {
  Response.Write("ACCESS=GRANTED");
  Response.Write("&loginname=" + myName);
  Response.Write("&content=" + Server.UrlEncode(content));
} else {
  Response.Write("ACCESS=DENIED");
}
}
</script>
```

15. The ASP.NET code's finished now, so save it in `wwwroot` as `login.aspx`, and take it for a test run in your browser. If you simply call up the page URL with no query variables attached, you should get a simple ACCESS=DENIED response.

Try it again with a valid username/ password pair (for example, try calling up the page with ?username=pallav &password=nadhani attached to the URL, as shown below) and you can expect quite a different result:

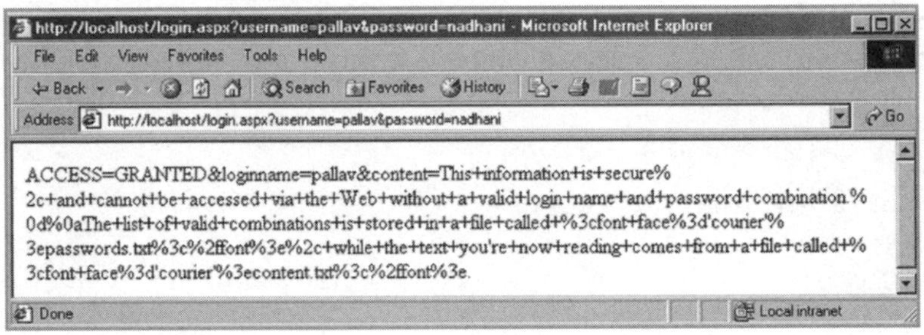
http://localhost/login.aspx?username=pallav&password=nadhani - Microsoft Internet Explorer
File Edit View Favorites Tools Help
Back Search Favorites History
Address http://localhost/login.aspx?username=pallav&password=nadhani
Go
ACCESS=GRANTED&loginname=pallav&content=This+information+is+secure%2c+and+cannot+be+accessed+via+the+Web+without+a+valid+login+name+and+password+combination.%0d%0aThe+list+of+valid+combinations+is+stored+in+a+file+called+%3cfont+face%3d'courier'%3epasswords.txt%3c%2ffont%3e%2c+while+the+text+you're+now+reading+comes+from+a+file+called+%3cfont+face%3d'courier'%3econtent.txt%3c%2ffont%3e.
Done
Local intranet

Building the Flash front-end

Now that the bare bones of the application are all in place, it's time for us to finish off by giving it a nice Flash interface and presenting the content in a more aesthetically pleasing way than the browser's managed to.

16. Create a new Flash document called `login.fla`, and create a new movie clip called LoginForm. We'll create the whole interface in here, so that it's nice and portable for use in the future. You may want to start off by making a background for the user interface – you can see mine in the screenshot here:

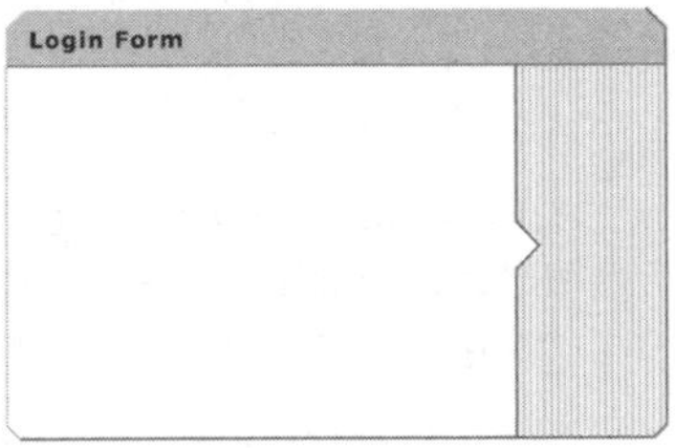
Login Form

I created it on three layers, which I then grouped in a layer folder called Background Elements. Note that all three layers are defined right through to frame 24.

17. The next step is to add three new layers called Actions, Frame Labels, and Form Elements, and add keyframes and frame labels as shown here:

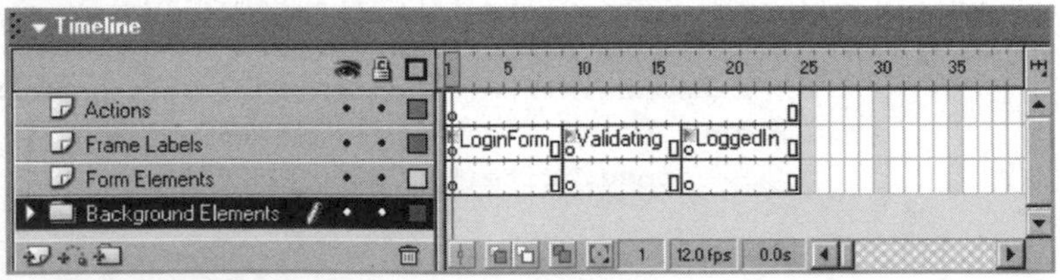
Timeline
Actions
Frame Labels
Form Elements
Background Elements
LoginForm
Validating
LoggedIn
12.0 fps
0.0s

18. Frame 1 will serve as our login form, and the Form Elements layer will need to contain the following elements: a dynamic text field (Var: tbStatus), a pair of input text fields (Var: username and Var: password respectively), and a button (instance name: go_btn). You can also add a couple of static text fields to label the input text boxes:

19. Frame 9 (labeled as Validating) just contains a single looping movie clip, which just shows a clock hand that rotates while we're waiting for the server to respond:

20. Frame 17 (labeled as LoggedIn) contains three elements: a static text field to proclaim the fact that our users have logged in successfully, a multi-line dynamic text field (instance name: content_txt, Var: content) to show the secure content, and a ScrollBar component, which we've dropped onto the dynamic text field so that we can use it to scroll up and down the secure content:

21. Now we just need to add in some actions to control what happens when we run the movie. Firstly, we write a handler function for the Go button's onRelease event:

```
go_btn.onRelease = function() {
  if (userName == undefined || password == undefined) {
    tbStatus = "Please enter both fields";
  } else {
    loadVariables("http://localhost/login.aspx",_parent._parent,
                   ➡ "POST");
    gotoAndStop("Validating");
  }
};
```

We check that both fields have been filled in, and use the loadVariables action to POST their values to the ASP.NET page – more on this in a moment. We jump to the rotating clock hand while we wait for a response.

22.   Now we need to define what happens when the LoginForm receives data: it checks the value of ACCESS, and either jumps ahead to the LoggedIn frame, or back to the LoginForm:

```
onData = function() {
  if (ACCESS == "GRANTED") {
    gotoAndStop("LoggedIn");
  } else {
    tbStatus = "Invalid Login!!!";
    gotoAndStop("Loginform");
  }
};
```

We wrap things up by stopping the playhead – otherwise the movie would end up looping endlessly through each of the three screens:

```
stop();
```

Is that really it? What about calling up the username and password to send to the server? What about putting the secure content in the multi-line text field? In fact, we've taken care of both already.

In this example, I've deliberately used the `loadVariables()` action, which works in much the same way as `loadVars.load()`, but also lets us tell it where to get and set variables. In this case, `_parent._parent` is a relative path from go_btn to the root timeline of the LoginForm movie clip itself.

This is where we defined the `username` and `password` variables (by attaching them to the corresponding input text fields), so these values will both be sent to the server along with the page request. Likewise, when we get a response from the server, the URL-encoded value of the variable `content` will automatically be shown in the multi-line text field.

So, it's time to put our login system to the test. We've hard-wired the `localhost` path into the FLA, and everything else is in place on the server, so we should be able to simply hit CTRL+ENTER and test run `login.swf` from wherever it happens to be.

Now you just need to go and create something worth keeping secret! In the next section, we're going to turn things around, and look at how we can use ASP.NET to write data into files on the server.

Building a hit counter

To write data into a file, we use the `StreamWriter` class (defined in .NET's `System.IO` namespace) in much the same way as we did the `StreamReader` class earlier on. Now, by writing data to the server whenever someone accesses a particular page on our site, we can create a simple hit counter, to keep track of how many times the page has been requested.

Strictly speaking, it's the server that keeps track of this number: the hit counter SWF itself just has to tell the server to update a stored value, retrieve the new count, and show users what it is.

So, we're going to need the following: a text file on the server that can store the number of hits received; an ASP.NET page to retrieve that number, update it, and send the updated value back to (a) the client and (b) the text file; a Flash movie to call up the ASPX and display the current hit count.

Setting up the hit count

Since we're going to rely on ASP.NET to put data in our text file, this first bit's very easy: we just need to create an empty text file called `hitCount.txt` in C:/MyData. In fact, it'll help us test things later on if we have just a little sample data in here, so you might like to put a few entries in:

```
hitCount.txt - Notepad
File  Edit  Format  Help
home:100
gallery:200
news:300
END
```

Building the ASP.NET page

Next, we need to write the ASP.NET page that will access and update these values.

1. Create a text file in wwwroot called `hitCounter.aspx`, and enter the following code:

```
<%@ Page Language="c#" debug="true" %>
<%@ Import NameSpace="System.IO" %>

<script runat=server>
  void page_load(Object sender , EventArgs e) {
    // main page code goes in here
  }
</script>
```

Once more, we begin with the standard ASP.NET template, and since we're still working with files, we still need to include the namespace `System.IO`. As usual, all the following code needs to be added into the `page_load` function.

2. First, we need to initialize a few variables that will come in useful later on:

```
string hitsFile = "C:/MyData/hitCount.txt";
string newContents = "";
string pageName = Request ["page"];

int currentHits = 0;
string[] lines;
```

We start off with a few string variables, which we'll use respectively to store the name of the hit count file, its contents, and the name of the page for which we want to register a fresh hit.

The first and last of these are fairly self-explanatory, but what's the second one for? Well, since we can't modify the contents of the file directly, we need to read them into the newContents variable, modify them there, and recreate the file by erasing all its old contents and replacing them with the data in newContents.

We also declare an integer called currentHits (to keep track of the current hit count for the specified page) and a string array called lines (to hold each pair of colon-separated values in turn, just as we did in the login example).

3. Following this, we're ready to open up the hit count file so we can find out what the specified page's current hit count stands at:

```
FileStream fs = new FileStream(hitsFile,FileMode.Open);
StreamReader sr = new StreamReader(fs);
String strLine = sr.ReadLine();
```

As before, we make a FileStream object and open up the file in FileMode.Open mode. We pass the FileStream fs into a new StreamReader object sr, which can now be used to sift through the file's contents. We pull the first line into a new string variable called strLine.

4. Now we start up a while loop, and cycle through each line in the file until we hit the one that reads "END":

```
while (strLine != "END") {
   lines = strLine.Split(':');

   if (lines[0] == strPageName) {
      currentHits = Convert.ToInt32(lines[1]) + 1;
      newContents += lines[0] + ":";
      newContents += currentHits + '\n';
   } else {
      newContents += strLine + '\n';
   }
   strLine = sr.ReadLine();
}
```

The first thing we do with each line is to split it in two, using ':' to separate terms. We use the Split() function to separate the values and store them in the string array lines, so that lines[0] contains the counter name, and lines[1] the corresponding hit count.

We now compare the strings to find out if the counter we're looking at is the one we actually want to update. If it is, we extract the hit count, add 1 to its value, and store the result in the variable currentHits. We then use that result to create a new name:count pair, and add it to newContents. If it's not the one we're interested in, we just add strLine and a newline character to the end of newContents and move on to look at the next line.

5. Now we're done reading the file, we can test the value of currentHits to check whether we've found a match:

    ```
    if (currentHits < 1) {
      currentHits = 1;
      newContents +=  strPageName + ":1" + '\n';
    }
    ```

    If the counter we're looking for doesn't exist, the currentHits value will still be set to its original value of 0. In that case, we bump it up to 1, and add the new name:count pair to the end of the newContents string.

6. We wrap up this part of the code by adding "END" to the newContents string, and closing the StringReader object:

    ```
    newContents += "END";
    sr.Close();
    ```

7. Now it's time to take all the data stored in variable newContents and put it back into hitCounter.txt:

    ```
    fs = new FileStream(hitsFile, FileMode.Create);
    StreamWriter sw = new StreamWriter(fs);
    ```

    In order to replace the original contents, we recreate the file by opening it with a FileStream in FileMode.Create mode. Once again, we use a FileStream object to open the file; this time though, we follow up with a StreamWriter object, so that we can write data *into* the file.

8. Now we just need to write all the data from newContents into the file and close the StreamWriter when we're done. We do this by calling the StreamWriter object's WriteLine() and Close() methods:

    ```
    sw.WriteLine(newContents);
    sw.Close();
    ```

9. For our final step, we send the new hit count for the requested counter back to the client, in the form of a name-value pair:

    ```
    Response.Write("&hits=" + currentHits);
    ```

To make sure the page is up and running okay, save the ASPX again, and point your browser at http://localhost/hitCounter.aspx?Page=home. Now open up `hitCount.txt`, and you should see that the hit count for page `home` has increased by 1:

Close `hitCount.txt` and try this again with a page that *doesn't* exist. For example, you could point your browser at http://localhost/ch3/Counter.aspx?Page=MyCV. Open up `hitCount.txt` once again, and you should see the new counter that's been created for you automatically.

Now that we have the ASP.NET page ready, we're ready to build the Flash client.

Building the Flash front-end

This is going to be responsible for sending the page name to `counter.aspx`, which in turn updates the hits for this page and returns the current number of hits to be displayed by Flash.

1. Create a new Flash document and save it in `wwwroot` as `Counter.fla`. Create a new layer called `Textbox`, and add a dynamic text field with the instance name `tbHits`.

2. Now add another layer called `Actions`, and attach the following ActionScript to the first keyframe:

    ```
    tbHits.text = "Loading...";
    objlv = new LoadVars();
    myDate = new Date();
    myPage = "Home";
    ```

continues overleaf

```
                objlv.load("http://localhost/HitCounter.aspx?Page="
                                  ➥ + myPage + "&trash=" + escape(myDate));

            objlv.onLoad = function(success){
              if (success==true){
                //If the movie successfully got the data
                tbHits.text = objlv.hits;
              }
              else{
                tbHits.text = "Error";
              }
            };
```

We create a LoadVars object and use its load method to retrieve the data for myPage
(using myDate to provide us with a trash value that avoids the risk of page caching).

After that, we define an onLoad event handler function, which sets the value of the counter
once the data has been successfully returned from the server. If we receive an error, we
display an error message instead.

3. Save the FLA and give it a test run – you should now
    see an accurate update of the number of page hits
    displayed:

Okay, it's nothing much to look at, but the principle is what counts here: we've got a Flash movie
that shows a different number each time you run it – now that you can access the hit count from
ActionScript, you can display it in any number of ways. Here's a picture of one example that you
can find in the download bundle – try inventing more for yourself.

Building a news reader

So far in this chapter, we've dealt exclusively with files on the server that contain flat data. We've been able to create new ones, open existing ones, and append data to them. Now, we're going to see how we can open a physically present XML file at the server and load its contents into an XMLDocument object.

In the next example, we'll create a searchable news reader, featuring a Flash interface and an XML data store. Flash will offer us a search form, where users can enter specific keywords to search on. This will be passed onto an ASP.NET page, which will be responsible for opening the XML file that contains the list of news, going through each piece of news, and returning a short-listed set of news items to the Flash movie.

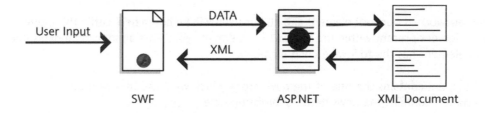

Why do this instead of getting Flash to do it? One, we're doing things on the server side, so it's a lot less load on our Flash file, and a lot quicker. Two, this approach will allow us to look at dealing with XML files generated by ASP.NET itself.

Later on, we'll add a Flash admin tool, which we can use to add news stories to the XML file. First though, let's put together the basic system that we'll use to read and display the news.

Defining the news stories

The full list of news items we're going to be viewing will be stored in a static XML file called news.xml. It'll have the following structure:

```
<newsdoc>

  <news>
    <title>News title comes here</title>
    <date>15th July, 2002</date>
    <shortdesc>
      Short description about the news.
    </shortdesc>
    <longdesc>
      The Complete Story comes here.
    </longdesc>
```

continues overleaf

```
                    </news>

                    <news>
                       <title>Another News title comes here</title>
                       <date>2nd June, 2002</date>
                       <shortdesc>
                          Short description about the news.
                       </shortdesc>
                       <longdesc>
                          The Complete Story comes here.
                       </longdesc>
                    </news>

                 </newsdoc>
```

Here, `<newsdoc>` is our root element and all our news will be contained within this element. Each `<news>` element present within the `<newsdoc>` element represents an individual news item. The `<news>` element has the following child elements:

- `<title>` contains the title of the news story, which we'll use as a caption.
- `<date>` contains the news item's submission date.
- `<shortdesc>` contains a summary of the story, to be shown in the story listing.
- `<longdesc>` contains the full story, to be displayed in the main news page.

Go ahead and create a `news.xml` document for yourself, and add in some news items of your own. Save it in the usual place – `C:/MyData` – and we're all set to carry on.

Building the ASP.NET news reader page

The ASP.NET page `news.aspx` will take the search string sent to it by the Flash front-end, look through the news nodes in `news.xml`, and send back any items it finds whose titles contain an instance of the search string.

1. Create a new file called `readNews.aspx`, and save it in your `wwwroot` folder. Add the following code:

    ```
    <%@ Page Language="c#" debug="true" %>
    <%@ Import NameSpace="System.Xml" %>

    <script runat=server>
      void page_load(Object sender , EventArgs e) {
         // main page code goes in here
             }
    </script>
    ```

We begin with the page and import directives we'll need for our page to work. As usual, we're using C# as the language, and in this case we need `System.Xml` as we're going to be working with XML.

2. We start by declaring a string variable called `strOutput`; we'll use this to hold the XML data we want to send back. We then obtain the search string, put it in another string variable called `strSearch`, and get rid of any URL encoding it may contain:

```
string strOutput;
string strSearch = Request["Search"];
strSearch = Server.HtmlEncode(strSearch);
```

`Server.HtmlEncode()` converts URL-encoded characters in the `strSearch` string into spaces, slashes, apostrophes, and other characters that we (and the XML parser) can make sense of.

3. Next, we create an `XmlDocument` object and load in the contents of our XML news file:

```
XmlDocument myXml = new XmlDocument();
myXml.Load("C:/MyData/News.xml");
```

4. Now we check whether the search string is empty. If it is, we use the XMLDocument's `OuterXml` property to get an XML string that describes the complete document, and store it away in `strOutput`:

```
if (strSearch == null) {
   strOutput = myXml.OuterXml;
} else {
```

5. If not, we're looking at slightly more work. We start by declaring some variables:

```
string strtitle, strlongdesc;
bool foundInTitle, foundInDesc;
XmlNode rootnode = myXml.DocumentElement;
XmlNode newsnode;

strOutput = "<newsdoc>";
```

We'll use the two strings to hold title and description text for each of the news nodes we take a look at. The two Booleans will help us test whether the search term shows up in either string. Then we store the XML document's root node in `rootnode`, and declare another XmlNode called `newsnode` ready for later on. Finally, we start putting data into `strOutput`, beginning with a `newsdoc` tag for the top of the XML document we want to send back.

6. Now we have to loop through each of the document's news nodes, checking whether their titles or descriptions contain the search term:

```
for (int i=0; i<rootnode.ChildNodes.Count; i++) {
   newsnode = rootnode.ChildNodes[i];
   strtitle = newsnode.FirstChild.FirstChild.Value;
   strlongdesc = newsnode.LastChild.FirstChild.Value;

   foundInTitle = strtitle.IndexOf(strSearch)>-1;
   foundInDesc = strlongdesc.IndexOf(strSearch)>-1;

   if (foundInTitle||foundInDesc) {
      strOutput += newsnode.OuterXml;
   }
}
```

We use `newsnode` to contain each news element in turn, and the `IndexOf()` function to find out whether our search term occurs in either `strtitle` or `strlongdesc`. If so, we add the full XML of `newsnode` to the end of our output string.

7. Before we leave the `else` block behind, we tack a closing `newsdoc` tag on the end of the output string:

```
   strOutput += "</newsdoc>";
}
```

8. Finally, we set the content type (so that the client knows that it's being sent an XML document), and write the output string into the Response stream:

```
Response.ContentType = "text/xml";
Response.Write(strOutput);
```

As a test to make sure everything's working okay, fire up your browser with the following in the address bar: http://localhost/News.aspx. You should get output similar to what's shown below, giving you the full contents of the news.xml file:

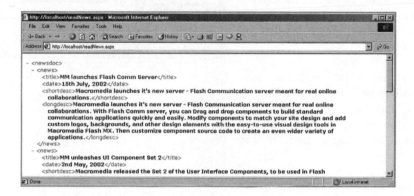

Now try adding a search term to the URL – for example, you might search on stories that mention Macromedia: http://localhost/News.aspx?search=Macromedia. You should find that ASP.NET has filtered out all the stories that don't feature this word in either their title text or their description text. Great – now let's add in a proper interface.

Building the basic Flash front-end

The Flash front-end for our basic news reader will just need to call up XML data from the ASP.NET page we just built, and display it in a user-friendly fashion. Before we get stuck into fancy features like search capabilities and admin screens, let's get our first hurdle out of the way and see how we're going to present the news.

1. Create a new Flash document called news.fla with stage dimensions of 450 by 300 pixels. If you want to create a background for the interface, store it away in a locked layer (or layer folder) so that it doesn't interfere with our other elements.

2. Create a new layer called News Reader, and make a new movie clip with the same name. This will contain all the elements we need to read news items from the XML document, plus a few more that we'll be using later on. Here's how I've set up the News Reader movie clip:

There are three layers here:

Content contains a multi-line dynamic text field, instance name news_tb (which will act as a container for all our news items), and a vertical ScrollBar component that will allow us to control it).

Controls contains two buttons: add News_btn (which we'll use later to add in news items) and back_btn (which will appear in the detailed news screen, allowing users to navigate back to the listings).

Search contains an input text field with Var set to search (where users will enter terms to search on), a button search_btn (for triggering search), and a static text label.

3. Now we head back to the main timeline, and add a couple of new layers there. The first is called User Feedback, and contains a looping movie clip (instance name clock_mc) and a dynamic text field (with Var set to errorMessage).

4. The second new layer is called Actions, and that's where we're going to add the script that'll make our news reader work. Select frame 1 in this layer, open up the Actions panel, and add the following code:

```
reader_mc.news_tb._visible = false;
reader_mc.back_btn._visible = false;

myXml = new Xml();
myXml.ignoreWhite = true;

myXml.load("http://localhost/news.aspx");

myXml.onLoad = function(success) {
clock_mc._visible = false;
  if (success && myXml.status == 0) {
newsnodes = myXml.firstChild.childNodes;
reader_mc.listItems(newsnodes);
        } else {
showError(success);
}
}
```

We start by hiding the news textbox and back button, while we load up our XML from the server. Once it's loaded, we hide the clock, and check to see whether the data loaded successfully. If so, we pass a list of news nodes into a function called listItems(), which we'll define in a moment. If not, we assume that the document is either malformed or just failed to load, so we call another function called showError(), using success to indicate which of these errors occurred.

5. Now we have to define the functions that'll handle this information and let users control what's displayed in the news reader movie clip. We start with a function that creates a list of items in the news textbox:

```
reader_mc.listItems = function(nodes) {
 var list="";

for (i=0; i<nodes.length; i++) {
titleNode = nodes[i].childNodes[0]
dateNode = nodes[i].childNodes[1]
summaryNode = nodes[i].childNodes[2]

list += "<A HREF='asfunction:showStory,"+i+"'><B>";
list += titleNode.childNodes[0].nodeValue;
list += "</B></a>";
list += "<BR>";
```

continues overleaf

```
            list += dateNode.childNodes[0].nodeValue;
            list += "<BR>"
            list += summaryNode.childNodes[0].nodeValue;

            list += "<A HREF='asfunction:showStory,"+i+"'><B>";
            list += " &lt;more&gt;"
            list += "</B></a>";

            list += "<BR><BR>";
        }
        with(reader_mc) {
            news_tb.htmlText = list;
            news_tb._visible = true;
        }
    }
```

The main part of the function loops through the provided list of nodes, using titles, dates, and summaries to produce a nicely formatted list of news items, complete with asfunction hyperlinks that will call the ActionScript function showStory when they're clicked on. We send the finished list to news_tb, and make sure the textbox is visible.

asfunction is a special tag that we can use within <A HREF> tags in a Flash movie to invoke a specific ActionScript function. The syntax used is:

    asfunction:functionname, "parameter"

where *functionname* is the name of the function to be invoked when the link is clicked, and *parameter* is a string value that will be passed to the function. So, now that we've given users a way to invoke the showStory() function, we'd better define it!

showStory() just takes information from a specified node in the loaded XML document and presents it as a complete news story in the news textbox.

```
    reader_mc.showStory = function(storyNumber) {
        titleNode = newsnodes[storyNumber].childNodes[0];
        dateNode = newsnodes[storyNumber].childNodes[1];
        storyNode = newsnodes[storyNumber].childNodes[3];

        var story = "";
        story += "<B>"
        story += titleNode.childNodes[0].nodeValue
        story += "</B>";
        story += "<BR>";
        story += dateNode.childNodes[0].nodeValue
        story += "<BR>";
```

continues overleaf

```
story += storyNode.childNodes[0].nodeValue;

with(this) {
   news_tb.htmlText = story;
   back_btn._visible = true;
}
}
```

Again, it's mainly concerned with digging into the XML node structure, retrieving the values we're interested in, and adding them into a variable with a nice bit of HTML formatting to keep things looking nice. Once we've assigned the story text to the news textbox, we make sure the Back button is visible so that users can return to the original list view.

6. Of course, we'll need to wire up that button if it's going to do anything at all:

```
reader_mc.back_btn.onRelease = function() {
   // Return to summary list
   reader_mc.listItems(newsNodes);
   this._visible = false;
}
```

Simple enough, it calls the listItems() function again (replacing the displayed content) and then makes itself invisible. That's it.

7. Finally, we need to deal with those darned error messages. As you may recall, we called showError() with success as sole argument. If the argument value is 0, we know that the XML document failed to load; otherwise we assume that it loaded, but was malformed:

```
showError = function(errorType) {
   // Display error info in textbox
   switch (errorType) {
   case 0: // The document failed to load
     errorMessage = "An error occurred while reading";
     errorMessage += " from the XML document";
     break;
   case 1:    // The document loaded, but was malformed
     errorMessage = "Error: malformed XML document";
     break;
   default:
     errorMessage = "An unknown error has occurred";
   }
}
```

8. Whatever string we store in errorMessage will show up on the stage via the textbox we placed in the User Feedback layer. However, we only want it to display the message for a short while after the error occurs. For that reason, we define one more function, which will take care of blanking error messages after 20 frames:

```
    onEnterFrame = function() {
  wasMessage = isMessage;
  isMessage = (errorMessage != "");

  if (isMessage && !wasMessage) {
    delay = 20;
  } else if (isMessage && wasMessage) {
    delay--;
  }
  if (delay<0) {
    errorMessage = "";
    isMessage = false;
  }
}
```

That's all the code we need to make the basic news reader function as intended. Once you've saved the FLA, hit CTRL+ENTER to test it, and you should be able to browse each of the news stories from the XML file, both in summary form and in full.

Adding search functionality

Well, we've managed to view the complete document, but what about that search feature we mentioned earlier? Both screens already feature a search interface, so what else do we need to do to make it work? Well, not a lot as it happens.

1. In fact, this is all the code we need to wire up the search button:

```
reader_mc.search_btn.onRelease = function() {
  // Replace loaded XML with response from ASPX
  url = "http://localhost/news.aspx";
  url += "?search=" + reader_mc.search;
```

continues overleaf

```
    _root.myXml.load(url);
}
```

We just call the load method on myXml again, this time adding our search text to the end of the URL as a query string.

Now try running the movie again. Enter a search string and click on the Go button, and you'll see the rotating clock once again while the data's fetched in from the server. Once the server responds with the selected nodes of XML data, the movie displays them all (or 'it' in this case) in summary as before, complete with a clickable link to the full story.

Building an admin section for the news reader

With the basic news reader application up and running, it's time to move on to the admin interface. The admin interface will be available to anyone pressing the Add News button in the movie. All the same, we don't want just anyone adding news items, so we'll need to insist that a valid username and password be supplied along with the details of the news story; otherwise the story won't be added to news.xml.

Building the ASP.NET admin page

We're going to start by creating a brand new ASP.NET page. This page will be responsible for adding items to the news.xml file, and sending a response to the client that indicates whether or not it's succeeded.

1. Create a new text file and save it in the wwwroot folder as addNews.aspx. Now enter the following code:

    ```
    <%@ Page Language="c#" debug="true" %>
    <%@ Import NameSpace="System.Xml" %>

    <script runat=server>
        void page_load(Object sender , EventArgs e) {
            // main code goes in here
        }
    </script>
    ```

We begin, as ever, with the page and import directives, and making sure we've included all the namespaces required for operations in this page: System.XML in this case.

continues overleaf

2. Now we look at the main code for the `page_load` function. First of all, we grab the username/password values submitted with the client request:

```
void page_load(Object sender , EventArgs e) {
    //Request the data
    string strUser = Request["Username"];
    string strPass = Request["Password"];
    if (strUser=="mylogin" && strPass=="mypassword") {
```

We check them against some predefined values to ensure that no unauthorized users can add news items – I've hard-coded these values into the ASPX simply for the sake of brevity.

3. If the username/password combination is correct, we run the following block of code:

```
string strtitle, strdate, strshortdesc, strlongdesc;
strtitle = Server.HtmlEncode(Request["title"]);
strdate = Server.HtmlEncode(Request["date"]);
strshortdesc = Request["shortdesc"];
strshortdesc = Server.HtmlEncode(strshortdesc);
strlongdesc = Request["longdesc"];
strlongdesc = Server.HtmlEncode(strlongdesc);
```

Here, we dig up all the information passed to the page from the Flash movie and store it in local string variables.

4. Following this, we create an instance of the `XmlDocument` object and use its `Load` method to load up the XML document `news.xml`.

```
XmlDocument myxml = new XmlDocument();
myxml.Load(Server.MapPath("news.xml"));
```

5. We then get a reference to the root element of the loaded `News.xml` document:

```
XmlNode rootnode = myxml.DocumentElement;
```

6. Now we use `CreateElement` to create a few element nodes and assign text values to them with the `InnerText` property:

```
XmlElement newsele, titleele, dateele,
    ➡ 0shortdescele, longdescele;
titleele = myxml.CreateElement("title");
dateele = myxml.CreateElement("date");
shortdescele = myxml.CreateElement("shortdesc");
longdescele = myxml.CreateElement("longdesc");
titleele.InnerText = strtitle;
dateele.InnerText = strdate;
```

```
shortdescele.InnerText = strshortdesc;
longdescele.InnerText = strlongdesc;
```

7. We append each of these nodes to the main document:

```
newsele = myxml.CreateElement("news");
newsele.AppendChild(titleele);
newsele.AppendChild(dateele);
newsele.AppendChild(shortdescele);
newsele.AppendChild(longdescele);
rootnode.AppendChild(newsele);
```

Note that we append them in a very specific order – that is, we first append the title element to the news node, and only then append the date, short description, and long description elements. Finally, we append the news element itself to the root node.

8. Now we save the updated XML Document, using the XmlDocument class `Save` method:

```
myxml.Save(Server.MapPath("News.xml"));
```

9. If everything goes okay, we send a status flag (containing the value 1) back to the client:

```
Response.Write("&status=1");
```

10. Now that we've finished dealing with what happens when a user provides us with a valid login/password combination, it's time to consider the other possibility:

```
        } else {
    Response.Write("&status=2");
        }
    }
</SCRIPT>
```

11. This `else` code block is executed if the client isn't authorized to add news items, so we just send back a status variable with the value 2.

Save your file in `wwwroot`, and make sure the page is running okay. You might try pointing your browser at the following URL:

http://localhost/AddNews.aspx?login=mylogin&password=mypassword&title=Mynews title&date=23September2002&shortdesc= Short Description&Longdesc=Long Description comes here

This should give you the following output:

Nothing much to look at, but open up C:/MyData/news.xml, and you should be able to see the latest fruit of your labors: a new news item! We've written XML data *into* the file.

Building the Flash admin interface

We now have all we need to usefully add an admin interface to the feature set of our Flash news reader.

1. The first step is to add a new layer on the root timeline, called News Admin. Create a new movie clip called Admin, and add an instance (called admin_mc) to the News Admin layer. Now open up the movie clip in situ, and add in the following elements:

   We've two buttons (back_btn and submitNews_btn), plus six input text fields (with Var set to tbAddLogin, tb AddPassword, tbAddTitle, tbAddDate, tbAddShortDesc, and tbAddLongDesc respectively) and a bunch of labels.

   The tbAddPassword box will need its input type setting to Password, in order to have asterisks shown (rather than the actual characters) when the user inputs their password.

2. Now we need to wire up our admin screen to the rest of the movie. Select frame 1 on the Actions layer, and make the following changes to the code in the Actions panel:

```
admin_mc._visible = false;
reader_mc.news_tb._visible = false;
reader_mc.back_btn._visible = false;

// Create LoadVars object for submitting new stories
myNews = new LoadVars();
// Create Xml object for reading news stories
myXml = new Xml();
myXml.ignoreWhite = true;
```

continues overleaf

```
// Load complete news document
myXml.load("http://localhost/news.aspx");
```

We start by making sure the admin screen is invisible – we don't want users to see it unless they're specifically trying to add a news item. Then we create a `LoadVars` object, which we'll use later on to submit story details to the ASPX admin page.

3. Now we must add a few handler functions, so that we can navigate to and fro between the reader and admin pages. First, there's the add news button inside `reader_mc`, which needs to make the reader invisible, and make the admin screen visible:

```
reader_mc.addNews_btn.onRelease = function() {
   reader_mc._visible = false;
   admin_mc._visible = true;
}
```

4. The admin screen's Back button does the opposite, making `admin_mc` invisible, and `reader_mc` visible again:

```
admin_mc.back_btn.onRelease = function() {
   // Return to summary list
   admin_mc._visible = false;
   reader_mc._visible = true;
}
```

5. Now that users have a way to access the admin screen, we need to wire up its 'submit news' button, so that all the user-supplied text values will be sent to the admin ASPX:

```
admin_mc.submitNews_btn.onRelease = function() {
   with (admin_mc) {
     myNews.username = tbAddLogin;
     myNews.password = tbAddPassword;
     myNews.title = tbAddTitle;
     myNews.date = tbAddDate;
     myNews.shortdesc = tbAddShortDesc;
     myNews.longdesc = tbAddLongDesc;
     myNews.trash = new Date();
     _root.clock_mc._visible = true;
     _visible = false;
     myNews.sendAndLoad("http://localhost/addNews.aspx",
                    ➥ myNews, "POST");
   }
}
```

We now use the `LoadVars` object `myNews` that we created earlier, and store all the user-supplied values as properties inside it. We make the clock visible and hide the admin screen, while we `sendAndLoad()` these values to the server.

6. When Flash receives a response, we need to hide the clock, and check whether the request was successful:

```
myNews.onLoad = function(success) {
  _root.clock_mc._visible = false;
  if (success && myNews.status != "2") {
    errorMessage = "News successfully added.";
    myXml.load("http://localhost/news.aspx");
    reader_mc._visible = true;
  } else {
    showError(success+2);
    admin_mc._visible = true;
  }
};
```

If all went to plan, we show a message to that effect, reload the complete XML file (thereby updating the list with our new item), and make the news reader visible. Otherwise, we call `showError()` and show the admin screen again.

7. Of course, this time around, the possible errors we're considering are slightly different from before. If `success` is false, it indicates that we failed to write data to the server, whereas if it's true, we can only be calling `showError()` because the ASPX returned a status value of 2 (indicating that we're not authorized to add news items). All this means that we need to add a few extra lines to the definition for our `showError()` function:

```
showError = function(errorType) {
  switch (errorType) {
    case 0:    // The document failed to load
      errorMessage = "An error occurred while"
      errorMessage += " reading from XML document";
      break;
    case 1:    // The document loaded, but was malformed
      errorMessage = "Error: malformed XML document";
      break;
    case 2:    // The document failed to save
      errorMessage = "An error occurred while"
      errorMessage += " writing to XML Document.";
      break;
    case 3:    // The user was not authorized to add news
      errorMessage = "Invalid login-password"
      errorMessage += " combination. Please re-enter";
      break;
    default:
      errorMessage = "An unknown error has occurred";
  }
}
```

Now test the movie one last time, and try out the new feature. Assuming everything's gone to plan, you should be able to click back and forth between the news reader and admin screens, and add in news items of your own. Don't forget the values we hardwired earlier for authentication: `mylogin` and `mypassword`, both of which are case-sensitive.

Here's what a new item might look like on the admin screen:

Now click on GO! and you'll see the news story listed along with all the others, in summary and in full

We've now seen a few of the ways in which we can use files on the server to store data for our Flash.NET applications. Considering what we were doing in the examples there, the files served their purpose; but what about using information *about* the files?

Working with information about files

Earlier on, we looked at using the `FileStream` class from the `System.IO` namespace to work with data stored in files on the server. Well, there are several other classes in `System.IO` that we can make good use of.

For example, `FileInfo` and `DirectoryInfo` both contain properties and methods that tell us all about specified files and directories: we can find out what they're called, how big they are, and in the case of directories, what files and other directories they contain.

Image gallery

In this example, we're going to create an image gallery that will automatically display all the JPEG images contained in a specific folder on the server.

The ASP.NET file

We'll start by writing an ASP.NET web service that sends out the list of files from the specified folder, and then import that list into Flash.

1. Open Notepad, and enter the following code:

```
<%@ WebService Language="c#" class="PicList" %>
using System.IO;
using System.Web.Services;

public class PicList: System.Web.Services.WebService
{
  [WebMethod]
  public string[] getPicList() {
    string dirName = Server.MapPath("images");
    DirectoryInfo myDirInfo = new DirectoryInfo(dirName);
    FileInfo[] myFileInfo = myDirInfo.GetFiles();
    string[] fileNames = new string[myFileInfo.Length];
    for (int i=0; i<myFileInfo.Length; i++) {
      fileNames[i] = myFileInfo[i].Name;
    }
    return fileNames;
  }
};
```

Ultimately, all this web service does is to look for a folder called images, pick up the name of each file present in the folder and add it to a string array called fileNames. It then sends this array back to the server.

I've highlighted the crucial lines here, which create a DirectoryInfo object called myDirInfo, pull out an array of FileInfo objects (using its GetFiles() method) and retrieve the name property for each element in that array.

2. Save the file in your wwwroot folder as picList.asmx. Now create a folder called images in the same place, and put some JPEG image files inside.

3. Now point your browser at http://localhost/ piclist.asmx/getPicList? and you should get something like this (depending, of course, on what JPEG files you have in your own images folder):

As you can see, the ASP.NET web service has automatically converted our fileNames string array into an XML document, saving us the trouble of encoding it for ourselves.

```xml
<?xml version="1.0" encoding="utf-8" ?>
- <ArrayOfString
    xmlns:xsd="http://www.w3.org/2001/XMLSchema"
    xmlns:xsi="http://www.w3.org/2001/XMLSchema-
    instance" xmlns="http://tempuri.org/">
    <string>08040003.jpg</string>
    <string>08040005.jpg</string>
    <string>08040010.jpg</string>
    <string>08040014.jpg</string>
    <string>08040016.jpg</string>
    <string>08040017.jpg</string>
    <string>08040018.jpg</string>
    <string>08040019.jpg</string>
    <string>08040020.jpg</string>
    <string>08040022.jpg</string>
    <string>08040023.jpg</string>
    <string>08040024.jpg</string>
    <string>08040025.jpg</string>
    <string>08040026.jpg</string>
    <string>08040027.jpg</string>
</ArrayOfString>
```

The Flash movie

Now let's create the Flash client, which will call up the web service, and use the list of files it returns to present a gallery of all the JPEGs in the images folder.

1. Create a new movie, save it as picBrowser.fla, and set the stage size to 400x300 pixels.

2. First of all, we need to create a container for each loaded image, so make a new movie clip called MovContainer and draw a filled gray rectangle, 300 pixels wide and 225 high. Place an instance on the main timeline and call it container.

3. Next, we need to frame the loaded image, so create a new movie clip called MovFrame and draw a rectangle in it, 300 x 225 pixels again. Add an instance to the main timeline, and make sure it lines up with the container movie clip.

4. Now we need two buttons, so that users can navigate from one image to another. Create two buttons, with left and right arrows, and give them the instance names btnNext and btnPrev respectively.

5. Finally, we need some way to show the user messages, so add a dynamic textbox over the top of the frame, and use the Property inspector to set Var to txtMessage.

Your stage should now look something like this:

Now let's write the ActionScript to make the movie functional.

6. Create a new layer called Actions. Select the first frame of this layer, and add the following code:

```
myxml = new XML();
myxml.ignoreWhite = true;
myxml.load("Piclist.asmx/getPicList");
myxml.onLoad = readList;
```

7. We start by calling our ASP.NET web service to load in the list of files in our images folder. As you can see, we give the URL as `piclist.asmx/getpicList` and not `Piclist.asmx` (as we would have done to call a normal ASP.NET page). This just tells ASP.NET that we want to call the `getPicList` method of the `piclist` web service.

8. Next, we set the variable `currImg` to 1. We'll use this value to keep track of which image we're looking at. We disable the 'Previous' button, since we know we'll be looking at the very first image in the list, and display a loading message.

```
var currImg = 1;
btnPrev.enabled = false;
txtMessage = "Loading image list...";
```

9. We now define the `readList()` function, which is invoked when we receive XML data from the server. If the XML loads successfully, we pluck out our list of image names, store them in an array, and show the first image.

```
function readList(success) {
   if (success == true) {
      //Remove the loading message
      txtMessage = "";
      //Parse the received XML and store in an array
      for (i=0; i<myxml.firstChild.childNodes.length; i++) {
         arrImages[i] = myxml.firstChild.childNodes[i]
            ➥ .firstChild.nodeValue;
```

continues overleaf

```
    }
    showImage(currImg);
```

If not, we show an error message:

```
    } else {
      //Output an error message
      txtMessage = "An unknown error occurred!!!";
    }
  }
```

10. The `showImage()` function is responsible for loading in each new image, and displaying a name and number at the top of the stage:

```
function showImage(imgIndex) {
  txtMessage = imgIndex + ". " + arrImages[imgIndex];
  //Load this image into the movie clip
  container_mc.loadMovie("images/"+arrImages[imgIndex]);
};
```

11. Finally, we have an `onRelease` event handler function for each of the buttons:

```
btnNext.onRelease = function() {
  if (currImg<myxml.firstChild.childNodes.length) {
    showImage(++currImg);
    btnPrev.enabled = true;
  } else {
    this.enabled = false;
  }
};

btnPrev.onRelease = function() {
  if (currImg>0) {
    showImage(--currImg);
    btnNext.enabled = true;
  } else {
    this.enabled = false;
  }
};
```

Apart from updating `currImg` and calling the `showImage()` function, these handler functions make sure that the buttons are enabled and disabled as appropriate to let the user navigate from one end of the image list to the other, and no further.

All that's left now is to publish the movie to wwwroot and call it up from your browser. Make sure you have a collection of JPEG images (ideally all 300x225 pixels in size) in a folder called images, just under wwwroot, an you can expect to see results like this:

A simple web service like the one we've used here can be very useful in all sorts of situations, since it can be accessed by any client that has a direct line of sight to your web server. But we're not the only ones who can write web services – there are plenty more out there on the Web, and they too can be a fantastic source of data for our apps.

Working with data from the Web

We've already seen how to load XML data into Flash from files on our server machine, and from ASP.NET pages and web services on the local server. When it comes to loading XML from other sources though, it's a different ballgame. The sandbox security restrictions of the Flash Player won't let you load XML from anywhere outside the domain of the host server (the server responsible for sending out the SWF file in the first place).

Fortunately, these constraints only apply to the Flash player. We can still load data from other sites into Flash, but we need to go via an ASP.NET page that's in the same domain. It will act as middleman, loading data from the external resource and then relaying it to the SWF.

ASP.NET lets us use the WebRequest and WebResponse objects (defined in the System.NET namespace) in conjunction with the stream reader objects we used earlier to connect to web-based resources. Let's look at an example that makes use of them.

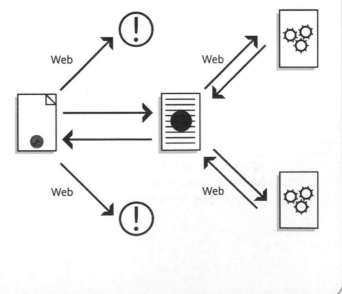

Using TerraServer

We're going to use Microsoft's TerraServer web service to power a town-locator tool, which will let users type in the name of a town or city and show them where in the US they can find places with that name. We'll use the web service to retrieve latitude and longitude values for each location, and then use Flash to show that point on a map.

There are three parts to this application:

- The Flash movie, which lets the user input the name of the place they're interested in locating, and then shows its location on the map.

- The ASP.NET page, which takes a place name (as submitted with the page request), uses it to call up the TerraServer web service, picks up the response and passes it back to Flash.

- The TerraServer web service itself, which you can access online at http://terraserver.homeadvisor.msn.com/TerraService.asmx.

It's all too easy to forget about the last part of an application like this, but it's actually the most important – a problem at the web service can make or break your app. Your own files may be working perfectly, but if the server at the other end has been taken down for maintenance, that'll count for nothing – the app just won't work!

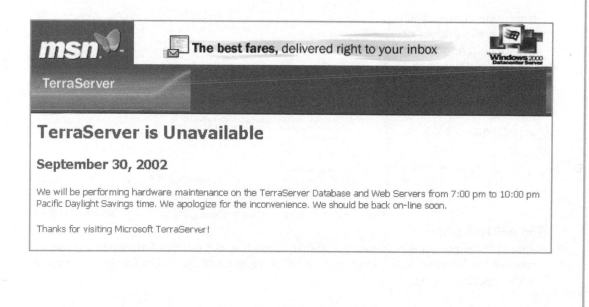

msn The best fares, delivered right to your inbox

TerraServer

TerraServer is Unavailable

September 30, 2002

We will be performing hardware maintenance on the TerraServer Database and Web Servers from 7:00 pm to 10:00 pm Pacific Daylight Savings time. We apologize for the inconvenience. We should be back on-line soon.

Thanks for visiting Microsoft TerraServer!

So, before you go any further, call it up for yourself, check that everything looks okay, and maybe even try out the test page to call a few of the web methods:

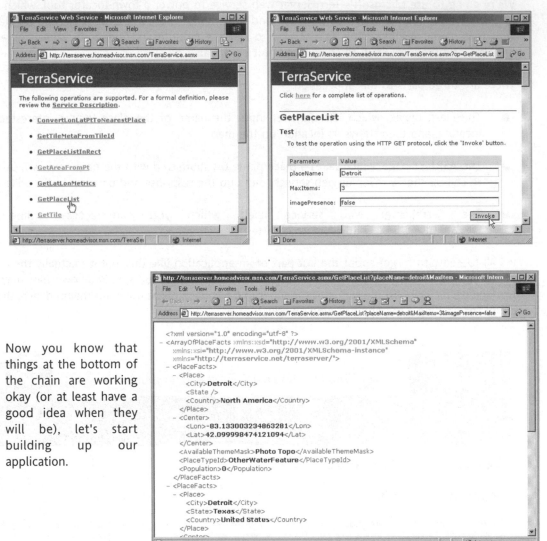

Now you know that things at the bottom of the chain are working okay (or at least have a good idea when they will be), let's start building up our application.

The ASP.NET page

First of all, we're going to create the ASP.NET page that will call the TerraServer web service and retrieve the information we want: namely latitude and longitude values for each location it finds with a specified name.

1.   Create a new text document and save it in wwwroot as placeLocator.aspx. Now add the following code:

```
<%@ Page language="C#" %>
<%@ Import namespace="System.Net" %>
<%@ Import namespace="System.IO" %>

<script runat="server">
  void Page_Load(Object sender, EventArgs e) {

      string place = Request.QueryString["place"];
      WebResponse objResponse;

      string url,query;

      url = "http://terraserver.homeadvisor.msn.com/";
      url += "TerraService.asmx/GetPlaceList";

      query = "?placeName=" + place;
      query += "&MaxItems=10&imagePresence=false";
      WebRequest objRequest = System.Net.HttpWebRequest
                     ➥ .Create(url+query);
objResponse = objRequest.GetResponse();

using (StreamReader sr = new StreamReader(
                    ➥ objResponse.GetResponseStream()) ) {
    string result = sr.ReadToEnd();
    sr.Close();
}

//Close the response to free resources.
objResponse.Close();

Response.ContentType="text/xml";
Response.Write(result);
  }
</script>
```

We hook up to the TerraServer web service using the WebRequest and WebResponse objects.
We pass the place name as a query string and finally send the received output to the output
stream.

As a test to make sure that our ASP.NET Page is working okay, fire up your browser and enter http://local host/placeLocator.aspx?Place= Birmingham in the address bar. You should get an output like this:

As you can see, the web service has returned a list of all the places in the US named as Birmingham, along with some additional details. We are only concerned with the longitude and the latitude of the place, and we'll be using this information in Flash.

If you're accessing the Web via a 'proxy server' (most probably the case if your machine is part of a company's internal network or **intranet**), then you'll need to add one more line before the page works:

```
WebRequest objRequest = System.Net.HttpWebRequest
                    ➥ .Create(url+query);
objRequest.Proxy = new
                ➥ WebProxy("http://proxyAddress:portNumber/");
objResponse = objRequest.GetResponse();
```

You'll need to replace `proxyAddress` and `portNumber` with values specific to your system. If you don't happen to know the address and port number of your proxy server, you can check it out for yourself by looking in your Internet Explorer settings (under Tools > Internet Options > Connections > LAN Settings), or just ask your system administrator for the information.

The Flash Movie

Now let's create the front-end for our application.

1. Create a new Flash document and save it as `placeLocator.fla`. Set the stage dimensions to 700x500 pixels, and change the background color to blue.

2. The stage is very simple to set up: we just need a map (`map_mc`), a loading clock (`clock_mc`), an input text field (Var: `tbCity`), and a button (`submit_btn`). Here's how they should look once they're all set out:

    If you're using the map image that's included in the download files, you should make sure that it's 600 pixels wide and 400 pixels high, so that the default settings match up okay. If you opt to use your own map, you'll need to work out calibration settings for yourself.

3. The other thing we need to do before getting stuck into ActionScript is to create a movie clip that will serve as our marker, indicating where places are on the map.

As you can see, I've chosen to use a simple circle with a red-black radial fill, and set its Linkage properties to export the movie to ActionScript with the name MovPoint. It only needs to be 10 pixels across, but make sure the registration point is in the center of the circle, as this will be what we use to pinpoint our locations.

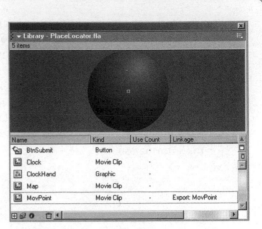

4. Now switch back to the main timeline and create a new layer called Actions. Add a keyframe in the first frame, and attach the following script:

    ```
    mapWidth =   600;
    mapHeight = 400;

    startLon = 126;
    endLon = 65;
    startLat = 50;
    endLat = 23;
    ```

    We begin by setting some variables that calibrate geographical coordinates to the pixel coordinates of our map. I've deliberately chosen to use a simple projection so that the calculations don't get needlessly complicated.

5. We hide the clock movie, and set up the XML object that we'll be using to gather our data:

    ```
    clock_mc._visible = false;

    myXML = new XML();
    myXML.ignoreWhite = true;
    myXML.onLoad = showPoints;
    ```

6. Next, we define a handler function for the button. When a user clicks on it, Flash will show the clock again, take the name of the location set in tbCity (via the input text box), and use it to load data from our ASP.NET page into myXML.

    ```
    btnSubmit.onRelease = function() {
      clock_mc._visible = true;
      myDate = new Date();
    url = "http://localhost/PlaceLocator.aspx";
    query = "?place="+tbCity+"&trash="+escape(myDate);
    ```

continues overleaf

```
                    myXML.load(url + query);
  };
```

7. Once Flash receives the data, the `myXML.onLoad` event will trigger the following function, `showPoints()`. This is responsible for most of the hard work involved in our application:

```
function showPoints() {
  clock_mc._visible = false;

  placeFacts = myXML.firstChild.childNodes;
```

The data's loaded now, so we hide the clock and make an array called `placeFacts` to hold all the document's `placeFacts` nodes. Next, we need to loop through each of those nodes:

```
for (i=0; i<placeFacts.length 1; i++) {
  centernode = placeFacts[i].firstChild.nextSibling;

  lon = centernode.firstChild.;
  lon = lon.firstChild.nodeValue;
  lon = Math.abs(lon);

  lat = centernode.firstChild.nextSibling;
  lat = lat.firstChild.nodeValue;
  lat = Math.abs(lat);

  // Attach a point movie clip and place it
  pointx = mapWidth * (lon-startLon)/(endLon-startLon);
  pointy = mapHeight * (lat-startLat)/(endLat-startLat);

  map_mc.attachMovie("MovPoint", "MovPoint"+i, i+100);
  map_mc["MovPoint"+i]._x = pointx;
  map_mc["MovPoint"+i]._y = pointy;
  }
}
```

For each one, we track down the `center` element, and pull out values for latitude and longitude. We then use our calibration values to convert these into coordinates on the stage, and finally attach MovPoint movie clips to the appropriate points on the map movie clip.

We're now ready to export and test the movie. Save the SWF into your wwwroot folder as placeLocator.swf, and point your browser at http://localhost/placeLocator.swf. Enter the name of a city and press the Go button:

You should see results similar to these:

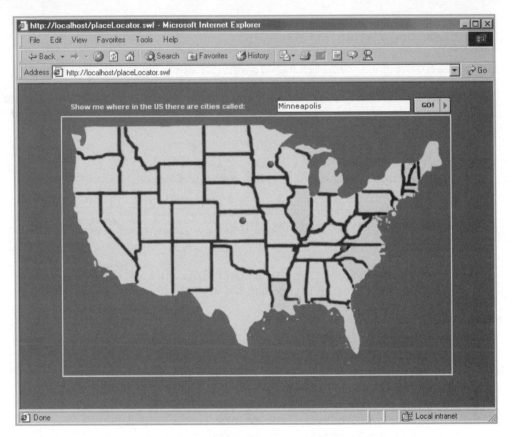

Summary

In the course of this chapter, we've looked at a few different ways that ASP.NET can tap into server files, reading data out of them and writing data back into them. Along the way, we've built some practical examples that demonstrate all these techniques, and include functionality that a Flash movie simply couldn't manage on its own. You may well find them useful for a variety of purposes, and should be able to use, re-use, and customize them all to your heart's content.

We've also seen how to access information about the server files, and finally struck out onto the Web in search of new and useful data.

So, we've begun to raise the bar on what's possible with Flash and .NET. We're going to raise it even further in the next chapter, when we'll take a look at some of the other places where we can access and store data. This is only the beginning...

chapter 4: **Databases**

If you're looking for effective ways to store data for your application, you can't afford to ignore databases. In many ways, they serve the same purpose as the files we used in Chapter 3: storing away data for as long as we like, in a place from which we can easily retrieve it when it's needed. So what's wrong with files – why should we bother using a database?

Well, the files we used in the last chapter all contained fairly small amounts of data. Whether it was flat data or XML, the data we stored was weighing in at just a few kilobytes. Even if you put an application like the news reader online, it'd probably be quite a while before the XML file storing all your news stories grew beyond a few tens of Megabytes – unless you allowed all your friends and colleagues to add items for themselves!

At that point though, however long it takes to reach, you might start to notice the app getting a little sluggish, as ASP.NET (or even worse, Flash) has to sift through a massive list of news stories looking for the one you want to read. If that's happening once a month for example, and none of your users mind too much if they lose all the month-old news stories, you're probably okay. You could maybe drop any stories that are more than a month old.

However, if you *need* to deal with lots of traffic and potentially huge quantities of data, you need a data store that's properly equipped to handle it, and not just a text file with a couple of `for` loops. That's where databases come in.

Understanding databases

The most common type of database you're likely to encounter is a **relational database**, which uses tables (of columns and rows, not the kitchen variety) to store data. A single database can contain several tables, each one representing a different set of information. By defining clear relationships between the different tables, the database can store huge amounts of complex information without bloating up nearly so fast as an equivalent XML file would.

For example, an online music store might use a relational database containing tables to represent CDs, customers, and customer purchases.

Customer#	Name	Phone
0	David	555-6541
1	Pallav	555-8281
2	Gregg	555-6732
3	Todd	555-1234

CUSTOMER TABLE

Purchase#	Customer#	Product#
0	3	4089
1	3	6572
2	1	3013
3	0	2558
4	2	3013

PURCHASE TABLE

Product #	Format	Title	Artist
2258	single	Up	Peter Gabriel
3013	single	Melody A.M.	Röyksopp
4089	double	Aphorodite's Child	Vangelis
6572	boxset	Andy Warhol	Velvet Underground

PRODUCT TABLE

Say we tried storing all this data as XML, as we've done in the last couple of chapters; maybe each `customer` element would contain a list of CDs bought. The only trouble is, if two customers bought the same CD, we'd end up duplicating all the information we had about that CD. So how about we turn it around, and list customers inside `cd` elements? We'd hit exactly the same problem: as soon as one customer buys two different CDs, we end up duplicating the customer details in two different `cd` elements.

Apart from this problem of **redundant** data adding to the size of the data file, there's a performance issue to consider too. What if you want to get information on a specific purchase? If it's right at the top of the XML document, then looping through one line at a time won't be a problem. But what if it's right at the end, and what if the document's so massive that it takes the server minutes or even hours to read through the thousands and thousands of preceding elements before giving you a result? By contrast, relational databases are specifically designed to make it as easy (and quick) as possible to track down specific rows of data.

Enough talk. Let's start making use of some of this fabled power and efficiency. In order to create a database and work with tables and records inside it, we need two things:

- A simple grasp of **SQL**, the standard language for making and manipulating databases

- A **database engine** program that will interpret the SQL commands and carry them out

We'll start off by dealing with the second of these – once the database engine is up and running, we can learn about SQL by seeing it in action.

Introducing MSDE

MSDE (short for 'Microsoft SQL Server Desktop Engine') is a free database engine from the same company that brought us ASP.NET. It's basically designed as a cut-down version of Microsoft's flagship database product, SQL Server, so that application developers can test their database code locally without having to sell their grandmothers to pay for multiple copies of the full version.

> *Microsoft SQL Server is the preferred database solution for most professional ASP.NET developers. You can find out about its features and even download a 120-day trial version from* www.microsoft.com/sql/. *For more information on MSDE, visit* www.microsoft.com/sql/techinfo/development/ 2000/MSDE2000.asp.

MSDE offers all the core features from SQL Server, so it has the advantage of being compatible with the database engines you're likely to find on a production grade .NET server. What's more, it comes as part of the .NET Framework SDK, so there's no need to track down a download site it's already there on your machine!

Installing and configuring MSDE

1. The first step here is to locate the MSDE setup files. Assuming you installed the .NET Framework SDK using the default options, you should find them in `C:\Program Files\Microsoft.NET\ FrameworkSDK\ Samples\Setup\msde\`.

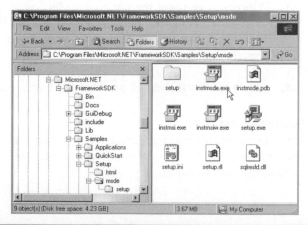

Now we're ready to configure and install the database engine.

2. Double-click on setup.ini and it should automatically open up in Notepad. The contents of this file control how MSDE will be installed. In this case they just specify an instance name of NetSDK; we'll be using this name later on to let ASP.NET know what database engine we want it to connect to.

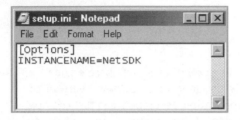 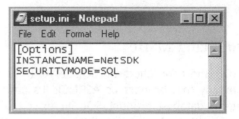

We just need to add one new line to the end: SECURITYMODE=SQL. This will make sure that can add and configure our own database logins (instead of leaving it to use the much less flexible security settings that are built into Windows itself).

> *Unlike other programs like Notepad or Flash, MSDE runs as a service. This means that instead of giving you a flashy interface in a window complete with an entry on the menu bar, it starts up automatically along with Windows, and lurks quietly in the background doing jobs for other programs.*
>
> *There are other ways to start and stop the MSDE service – look in* Control Panel > Administrative Tools > Services *under* MSSQL$NetSDK *if you're interested – but a good old-fashioned reboot is still the most straightforward.*

3. Once you've saved the setup.ini file, make sure you've shut down any other programs that are running, and double-click on instmsde.exe to run the MSDE setup program. It'll whirr and click its way through the automated install, and when it's done MSDE should be installed and ready to run.

4. Once the installation's finished, reboot your computer to start up MSDE.

Database security

One of the most important features that virtually all database engines include is built-in security. Rather than letting anybody muck around with their data, they insist on having users provide a valid login and password.

Right now there's only one user account set up in our MSDE instance: the system administrator's account (username: sa) and by default it has a blank password. Any user logged into the database using this account will have full rights to perform any database administration tasks: adding and dropping (in other words, deleting) databases, adding new login accounts, and setting permissions on them.

Obviously, leaving the sa password blank can pose a massive security risk, so it's important to change it as soon as possible. We can do this very easily from the Windows command prompt. Just press WINDOWS+R to call up the Run dialog, then type cmd and click on OK to call up the command prompt.

Now type in the following and hit ENTER to set the default sa password to secret:

```
C:\>osql -E -S (local)\NetSDK -Q "EXEC sp_password '','secret','sa'"
```

Leave the command prompt open, as we'll be using it again in just a moment.

Setting up a sample database

To complete the upcoming database examples, you need to install the sample pubs database included with the .NET Framework SDK samples. The database is modeled after a book publishing company, and is often used in SQL Server documentation. Unfortunately, the MSDE does not include visual utilities for administering databases, so we will need to use the OSQL command-line utility to complete this exercise.

1. Back at the command prompt, type in the following and hit ENTER, to change the working directory to the one we need:

   ```
   C:\>cd "C:\Program Files\Microsoft.NET\FrameworkSDK\Samples\Setup"
   ```

2. Now use the following command to set up the pubs database:

   ```
   C:\>osql -E -S (local)\\NetSDK -i instpubs.sql
   ```

   You'll probably now see a lot of numbers flow across your screen. Don't worry – this is perfectly normal. Eventually, you'll see a fresh command prompt C:\>, at which point the pubs database should be installed.

3. The last step is to create a database login and assign it permissions to the `pubs` database. Type in each of the following commands and hit ENTER after each line.

```
C:\>osql -E -S (local)\NetSDK -Q "sp_addlogin 'pubsadmin', 'password'"

C:\>osql -E -S (local)\NetSDK -d pubs -Q "sp_grantdbaccess 'pubsadmin'"

C:\>osql -E -S (local)\NetSDK -d pubs -Q "sp_addrolemember
                              ➥'db_owner', 'pubsadmin'"
```

The first statement creates a new login with the user name `pubsadmin` and password `password`. The second grants user `pubsadmin` access to the `pubs` database, while the third adds `pubsadmin` to the `db_owner` security role, giving it full control over the entire `pubs` database.

Now that we have all the privileges we need to run our examples, let's start playing with the `pubs` database.

Talking to databases with .NET

The .NET Framework has a pretty comprehensive set of tools for accessing and manipulating databases. Once again, we find they're all in the form of object classes – in this case, defined in a small group of namespaces whose names all begin with `System.Data`:

- `System.Data` contains lots of general data manipulation classes.

- `System.Data.SqlClient` provides classes that help us to create and use connections to SQL Server (and therefore to instances of MSDE as well).

- `System.Data.OleDb` provides classes for making and using OleDB connections, which sacrifice speed and power for compatibility with a broader range of database engines, including Access and Oracle.

Taken together, the classes defined in these (and a few other) `System.Data` namespaces are usually referred to as ADO.NET. They provide a consistent model of data access and data representation across all supported databases.

Since we'll be using MSDE, we're going to focus on the `System.Data.SqlClient` objects. However, you might want to bear in mind that most of the concepts and techniques we'll see can just as easily be applied to the equivalent OleDB objects, with hardly any changes made at all.

Connecting to the database

The first step in accessing any database is to create and open a database connection. In the following example we are going to demonstrate how to connect to our local instance of MSDE and open the sample pubs database.

Create a new text file, and save it as connecting.aspx in your wwwroot folder. Now add the following code:

```
<%@ Page Language="C#" %>
<%@ Import NameSpace="System.Data" %>
<%@ Import NameSpace="System.Data.SqlClient" %>

<script runat="server">
  void Page_Load(object sender, System.EventArgs e) {
    // change the following cnnString to match your
    // own database connection settings
    string cnnString="";
    cnnString += "server=(local)\\NetSDK;database=pubs;";
    cnnString += "uid=pubsadmin;pwd=password;";

    SqlConnection sqlCnn = new SqlConnection(cnnString);

    sqlCnn.Open();
    Response.Write("<p>Connection is open!</p>");

    sqlCnn.Close();
    Response.Write("<p>Connection is closed!</p>");
  }
</script>
```

Let's take a quick look at the most important lines of code here. Once we've imported the required namespaces, we declare a **connection string**. This lets ASP.NET know the location of the database engine, the name of the database to connect to, and the login credentials to use. Note that .NET treats backslashes as special control characters – we therefore need to double them up in the server name to avoid confusing it.

We then use the connection string to create an instance of the SqlConnection class; this gives us a fully configured connection object, but not an active connection just yet. We need to explicitly call its Open() and Close() methods to open and close the connection.

Now, point your browser at http://localhost/connecting.aspx. If the connection settings are correct, you should see the output "Connection is open!" and "Connection is closed!" appear in your browser.

Alternative connection strings

If you're using SQL Server Desktop, Standard or Enterprise Editions instead of the MSDE, you'll probably need to change the server name in the connection string. For a local instance of SQL Server, use:

```
server=(local);database=pubs;uid=pubsadmin;pwd=password;
```

To connect to an instance of SQL Server that's running on another machine, use the following, replacing MACHINENAME with the actual name of the machine:

```
server=MACHINENAME;database=pubs;uid=pubsadmin;pwd=password;
```

If SQL Server is running on another machine on your network, you may need to obtain a login and password from your local database administrator.

Retrieving data

Now that we can connect to a database, we can use the database connection to retrieve rows from a table. In this example, we'll use SQL's SELECT command to get author information from the authors table in the sample pubs database.

Create another new text file with the following code, and save it as authors.aspx.

```
<%@ Page Language="C#" %>
<%@ Import NameSpace="System.Data" %>
<%@ Import NameSpace="System.Data.SqlClient" %>

<script runat="server">
  void Page_Load(object sender, System.EventArgs e){
    string cnnString = "";
    cnnString += "server=(local)\\NetSDK;database=pubs;";
    cnnString += "uid=pubsadmin;pwd=password;";

    SqlConnection sqlCnn = new SqlConnection(cnnString);
```

continues overleaf

```
        sqlCnn.Open();

        string sql = "";
        sql += "SELECT au_fname, au_lname, phone FROM authors";

        SqlCommand sqlCmd = new SqlCommand(sql, sqlCnn);

        SqlDataReader authorReader = sqlCmd.ExecuteReader();

        while (authorReader.Read()) {
          Response.Write("<br>");
          Response.Write(authorReader.GetString(0));
          Response.Write(" ");
          Response.Write(authorReader.GetString(1));
          Response.Write(" : ");
          Response.Write(authorReader.GetString(2));
        }

        authorReader.Close();
        sqlCnn.Close();
      }
  </script>
```

The first dozen or so lines of code are just the same as our previous database connection example. We import the relevant namespaces and use a connection string to initialize a SqlConnection object. We then open the database connection, and declare a string to represent our SELECT query for author information.

SELECT returns data from one or more tables in a database – here's the basic syntax we use:

```
SELECT column_name_1, column_name_2, ...
FROM table_name
WHERE search_condition
```

In this example, we select the author's first name, last name, and phone number from the authors table. Various other pieces of information are also defined in the table, but these are the only ones we're interested in for now.

We then send the SQL command (or **query**) to the database by creating a SqlCommand object, specifying the query itself along with the relevant sqlCnn connection object.

To retrieve the results from our query, we use the ExecuteReader() method on the SqlCommand object. This returns a SqlDataReader object (which we call authorReader), designed to give us very fast (forward-only, read-only) access to all the rows of data returned from the database in response to our SQL query.

In the next few lines, we use a `while` loop to iterate through all these rows of data. We call the `Read()` method on `authorReader`, attempting to retrieve one line of data at a time, and checking the return value to see if we've succeeded.

We then use the `GetString()` method to access each of the three columns of data returned in any given row. Just as with an array, we reference the first column (author's first name) using index 0, the second (author's last name) using 1, and the third (phone number) using 2.

> *The SqlDataReader implements several more similar methods for retrieving other types of data. For example,* `GetBoolean()` *returns a Boolean,* `GetDateTime()` *returns a DataTime object,* `GetFloat()` *returns a floating point number, and* `GetInt32()` *returns a 32-bit signed integer.*

Once we've read the last record, `Read()` will return `false`, so we stop looping.

Finally, we close the `authorReader` and `sqlCnn` objects. In fact, if we should forget to do this, ASP.NET will close the connections for us automatically. All the same, it's good practice to tidy up like this, as the sooner you can free up system resources, the more efficient (not to mention considerate) your programs will be.

Running this sample ASP.NET page should produce output similar to this:

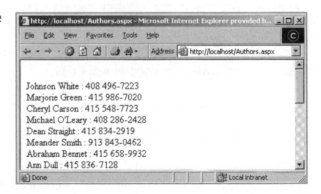

Inserting data

Now let's look at how to use ADO.NET to insert new rows of data into a database table. In this example we will look at SQL's `INSERT INTO` command and use it to add a new row of book publisher information to the `publishers` table in the sample `pubs` database.

Create a new text file with the following code and save it as `publishersInsert.aspx`.

```
<%@ Page Language="C#" %>
<%@ Import Namespace="System.Data" %>
<%@ Import Namespace="System.Data.SqlClient" %>

<script runat="server">
  void Page_Load(object sender, System.EventArgs e) {

    string cnnString = "";
    cnnString += "server=(local)\\NetSDK;database=pubs;";
    cnnString += "uid=pubsadmin;pwd=password;";

    SqlConnection sqlCnn = new SqlConnection(cnnString);

    string sql = "";
    sql += "INSERT INTO publishers";
    sql += " (pub_id, pub_name, city, state, country)";
    sql += " VALUES";
    sql += " ('9991', 'Music City Publishers',";
    sql += " 'Memphis', 'TN', 'USA')";

    SqlCommand sqlCmd = new SqlCommand(sql, sqlCnn);

    sqlCnn.Open();
    int rowsAdded = sqlCmd.ExecuteNonQuery();
    Response.Write("Rows Added: " + rowsAdded);
    sqlCnn.Close();
  }
</script>
```

The first difference you should notice is that our SQL command has changed to an INSERT INTO statement. This is a command that's used to add new rows to an existing table. Here's the basic syntax we use:

```
INSERT INTO table_name (column_name_1, column_name_2 [, ...n])
VALUES (value1, value2 [, ...n])
```

The publishers table has five columns:

- pub_id contains each publisher's unique identifier
- pub_name contains each publisher's company name
- city contains the name of the city in which the publisher is based
- state contains the name of the publisher's state
- country contains the name of the publisher's country

In this example, we want to add a new record to the table, for publisher called 'Music City Publishers' based in Memphis, TN USA. To do so, we choose a unique publisher identifier and insert the row using the following command:

```
INSERT INTO publishers (pub_id,pub_name,city,state,country)
VALUES ('9991','Music City Publishers','Memphis','TN','USA')
```

> *Many database tables contain a special integer or numeric column declared with an **identity** property. This instructs the database engine to automatically increment the column value every time a new row is added. By doing this, we can make sure that every row in the table has a unique value for the associated column.*

After creating the `SqlCommand` object and opening the database connection, the next step is to execute the SQL `INSERT INTO` command. This time around, we use the `SqlCommand`'s `ExecuteNonQuery()` method, which is optimized for executing SQL commands that don't return any data rows. However, for certain commands (this one included) it *will* return the number of rows affected – we store this number away in a variable named (imaginatively enough) `rowsAffected`.

Finally, we use `Response.Write()` to write the results of our executed SQL command to the browser and then close the database connection. Running this sample ASP.NET page should produce output like this:

Updating data

Next let's look at how to update table data. In this example, we'll look at the SQL `UPDATE` command and use it to change the information we inserted into the `publishers` table the last time around.

Create a new text file with the following code and save it as `publishersUpdate.aspx`.

```
<%@ Page Language="C#" %>
```

```
<%@ import Namespace="System.Data" %>
<%@ import Namespace="System.Data.SqlClient" %>

<script runat="server">
  void Page_Load(object sender, System.EventArgs e) {
    string cnnString = "";
    cnnString = "server=(local)\\NetSDK;database=pubs;";
    cnnString += "uid=pubsadmin;pwd=password;";

    SqlConnection sqlCnn = new SqlConnection(cnnString);

    string sql = "";
    sql += "UPDATE publishers";
    sql += " SET city = 'Nashville'";
    sql += " WHERE pub_id = '9991'";

    SqlCommand sqlCmd = new SqlCommand(sql, sqlCnn);
    sqlCnn.Open();
    int rowsUpdated = sqlCmd.ExecuteNonQuery();

    Response.Write("Rows Updated: " + rowsUpdated);

    sqlCnn.Close();
  }
</script>
```

When you analyze the code in this example you should see that little has changed from our previous example on inserting rows except the SQL statement itself. In this case, we use the SQL UPDATE command to update the publisher we added in the previous example. Here's the basic syntax for the SQL UPDATE command:

```
UPDATE table_name
SET column_name_1 = value1, column_name_2 = value2, ...
WHERE search_criteria
```

In our example, we are updating the city location of Music City Publishers, changing it from Memphis to Nashville. To ensure that we only update Music City Publishers and not any other publisher in the table, we specify the publisher's unique identifier in the WHERE clause.

```
UPDATE publishers
SET city = 'Nashville'
WHERE pub_id = '9991'
```

The UPDATE statement can be used to update more than one row of data at a time, depending on the search conditions specified in the WHERE clause. For example, to change all the publishers in the database with the country code 'USA' to 'US', we could use the following SQL UPDATE statement:

```
UPDATE publishers
SET country = 'US'
WHERE country = 'USA'
```

To summarize, we start by defining the database connection, the SqlCommand instance, and then execute the command using ExecuteNonQuery(), since we're not expecting to get any rows of data back. We then send the results back to the browser, so running this page should give you a result like this:

Deleting data

Rounding off our quick tour of database basics, let's see how to delete records from a table. In this example, we'll see how to use SQL's DELETE command to remove the row of publisher data that we played with in the last couple of examples.

Create a new text file with the following code and save it as publishersDelete.aspx.

```
<%@ Page Language="C#" %>
<%@ Import NameSpace="System.Data" %>
<%@ Import NameSpace="System.Data.SqlClient" %>

<script runat="server">
  void Page_Load(object sender, System.EventArgs e) {
    string cnnString = "";
    cnnString = "server=(local)\\NetSDK;database=pubs;";
    cnnString += "uid=pubsadmin;pwd=password;";

    SqlConnection sqlCnn = new SqlConnection(cnnString);

    string sql = "DELETE FROM publishers"
       + " WHERE pub_id = '9991'";
SqlCommand sqlCmd = new SqlCommand(sql, sqlCnn);
    sqlCnn.Open();
```

continues overleaf

```
        int rowsDeleted = sqlCmd.ExecuteNonQuery();

        Response.Write("Rows Deleted: " + rowsDeleted);
    sqlCnn.Close();
      }
</script>
```

Again, little has changed from our previous examples, except for the SQL statement itself. In this case, we use DELETE to update the publisher we added in the previous example. Here's the basic syntax we use for this command:

```
DELETE FROM table_name
WHERE search_criteria
```

In this example, we want to delete Music City Publishers from the publishers table. To make sure that we only delete Music City Publishers (and none of the other publishers in the table), we need to specify the publisher's unique identifier in the WHERE clause:

```
DELETE FROM publishers
WHERE pub_id = '9991'
```

> *Use statements like this with caution:* DELETE *can easily be used to remove more than one row of data at a time, and the number of records it wipes depends entirely on the conditions you specify in the* WHERE *clause. If you don't specify a* WHERE *clause (or simply forget), then it'll quite happily delete every row from the table!*

Once again, we began by defining the database connection and SqlCommand instance, then executed the command using the ExecuteNonQuery() method and wrote the results to the browser using Response.Write(). Run this page from your browser, and you should see the following:

Message board sample application

Now that we've looked at the basics of database access from ASP.NET, it's about time we brought Flash back into the story. In this section, we're look at putting these and other DB techniques into practice as we explore a Flash-fronted database-driven message board example.

Design goals and requirements

Before we start building our message board, let's set out some clear goals and requirements for the application, so that we can design the best possible solution. To keep things as simple as possible, here's a list of the requirements I've already identified, along with corresponding design decisions.

1. **Allow users to browse all messages that have been added to a message board.** Use Flash MX to provide a user interface for browsing a list of discussion topics. Selecting a given message in the list will let users view full message details, such as the message text, the username of whoever posted the message, and the date on which the message was posted. Use ASP.NET to provide the list of messages and message details in an XML format.

2. **Allow new users to register under a unique user name, with a minimum length of three characters, a password with a minimum length of four characters, and a unique e-mail address.** Use Flash MX to provide an interface for submitting registration information. Use ASP.NET to accept the registration information and provide appropriate feedback regarding the success of the user registration.

3. **Allow registered users to log in to the message board.** Use Flash MX to provide an interface for submitting user credentials to be validated. Use ASP.NET to accept the form submission and provide appropriate feedback regarding the success of the user validation.

4. **Allow registered users to add new discussion topics or reply to existing messages.** Use Flash MX to provide an interface for submitting new messages. Use ASP.NET to capture the new message submission and provide appropriate feedback regarding the success of the update.

5. **Must be quick to load and very responsive to users browsing or adding messages.** Use Flash MX to provide a dynamic interface, which will communicate with ASP.NET in such a way as to load only the *minimum* number of messages required to populate the current message list.

6. **Must support thousands of messages and hundreds of users.** Use SQL Server (or MSDE) database for storing registered user information and messages.

This last requirement is where storing messages and users in a text or XML file would totally fail to be an appropriate solution. This is even more true taking into consideration number 5, where we see that the interface must be quick to load and responsive to user interaction.

To keep interactions between the Flash MX interface and the ASP.NET database access code as simple as possible, we're going to build the ASP.NET as a web service. This way, all our DB access code will be contained in one file, and we can simply use Flash's XML object to call up its different methods as and when required.

Designing the database

Our first step in figuring out how the database will hang together is to design the tables that our message board application will need to use. Remember, we have two basic forms of information: messages and user registrations. It therefore makes sense to design two tables: one for messages and one for user registrations.

Consider the following diagram.

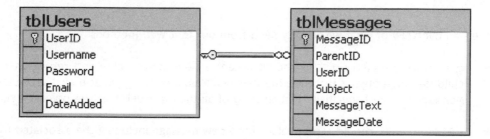

In tblUsers, UserID is marked out as the **primary key** for the table. This guarantees that values stored in the UserID column will be unique for each and every row in the table. To make sure that our tblMessages data stays consistent, we shouldn't allow any values of UserID that don't appear in the tblUsers table.

Any given user may post more than one message, so we can say that the tblUsers table has a 'one-to-many' relationship with tblMessages table. To enforce this relationship and keep data in tblMessages consistent with tblUsers, we create a Primary Key/Foreign Key (PK/FK) relationship based on the UserID column in both tables.

The UserID column in tblMessages has a Foreign Key constraint that points to the Primary Key of tblUsers. As you'll see later, a PK/FK relationship also facilitates queries that require data from two or more tables to be 'joined' together to create a single set of results.

In designing the tblMessages table, we use MessageID as the primary key, guaranteeing that each message will have a unique identifier. Message boards usually support hierarchies of parent-child messages (or **threads**), so we also have a self-referencing ParentID column, which we'll use to store the MessageID of the parent message.

Designing the ASP.NET web service

We now need to determine what methods our web service will need to expose. Thinking back to the list of application requirements, we need to ask: what actions will require information to be sent to and from the server? At the very least, we'll need to be able to do the following:

- Retrieve existing messages
- Add new messages
- Register new users
- Validate existing users' credentials

Our web service will need one method for each of these basic user actions. The next step is to decide what parameters (if any) each method will accept, and what results (if any) each one will return.

Here's an overview of what we actually need from our four web methods:

- `getMessagesByParentID()` should accept a `MessageID` value and return an array of child `Message` objects that have the specified `MessageID` logged as their `ParentID`. If the `MessageID` is not specified, then an array of all the top-level `Message` objects is returned.

- `addMessage()` should accept values for a new message including the associated user, the message topic/subject, message text, and the associated parent message (if any); it should return a `Message` object representing the newly created message.

- `addUser()` should accept values for a new user including the username, password, and e-mail address; it should return an `MUser` object representing the newly created user. This method should not allow duplicate user names or e-mail addresses to be created, and should enforce minimum user name and password lengths.

- `validateUser()` should accept users' logon credentials and return an `MUser` object. If the credentials match what's stored in the database, the properties of this `MUser` object will be populated; if not, the object will be empty.

You'll have noticed that some of our web methods return instances of objects called `MUser` and `Message`. These are custom classes that we'll develop to represent a single row from the `tblUsers` and `tblMessages` tables respectively. Fortunately for us, whenever an ASP.NET web service returns data in the form of an object, it's converted automatically into XML. This means that we can easily access even the most advanced web methods, using techniques that we've learned over the last few chapters.

Designing the Flash MX solution

As mentioned previously, our Flash MX solution will be interacting with our message board web service. Since a web service always returns data in the form of XML, we'll use Flash MX's built-in XML object to request web service methods and parse the results.

Once again, on reviewing the application requirements, it turns out we're going to need to do the following with our Flash interface:

- Display a list of existing messages
- View details for a selected message
- Provide a form to add new messages, and prevent users from using the form unless they're registered and signed in
- Provide a form to allow registered users to sign in
- Provide a form to allow new users to register

Since the messages will be hierarchical in nature, we're going to use the FTree component (as supplied in the Flash UI Components Set 2).

> *If you don't already have these components installed on your machine, you can download them from Macromedia's website. Just visit the Flash MX downloads page at http://www.macromedia.com/software/flash/download/ and follow the link to the Macromedia Flash Exchange.*

Building the message board database

The first step in implementing the database solution is to create a new database to hold the tables we will be creating. We will be executing commands using the OSQL command-line utility, just as we did earlier in the chapter when setting up MSDE.

Open an MS-DOS command window, type the following command and press ENTER.

```
C:/>osql -E -S (local)\NetSDK -Q "CREATE DATABASE MsgDB"
```

The command creates a new database called MsgDB. On successfully creating the new database, you should receive messages at the command prompt similar to the following:

```
The CREATE DATABASE process is allocating 0.63 MB on disk 'MsgDB'.
The CREATE DATABASE process is allocating 0.49 MB on disk
'MsgDB_log'.
```

> *The* `MsgDB_log` *database created in this step is a special transaction log database used by* `MsgDB` *to keep track of all the* `INSERT`, `UPDATE` *and* `DELETE` *commands that get executed. If the database engine fails to complete an* `INSERT`, `UPDATE` *or* `DELETE` *command, it can use the log data to cancel any changes it's already made, and 'roll back' the database to whatever state it was in before the command was issued. Think of it as an automatic and intelligent 'undo' feature.*

The next step is to create a SQL script for creating the `tblMessages` and `tblUsers` tables we discussed earlier. Open Notepad, place the following SQL statements into the text file, and save it in the root directory of your `C:` drive as `tables.sql`.

```
CREATE TABLE [dbo].[tblMessages] (
   [MessageID] [int] IDENTITY (1, 1) NOT NULL ,
   [ParentID] [int] NOT NULL ,
   [UserID] [int] NOT NULL ,
   [Subject] [varchar] (50) NOT NULL ,
   [MessageText] [varchar] (1024) NOT NULL ,
   [MessageDate] [datetime] NOT NULL
) ON [PRIMARY]
GO

CREATE TABLE [dbo].[tblUsers] (
   [UserID] [int] IDENTITY (1, 1) NOT NULL ,
   [Username] [varchar] (25) NOT NULL ,
   [Password] [varchar] (15) NOT NULL ,
   [Email] [varchar] (100) NOT NULL ,
   [DateAdded] [smalldatetime] NOT NULL
) ON [PRIMARY]
GO

ALTER TABLE [dbo].[tblMessages] WITH NOCHECK ADD
   CONSTRAINT [PK_tblMessages] PRIMARY KEY  CLUSTERED
   (
     [MessageID]
   )  ON [PRIMARY]
GO

ALTER TABLE [dbo].[tblUsers] WITH NOCHECK ADD
   CONSTRAINT [PK_tblUsers] PRIMARY KEY  CLUSTERED
```

continues overleaf

```
    (
      [UserID]
    )  ON [PRIMARY]
GO


ALTER TABLE [dbo].[tblMessages] WITH NOCHECK ADD
  CONSTRAINT [DF_tblMessages_ParentID] DEFAULT (0) FOR [ParentID],
  CONSTRAINT [DF_tblMessages_MessageDate] DEFAULT (getdate()) FOR
[MessageDate]
GO


ALTER TABLE [dbo].[tblUsers] WITH NOCHECK ADD
  CONSTRAINT [DF_tblUsers_DateAdded] DEFAULT (getdate()) FOR
[DateAdded]
GO


ALTER TABLE [dbo].[tblMessages] ADD
  CONSTRAINT [FK_tblMessages_tblUsers] FOREIGN KEY
  (
    [UserID]
  ) REFERENCES [dbo].[tblUsers] (
    [UserID]
  )
GO
```

Now we need to use the OSQL utility to execute the saved SQL scripts. From the command prompt, type the following command:

```
C:/>osql -E -S (local)\NetSDK -d MsgDB -i C:\tables.sql
```

The last step is to create a new login and give it necessary permissions on our MsgDb database. Type in each of the following commands and press ENTER after each one:

```
C:/>osql -E -S (local)\NetSDK -Q "sp_addlogin 'mbuser', 'mbpass'"

C:/>osql -E -S (local)\NetSDK -d MsgDB -Q "sp_grantdbaccess 'mbuser'"

C:/>osql -E -S (local)\NetSDK -d MsgDB -Q "sp_addrolemember
'db_owner', 'mbuser'"
```

Now that we've finished setting up the database, we're ready to move on up the food chain, and start building the ASP.NET web service that'll hook it all up to the Web. Before we do though, let's spend a few moments going through the SQL commands we used above.

It's not vital for you to understand every last line here (so feel free to skip this bit if you like), but you may find it useful anyway, especially if you want to start creating your own databases.

Understanding the SQL setup code

The initial set of statements down to the first GO command creates the tblMessages table. Each column is assigned a name, a data type, and a NULL setting.

- The first column, MessageID, is declared with the int data type, which denotes a 32-bit integer. We also assign the IDENTITY property – as mentioned earlier, this tells the database engine to assign a new, unique value to this column every time a new row is added. The NOT NULL setting tells the database engine to reject new rows for which there's no MessageID value – in other words, it's a required field.

- The ParentID and UserID columns are also declared as integers that do not allow NULL values.

- The Subject column is declared as a varchar(50) data type, which means it can hold strings of various lengths up to 50 characters. A varchar data type can be declared with a length of 1 to 8000 characters (except for versions of SQL Server earlier than 7.0, which have a maximum length of 255).

- The MessageText column is declared with a maximum size of 1,024 characters.

- Finally, we declare a MessageDate column with a data type of datetime. This can store date and time data with an accuracy of just a few milliseconds.

The next set of statements down to the GO command is responsible for creating the tblUsers table. Each column is defined similarly to the tblMessages table, but the smalldatetime data type used for the DateAdded column is worthy of note. It's similar to datetime, but takes up less space on the disk. The trade-off is that it's less accurate, storing date and time data with accuracy to the nearest minute.

The next set of statements creates a Primary Key constraint on the MessageID column of the tblMessages table. This serves as an additional step to make sure that each row contains a unique value for MessageID. It also causes the database engine to generate an index on the column, allowing for more efficient queries based on the MessageID column.

```
ALTER TABLE [dbo].[tblMessages] WITH NOCHECK ADD
   CONSTRAINT [DF_tblMessages_ParentID] DEFAULT (0) FOR [ParentID],
   CONSTRAINT [DF_tblMessages_MessageDate] DEFAULT (getdate()) FOR
[MessageDate]
GO
```

In the above set of statements, we are generating DEFAULT constraints for the ParentID and MessageDate columns in the tblMessages table. These tell the database engine to substitute a specific value whenever a new row is added and that column is null: in other words, ParentID will now default to 0, and MessageDate will default to the current date.

```
ALTER TABLE [dbo].[tblMessages] ADD
   CONSTRAINT [FK_tblMessages_tblUsers] FOREIGN KEY
   (
     [UserID]
   ) REFERENCES [dbo].[tblUsers] (
     [UserID]
   )
GO
```

In the final set of statements, we define the Primary Key/Foreign Key (PK/FK) relationship between our two tables, based on the UserID column in each one. This will guarantee that no new rows are added to tblMessages unless they have a UserID that matches up with one in tblUsers. It also guarantees that no rows in tblUsers can be deleted as long as there are messages in tblMessages associated with their UserID – otherwise, we could end up with "orphaned" messages in tblMessages.

Building the message board web service

Now it's time to set up our message board web service. As we decided at the design stage, we're going to implement two custom classes and four web methods.

First of all, we need to create a new text file and save it as messageService.asmx in the usual wwwroot folder.

Now add in the following code:

```
<%@ WebService language="C#" class="MessageBoard.messageService" %>

using System;
using System.Web.Services;
using System.Xml.Serialization;
using System.Data;
using System.Data.SqlClient;
```

continues overleaf

```
using System.Collections;
namespace MessageBoard {
   // class definitions will go here
}
```

The first line declares the web service attributes: we are using C# and the class should be compiled as `MessageBoard.messageService`.

Next, we declare the namespaces that we will be using. All web services need `System`, `System.Web.Services` and `System.Xml.Serialization` to work, while `System.Data` and `System.Data.SqlClient` namespaces are needed to communicate with our `MsgDB` database.

Next we declare the `System.Collections` namespace, which will be handy later when we're building a list of messages.

Finally, we declare our own `MessageBoard` namespace.

Custom classes

The next step is to develop our custom `MUser` and `Message` classes. You'll need to add the following lines of code *inside* the `MessageBoard` namespace code block:

```
namespace MessageBoard {

  public class Message {
    public Message() {
      MessageID = 0;
      ParentID = 0;
      ChildCount = 0;
      SubjectText = "";
      MessageText = "";
      MessageDate = "";
      UserID = 0;
      Username = "";
    }

    [System.Xml.Serialization.XmlAttribute()]
    public int MessageID;
    [System.Xml.Serialization.XmlAttribute()]
    public int ParentID;
    [System.Xml.Serialization.XmlAttribute()]
    public int ChildCount;
    [System.Xml.Serialization.XmlAttribute()]
    public string SubjectText;
    [System.Xml.Serialization.XmlAttribute()]
```

continues overleaf

```
        public string MessageDate;
        [System.Xml.Serialization.XmlAttribute()]
        public int UserID;
        [System.Xml.Serialization.XmlAttribute()]
        public string Username;
        [System.Xml.Serialization.XmlText()]
        public string MessageText;
    }

  }
```

Here, we declare a public class called Message, followed by a Message class constructor, where we initialize each of the property values. After the constructor, we declare all our public properties. Each one has a System.Xml.Serialization attribute associated with it; this tells ASP.NET that when it returns the object and converts it into XML, it should render these properties as XML attributes, rather than as element text.

Note that we declared the MessageDate property as a string. We're only intending to use this property for display purposes, so there's no need to bother with anything more complex.

Now let's define the MUser class:

```
    public class MUser {
      public MUser() {
        UserID = 0;
        Username = "";
        Password = "";
        Email = "";
        DateAdded = "";
      }

      [System.Xml.Serialization.XmlAttribute()]
      public int UserID;
      [System.Xml.Serialization.XmlAttribute()]
      public string Username;
      [System.Xml.Serialization.XmlAttribute()]
      public string Password;
      [System.Xml.Serialization.XmlAttribute()]
      public string Email;
      [System.Xml.Serialization.XmlAttribute()]
      public string DateAdded;
    }
  }
```

continues overleaf

This is defined in much the same way as the Message class. There's a constructor to initialize property values, followed by properties declared with XML serialization attributes.

The web service class

The next step is to develop the web service class itself. Once again, add the following lines of code inside the MessageBoard namespace block (but *above* the Message class definition):

```
namespace MessageBoard
{
    public class messageService : System.Web.Services.WebService {
        private string cnnString = "server=(local)\\NetSDK;"
        cnnString += "database=MsgDB;"
        cnnString += "uid=mbuser;pwd=mbpass;";

        // web methods will go here
    }
    public class Message {
        public Message() {
...
```

The first new line declares a public class called messageService that derives functionality from the System.Web.Services.WebService class.

> It's not obligatory for a web service to derive from the Web Service *class. However, it does give us access to objects such as* Application, Session, User, *and* Context, *should we need them.*

The first line of code inside the messageService class declares a private string containing our database connection settings. Since the string is declared private, it will be available to all our web methods that we will create, but it's not exposed outside of the class. This allows us to keep up with our connection settings in one place, should we ever need to update it in the future.

getMessagesByParentID()

Now let's jump into our first web method – getMessagesByParentID() – which lies at the heart of our web service, returning a list of all the messages with a specified parent. Add all the following code to the messageService class after the connection string and before the class's closing bracket.

We start by specifying the [WebMethod] attribute, telling ASP.NET that we want to expose the following function as a web method. The second line tells ASP.NET that we're defining a public function (meaning that it can be used by anyone) called getMessagesByParentID, which takes a single integer argument, stores it away as parentID, and returns an array of Message objects.

```
[WebMethod]
public Message[] getMessagesByParentID(int parentID) {
```

Now we set up the SQL command. We need a SELECT statement to retrieve all the messages whose parent has the specified value parentID. This means we'll either get back a list of original postings (if parentID is specified as 0) or all the messages sent in direct response to a particular post.

```
// Start building the SELECT statement
string sql = "SELECT ";

// List the message details we want to retrieve
sql += "tblMessages.MessageID, ";
sql += "tblMessages.ParentID, ";
sql += "tblMessages.UserID, ";
sql += "tblUsers.Username, ";
sql += "tblMessages.Subject, ";
sql += "tblMessages.MessageText, ";
sql += "tblMessages.MessageDate, ";
sql += "ChildMessageCount = COUNT(tblMsgs2.MessageID) ";

// State which table we want them retrieved from
sql += "FROM tblMessages ";
```

As well as retrieving all the details stored for each message in tblMessages, we need the Username associated with its userID value, as well as the number of child messages it has of its own.

To achieve the former, we specify a JOIN between our two tables. This is where our PK/FK relationship pays off: based on the UserID stored in tblMessages, we can reference and return any of the related user information in tblUsers.

```
sql += "INNER JOIN tblUsers ";
sql += "ON tblUsers.UserID = tblMessages.UserID ";
```

The syntax may seem a little baffling, but the concept is fairly simple. When MSDE sees that we're requesting a Username from tblUsers table, it'll know now which record to use: the one whose UserID matches the one in tblMessages.

So, the next question is: how do we return a count of child messages when we don't store a value for that in the tblMessages table? We've already used COUNT(tblMsgs2.MessageID) to set a value ChildMessageCount, but what on earth is tbMsgs2?

```
sql += "LEFT OUTER JOIN tblMessages tblMsgs2 ";
sql += "ON tblMsgs2.ParentID = tblMessages.MessageID ";
```

We use what's called a **self-join**. In simple terms, we ask the database engine to return 0 or more records (OUTER JOIN) for which the ParentID on the left side of the JOIN clause matches the MessageID on the right side. Since we're joining tblMessages to itself, we avoid naming conflicts by aliasing the joined table as tblMsgs2. This sets us up to use COUNT() to count the number of rows returned by the self-join.

Our WHERE clause ensures that we only retrieve messages where the ParentID matches the value passed to the method.

```
sql += "WHERE tblMessages.ParentID = "+ parentID;
```

The COUNT() function we used earlier on is known technically as an **aggregate function**, and these require us to declare a GROUP BY clause, listing all the selected fields that aren't based on aggregate functions.

```
sql += "GROUP BY ";
sql += "tblMessages.MessageID, ";
sql += "tblMessages.ParentID, ";
sql += "tblMessages.UserID, ";
sql += "tblUsers.Username, ";
sql += "tblMessages.Subject, ";
sql += "tblMessages.MessageText, ";
sql += "tblMessages.MessageDate ";
```

Finally, we use an ORDER BY clause to let MSDE know that we want results sent back in descending order of MessageDate.

```
sql += "ORDER BY ";
sql += "tblMessages.MessageDate DESC";
```

The next few lines should be familiar from our earlier examples. Now that we're done putting our SQL command into string variable sql, we initialize and open the database connection, and use the SQL query and connection object to declare a SqlCommand object. We then execute the command, giving us a SqlDataReader object called msgReader, leaving us all ready for action.

```
// Now we're ready to open the database connection
SqlConnection sqlCnn = new SqlConnection(cnnString);
sqlCnn.Open();
```

continues overleaf

```
                    // Execute the SQL command, returning a DataReader
                    SqlCommand sqlCmd = new SqlCommand(sql, sqlCnn);
                    SqlDataReader msgReader = sqlCmd.ExecuteReader();
```

Now we need to set up a list of Message objects. The only slight problem is that we don't know ahead of time how many messages our query might return, so we can't just set up an array as we might have done otherwise. Fortunately, there's another option.

The ArrayList object is part of the System.Collections namespace (which we declared at the start of the web service), and it's designed to help us store *arbitrary* numbers of items. Unlike an array, its internal storage will automatically grow to accommodate any new items we add.

```
                    // Create an ArrayList object to store each Message
                    ArrayList msgArrayList = new ArrayList();

                    while (msgReader.Read()) {
                     // Create a new Message object
                     Message msgItem = new Message();

                     // Set the Message properties with the current data row
                     msgItem.MessageID = msgReader.GetInt32(0);
                     msgItem.ParentID = msgReader.GetInt32(1);
                     msgItem.ChildCount = msgReader.GetInt32(7);
                     msgItem.UserID = msgReader.GetInt32(2);
                     msgItem.Username = msgReader.GetString(3);
                     msgItem.SubjectText = msgReader.GetString(4);
                     msgItem.MessageText = msgReader.GetString(5);
                     msgItem.MessageDate = msgReader.GetValue(6).ToString();

                     // Add the Message object to the ArrayList
                     msgArrayList.Add(msgItem);
                    }
```

For each row retrieved, we create a new Message object, set its properties from the values in msgReader, and add the finished message object to msgArrayList.

Once we're done accessing data, we close our database objects.

```
                    msgReader.Close();
                    sqlCnn.Close();
```

Unfortunately, ASP.NET web services can't return ArrayList objects, so we need to take all the elements from our flexible ArrayList and move them into a fixed Message array, which the web service *can* return.

This time, we know exactly what size our array needs to be, based on the `ArrayList`'s `Count` property. Finally, we loop through the `ArrayList`, assigning `Message` objects to our new array, and then return the array as our web service method output.

```
// Create an Array of Message objects
Message[] msgArray = new Message[msgArrayList.Count];
for (int i = 0; i < msgArrayList.Count; i++) {
 msgArray[i] = (Message) msgArrayList[i];
}
// Return the Array of Message objects
return msgArray;
}
```

addMessage()

Now add the following code to the `messageService` class, following straight on from our last block of code. This web method accepts a `ParentID`, `UserID`, subject, and text for a brand new message, which it adds to the `tblMessage` table in our database. It then returns the new message in the form of a `Message` object. Most of the code is along pretty much the same lines as our last web method, so I'll just point out the lines of special interest.

```
[WebMethod]
public Message addMessage(int parentID, int userID,
              ➥ string subjectText, string messageText) {

    // Initialize a new Message object
    Message msgItem = new Message();
    msgItem.ParentID = parentID;
    msgItem.UserID = userID;
    msgItem.SubjectText = subjectText;
    msgItem.MessageText = messageText;
```

The next two lines are of special interest. Single quotes have a very specific meaning in the context of a SQL statement, so if any occur in the text data that we send to the database, it will probably cause us major headaches. Fortunately, it's quite easy to fix this problem: we just need to replace each single quote with a *pair* of single quotes.

```
string subjectTextForSQL = subjectText.Replace("'", "''");
string messageTextForSQL = messageText.Replace("'", "''");
```

Use our values in an `INSERT INTO` command to add the message into `tblMessages` as a new record.

```
// Build the INSERT INTO statement
string insertSql = "INSERT INTO tblMessages ";
```

```
insertSql += "(ParentID, UserID, Subject, MessageText) ";
insertSql += "VALUES (" + parentID + ", " + userID + ", ";
insertSql += "'" + subjectTextForSQL + "', '";
insertSql += messageTextForSQL + "')";
// Open the database connection and execute the SQL command
SqlConnection sqlCnn = new SqlConnection(cnnString);
sqlCnn.Open();
SqlCommand sqlInsertCmd = new SqlCommand(insertSql, sqlCnn);
int rowsAdded = sqlInsertCmd.ExecuteNonQuery();
```

If the INSERT INTO is successful (that is, we've added a row to the table), we retrieve the new MessageID and MessageDate values from tblMessages, and update our Message object.

```
if (rowsAdded > 0) {
  // Retrieve the MessageID and MessageDate of the new row
  string selectSql = "SELECT MAX(MessageID) AS MessageID, ";
  selectSql += " MAX(MessageDate) AS MessageDate ";
  selectSql += "FROM tblMessages ";
  selectSql += "WHERE UserID = " + userID;

  SqlCommand sqlSelectCmd = new SqlCommand(selectSql, sqlCnn);
  SqlDataReader msgReader = sqlSelectCmd.ExecuteReader();

  if (msgReader.Read()) {
    msgItem.MessageID = msgReader.GetInt32(0);
    msgItem.MessageDate = msgReader.GetValue(1).ToString();
  }
  msgReader.Close();
}
```

Now we close the database connection and return the created Message object msgItem.

```
sqlCnn.Close();
return msgItem;
}
```

addUser()

Now let's get onto our next web service method. Place the following lines of code inside the messageService class, just after the addMessage() web method, and just before the class's closing bracket.

This method takes a user name, password, and e-mail address, uses them to create a new record in the tblUsers table, and sends back an MUser object that corresponds to the new user.

```
[WebMethod]
public MUser addUser(string userName, string password,
            ➥ string email) {
    MUser newUser = new MUser();
    newUser.Username = userName;
    newUser.Password = password;
    newUser.Email = email;
```

Once we've initialized a new `MUser` object called `newUser`, we build up a `SELECT` query, to check if a user is already registered with the same user name or e-mail address.

```
    string selectSql = "SELECT COUNT(*) AS UserCount "
    selectSql += "FROM tblUsers "
    selectSql += "WHERE Username LIKE '" + userName + "' "
    selectSql += "OR Email LIKE '" + email + "'";

    SqlConnection sqlCnn = new SqlConnection(cnnString);
    sqlCnn.Open();
    SqlCommand sqlSelectCmd = new SqlCommand(selectSql,sqlCnn);
```

The next line is of special interest. We want to check that the user name and e-mail address check returns a zero value. Otherwise, there must be at least one registration conflicting with the user name and/or e-mail address that we want to use.

```
    int userCount = (int) sqlSelectCmd.ExecuteScalar();
```

The `SqlCommand` object's `ExecuteScalar()` method returns whatever value is held in the first column of the first row of data returned by our `SELECT` command. If there are no matches at all, we end up with `userCount` set to zero.

That being the case, we build and execute an `INSERT INTO` statement, to insert the new user information.

```
    if (userCount == 0) {
        string insertSql = "INSERT INTO tblUsers "
        insertSql += "(Username, Password, Email) "
        insertSql += "VALUES ('" + userName + "', "
        insertSql += "'" + password + "', "
        insertSql += "'" + email + "')";

        SqlCommand sqlInsCmd = new SqlCommand(insertSql, sqlCnn);
        int rowsAdded = sqlInsertCmd.ExecuteNonQuery();
```

Once again, if the `INSERT INTO` is successful, we retrieve the new `UserID` and update our `newUser` object.

```
if (rowsAdded > 0) {
    string newSql = "SELECT UserID FROM tblUsers "
    newSql += "WHERE Username LIKE '" + userName + "'";
    SqlCommand sqlGetCmd = new SqlCommand(newSql, sqlCnn);
    newUser.UserID = (int) sqlGetUserCmd.ExecuteScalar();
    newUser.DateAdded = DateTime.Now.ToString();
    }
}
```

Finally, we close the database connection and send back `newUser`.

```
sqlCnn.Close();
return newUser;
}
```

validateUser()

Now for our last web service method, which we'll use to validate existing users. Add the following code into the `messageService` class. It accepts parameters that specify the user name and password of the user to be validated, and returns an `MUser` object containing details of the validated user.

```
[WebMethod]
public MUser validateUser(string userName, string password) {

    // Initialize the MUser object to be returned
    MUser msgUser = new MUser();
    msgUser.Username = userName;

    // Open the database connection
    SqlConnection sqlCnn = new SqlConnection(cnnString);
    sqlCnn.Open();

    // Build SQL query to validate username and password
    string sql = "SELECT UserID, Username, Email, DateAdded ";
    sql += "FROM tblUsers ";
    sql += "WHERE Username LIKE '" + userName + "'";
    sql += " AND Password LIKE '" + password + "'";

    // Execute the SQL command, return a SqlDataReader object
    SqlCommand sqlCmd = new SqlCommand(sql, sqlCnn);
    SqlDataReader userReader = sqlCmd.ExecuteReader();
```

If successful, we populate msgUser with values retrieved from the database.

```
        // Check to see that a row was returned
        if (userReader.Read()) {
        // Username and password match, so set other properties
        msgUser.UserID = userReader.GetInt32(0);
        msgUser.Username = userReader.GetString(1);
        msgUser.Email = userReader.GetString(2);
        msgUser.DateAdded = userReader.GetValue(3).ToString();
        }
```

We then close the database connection and return the MUser object.

```
        userReader.Close();
        sqlCnn.Close();
        return msgUser;
    }
```

If you haven't done so already, save the latest changes. We're now ready to test the web service!

Testing the web service

Open up your browser and point it at http://localhost/messageService.asmx.

The first time you access the page, it will probably take a moment or two to appear, because ASP.NET is busy compiling the code. Once it's finished though, the page should appear with the following contents:

As usual, each web service method is listed as a link, so that we can simply click through to find out more. First of all then, click on the addUser link.

ASP.NET automatically builds a form with which to test the addUser method. Try it out with any valid username, password, and e-mail address (I've used 'BigDog', 'secret', and 'big@d.com') and then click the Invoke button. A separate browser window should now appear with XML output similar to this:

Note that the UserID attribute has a value of 1, while DateAdded shows the current date and time. When MSDE added the new user to the tblUsers table, it automatically assigned new values to the UserID and DateAdded columns. Since this is our first registered user, UserID has a value reflecting that – try it again, and you'll see the UserID value change to 2, 3, and so on.

Now let's try adding the same user again. Close the current XML window and click the Invoke button without changing any of the values. This time when the window appears, the XML output is somewhat different:

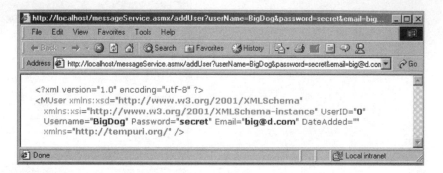

Notice the UserID value is 0? This is what we'll need to look for to know that there was a problem adding the user to the tblUsers table: the values for user name, e-mail address, or both *already exist*.

Each of the other methods on our web service functions in a fairly similar way – try validating our 'BigDog' user with the ValidateUser() method, and you'll get the same XML data as our first test produced, containing all the information we have on that user.

Now try out the addMessage() method, using the values shown below:

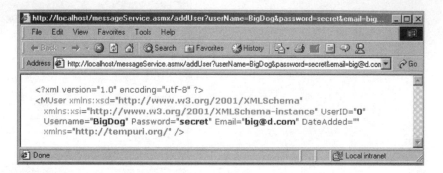

Hit Invoke, and you should get the following result:

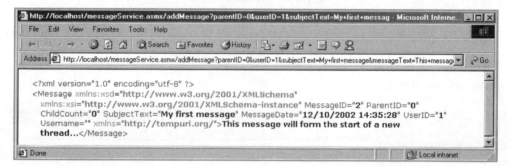

We can see that this message has a MessageID of 1 (it's the very first message we've added to the database), a ParentID of 0 (it's the first message in a thread), and a ChildCount of 0 (no other messages, so no children). We can also see that this message was posted by the user whose UserID value is 1 – that's BigDog to you and me.

Hit Invoke again, and you'll get almost exactly the same result:

The only difference is that MessageID is now set to 2, since this is the second message we've added to the database.

Now let's use the `getMessagesByParentID()` method to retrieve all the messages whose `ParentID` value is set to 0:

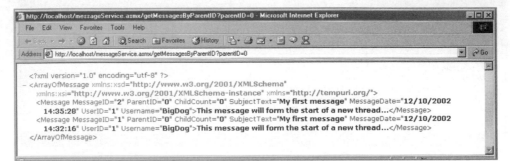

Here we see our two identical messages listed together. They're both at the start of their own new thread, which is why they both have a `ParentID` value of 0, and don't correspond to any other messages.

Building the message board interface

Now that all our back-end services are complete, we're ready to implement the Flash front-end. Start by creating a new movie project, and save it as `MessageReader.fla`.

Setting up the timeline

The first thing we need to do is set up the layers and frames. Create four new layers, and set them as shown below:

On the Labels layer, you'll need a total of six keyframes, with Frame Labels as follows:

- Frame 1: StartFrame
- Frame 11: ReadMessage
- Frame 21: NewMessage
- Frame 31: NewUser
- Frame 41: LoginForm
- Frame 51: NotLoggedIn

We'll use each of these frames represent the different 'views' that a user will see. For example, when a user selects a message to view we'll use ActionScript to move to frame 2.

Background and Main layers

Now that our layers and frames are set up, the next thing we need to do is add all the UI components. Here's how the basic layout of the stage should look once we're done:

Once you've put some background visuals and a title on the Background layer, you need to add a Tree component (instance name myTree) on the left-hand side, a dynamic text field (Var: txtLogin) in the top right corner, another along the bottom (Var: txtStatus) and five Push Button components, all on the Main layer.

Arrange the buttons along the bottom of the stage from left to right, and set their parameters as follows:

Button	Instance Name	Label	Click Handler
1	btnRefresh	Refresh	reloadTree
2	btnNewTopic	Start New Topic	newTopicClick
3	btnRegister	Register	registerClick
4	btnLogin	Login	loginClick
5	btnSignOut	Sign Out	signOut

As a final step, change the dimensions of the Tree component so that it fills up the left half of the stage with the top just below the title and the bottom just above the txtStatus dynamic text field.

Building the user forms

The UserForms layer is where we're going to keep our various views and forms, such as the message detail view, the login form, and the registration form. Click on frame 1, and add a static text field in the space on the right of the stage, reading "Select a message to view."

Now hide the Main layer, and select frame 11 on the UserForms timeline. We're going to set up the view message form here, so that it looks something like this:

We need four dynamic text fields on the right-hand side of the stage, with Var: set to txtSubject, msgDate, txt Username, and txtMessage respectively. Each of the first three needs to be labeled as shown, while the last one should be set to Multiline and given the instance name MessageText.

Drag a ScrollBar component onto the stage, and drop it on the right side of the txtMessage text field. Now select the ScrollBar – note that its Target parameter has been automatically set to MessageText – and set its instance name to scrMsgText.

Finally, add another PushButton to the stage, change its label to 'Reply', and set the click handler to replyClick.

Add New Message form

On frame 21 of the UserForms layer, we need to create the form we'll use to submit new messages:

The three dynamic text fields we use here should have Var: set to txtNewSubject, txtNewMessage, and txtNew Message Status respectively. The second should also be given the instance name NewMessageBox, and the lower two fields should both be Multiline. Again, drop a ScrollBar component on the message field so that it snaps to the right-hand side and targets the text field.

Finally, add two PushButton components, with click handlers `addMessage` (for the one labeled 'Submit') and `cancelClick` (for the one labeled 'Cancel').

Register form

Here's the form we'll use to register new users, which we'll place on frame 31 of the UserForms layer:

Place five dynamic text fields on the stage, and change their Var names to `txtRegUsername`, `txtRegPasword`, `txtRegPassword2`, `txtRegEmail`, and `txtRegStatus`. Both password fields should be set to Password mode in the Property inspector, and `txtRegStatus` should be Multiline. Again, we finish off the form with a couple of PushButton components, with handlers set to `addUser` and `cancelClick` respectively.

```
Register
User name: [            ]
 Password: [            ]
  Confirm: [            ]
   E-mail: [            ]
        [ Submit ]  [ Cancel ]
        ......................
        :                    :
        :                    :
        :                    :
        ......................
```

Login form

On frame 41 we'll have a login form, so that existing users can sign in:

We need three dynamic text fields, with Var set to `txtLoginUsername`, `txtLoginPassword`, and `txtLoginStatus` respectively. Again, the password field needs to be set to Password mode, and the status field should be Multiline.

Add another two PushButton components to the stage, and set their handlers to `submitLogin` and `cancelClick` respectively.

```
Login
User name: [            ]
 Password: [            ]
        [ Login ]  [ Cancel ]
        ......................
        :                    :
        :                    :
        :                    :
        ......................
```

Not Signed In form

For the last of our UI forms, we'll build a view on frame 51 to let users know that they need to be registered and signed in before they can add a new message:

All we need here are the two static text fields that make up the message.

```
      You Are Not Signed In
To add a new message, you must
be a registered user and signed in.

Click the Login button to  sign in or
the Register  button to create a
new account.
```

We are now ready to start coding the ActionScript for our movie.

Scripts for StartFrame (frames 1-10)

Select frame 1 on the Actions layer and attach the following code:

```
var currentMsgNode;   // the currently selected message node
var myDoc;            // XML doc used throughout
var Username;         // The logged in Username
var UserID;           // The logged in UserID

function init() {
  if (this.initialized == undefined) {
    this.initialized = true;

    myTree.setChangeHandler("messageSelected", _root);
    myTree.setNodeExpansionHandler("messageExpanded", _root);
    myTree.setStyleProperty("backgroundDisabled", 0xFFFFFF);

    signOut();
    reloadTree();
  }
}

init();
stop();
```

So far, we have declared the variables that we will reference throughout the remainder of the code. Next we define the code for our `init` function, which will be called exactly one time for the lifetime of the movie. Inside this, we set the functions that will be called by our Tree component when a user selects or expands a node.

We also define the `backgroundDisabled` property as the color white, which will reduce some of the flicker caused each time the Flash movie retrieves a new set of messages from our web service. The `signOut` and `reloadTree` functions should initialize the user information and start loading our first set of messages – we'll define them a little later on.

Finally, we call the `init` function and stop the movie.

signOut()

We'll call this function whenever a user signs out:

```
function signOut() {
  UserID = 0;
  btnSignOut._visible = false;
  btnRegister._visible = true;
  btnLogin._visible = true;
  txtLogin - "You are not Logged In";
  gotoAndStop("StartFrame");
}
```

The (signOut) function sets the UserID to 0, which will know to mean that the user is not currently signed in. Next, we make sure the Sign Out button is hidden, and that the Register and Login buttons are visible. We then set the Login status text to let the user know they are not currently logged in, and we set the current frame to StartFrame.

reloadTree()

This function is called when the movie first loads and after that, any time the user clicks the Refresh button to reload the list of messages.

```
function reloadTree() {
  myTree.removeAll();
  var rootNode = new FTreeNode("Message Board");
  var childNode = new FTreeNode("Loading, please wait...");
  rootNode.addNode(childNode);
  rootNode.setIsOpen(true);
  myTree.setRootNode(rootNode);
  currentMsgNode = rootNode;
  loadMessages("0");
}
```

Our first step is to remove all the nodes, if any, from the Tree component. The next step is to create the default root node with the caption "Message Board." Next, we create a new child node with the caption "Loading, please wait..." and add it to the root node.

Next, we make sure the root node is expanded and we add it to the Tree component. Finally, we set the currentMsgNode to the root node we just added, and we call the loadMessages function with a single parameter value of 0.

loadMessages()

This function's responsible for loading a message thread into the movie, by calling up the getMessagesByParentID web method on our web service:

```
function loadMessages(parentID) {
    myTree.setEnabled(false);
    myDoc = new XML();
    myDoc.ignoreWhite = true;
    var sUrl = "";
    // Uncomment the following line for debugging
    // sUrl += "http://localhost/";
    sUrl += "messageService.asmx";
    sUrl += "/getMessagesByParentID?parentID=" + parentID;
    myDoc.load(sUrl);
    myDoc.onLoad = childMessagesLoaded;
}
```

The (loadMessages) function takes one parameter, which is the MessageID of the parent node. If we want to load the top-level or 'root' messages, we call this function with an argument of 0.

The first thing we do is to disable the Tree control so that users can't accidentally cause another event to occur while the web service is being called and processed. Next, we declare a new instance of the Flash XML object, and set the ignoreWhite property to true. Now we need to build the URL for the web service.

The basic syntax to call a web service method using the GET method is as follows:

```
ServiceUrl/MethodName?QueryStringParameters
```

To call the getMessagesByParentID method, we use the following URL:

```
messageService.asmx/getMessagesByParentID?parentID=0
```

Finally, in the loadMessages function we use the XML object's load method to execute the URL and define what function to call when the web service returns all its data: childMessagesLoaded.

childMessagesLoaded()

This function really lies at the heart of our application's ability to load up messages returned by our web service.

```
function childMessagesLoaded(success) {
    if (success) {
        if (myDoc.status == 0) {
```

continues overleaf

```
           currentMsgNode.removeNodesAt(0,
              currentMsgNode.getNumChildren());

         var xmlRootNode = myDoc.firstChild;

         for(var i = 0; i<xmlRootNode.childNodes.length; i++) {
            var currentNode = xmlRootNode.childNodes[i];
            var nodeData = new Object();
            nodeData["Populated"] = true;
            nodeData["MessageID"] = currentNode.attributes.MessageID;
            nodeData["ParentID"] = currentNode.attributes.ParentID;
            nodeData["Username"] = currentNode.attributes.Username;
            nodeData["MessageDate"] = currentNode.attributes.MessageDate;
            nodeData["HasChildren"] =
                       ➥ Boolean(currentNode.attributes.ChildCount);
            nodeData["SubjectText"] = currentNode.attributes.SubjectText;
            nodeData["MessageText"] = currentNode.firstChild.nodeValue;

            var newTreeNode = new FTreeNode(nodeData["SubjectText"]);
            newTreeNode.setData(nodeData);
            if (nodeData["HasChildren"] == true) {
               var childNodeData = new Object();
               childNodeData["ParentID"] = nodeData["MessageID"];
               childNodeData["Populated"] = false;
               newTreeNode.addNode(new FTreeNode("Loading, please wait...")
                       ➥ .setData(childNodeData));
            }
            currentMsgNode.addNode(newTreeNode);
         }
      } else {
         showError("The MessageBoard data returned was not valid. " +
                    ➥ "Status code: " + myDoc.status);
      }
   } else {
      showError("Error retrieving the MessageBoard data.");
   }
   myTree.setEnabled(true);
   myTree.refresh();
}
```

The first thing we do is check the success of the XML load method, and that the document parse status is okay. Passing these two checks, we are ready to start parsing the XML and load up the returned messages.

We begin by removing any child nodes from the `currentMsgNode`. If you recall from the `reloadTree` function, there's always one child node in the beginning with the caption "Loading, please wait...." We then get the root node from the XML that was returned. Using a `for` loop, we iterate through all the message nodes and build our tree.

```
var currentNode = xmlRootNode.childNodes[i];
```

This line gets the current XML child node we want to examine. The next line creates a new object instance called `nodeData`, which we'll use to store all the properties of the message.

We set all the `nodeData` properties using the attributes of the XML node – all, that is, but the text of the message itself. We must get to that using the `firstChild.nodeValue` property, since the message text is contained between the `<Message></Message>` XML tags.

We now create a node for the Tree component, setting the caption to the subject of the message. The Tree node has the very cool ability of storing all the property information we just set using its (`setData`) method. As we will see later, we can retrieve all these properties again using the (`getData`) method.

If a message has child messages associated with it, then we need to indicate this and allow the user to retrieve those messages. To do this, we first check whether a given message has children. If so, then we create a new 'fake' tree node, much like we did in the (`reloadTree`) function with a caption of "Loading, please wait...." We also add data to the node so that we can later determine the `ParentID` to use when calling the `loadMessages` function.

Now we can add the new Tree node to the Tree component. Last, we enable the Tree once again and call the (`refresh`) method to ensure all the latest changes are visible.

messageExpanded()

So, what do we do when a user expands a message that has a 'fake' child message? The `setNodeExpansionHandler` value that we defined in the `init` function will call a function named (`messageExpanded`).

```
function messageExpanded(tree, msgNode) {
   currentMsgNode = msgNode;
   var nodeData = msgNode.getNodeAt(0).getData();

   if (nodeData["Populated"] == false) {
     loadMessages(nodeData["ParentID"]);
   }
}
```

The function needs to define two input parameters. The first is a reference to the Tree component and the second is a reference to the Tree node that was expanded. Using the second parameter, we set our currentMsgNode variable. Next, we get the node data of the first child node. If the Populated property value is false, then we know it's one of our "Loading, please wait..." nodes.

We can then call the (loadMessages) function passing the ParentID property value as our single parameter. The (loadMessages) function will call the getMessagesByParentID web service method with this value, returning all the child messages for the expanded message. Finally, childMessagesLoaded is called with the XML results, and the function populates this branch of our Tree with the newly returned messages! Using this technique, the number of messages retrieved from the server is minimized to what the user is interested in browsing!

messageSelected()

Now we're ready to code for when a user selects a message to view. We've already defined the function to be called as (messageSelected) using the Tree's (setChangeHandler) method. Here's the code:

```
function messageSelected(tree) {
  currentMsgNode = tree.getSelectedNode();
  var nodeData = currentMsgNode.getData();
  if (nodeData["MessageID"] != null) {
    txtSubject = nodeData["SubjectText"];
    msgDate = nodeData["MessageDate"];
    txtMessage = nodeData["MessageText"];
    txtUsername = nodeData["Username"];
    scrMsgText.setEnabled(false);
    scrMsgText.setEnabled(true);
    gotoAndStop("ReadMessage");
  } else {
    gotoAndStop("StartFrame");
  }
}
```

The function defines one input parameter, which is a reference to the Tree component affected. Using the (getSelectedNode) method, we can get a reference to the node the user clicked. The next step is to retrieve the node properties using the getData method. If the MessageID property is not null, we can proceed with setting our dynamic text fields with the property values.

After setting the variables, we can change the current frame to ReadMessage, which will display the dynamic text fields we just set. If the MessageID happens to be null, then the user must have clicked the root node, in which case we will change the current frame back to StartFrame.

Before moving on to the ActionScript associated with the other frames, we still have a few loose ends to tie up.

newTopicClick()

This function is called when the user clicks the New Topic button.

```
function newTopicClick() {
  if (UserID > 0) {
    currentMsgNode = myTree.getRootNode();
    txtNewSubject = "";
    txtNewMessage = "";
    txtNewMessageStatus = "";
    gotoAndStop("NewMessage");
  } else {
    gotoAndStop("NotLoggedIn");
  }
}
```

If the user is not logged in (UserID > 0), then we display the frame telling them they must be registered and logged in to add a new message. If the user is logged in, we first set the current message node variable to the Tree's root node so we later have the correct ParentID value of 0. Next, we initialize the dynamic text variables. Finally, we jump to the NewMessage frame.

registerClick()

This function is called when the user clicks the Register button. All it needs to do is initialize the form variables and jump to the NewUser frame.

```
function registerClick() {
  txtRegUsername = "";
  txtRegPassword = "";
  txtRegPassword2 = "";
  txtRegEmail = "";
  txtRegStatus = "";
  gotoAndStop("NewUser");
}
```

loginClick()

This function is called when the user clicks on the Login button. All it needs to do is jump to the LoginForm frame.

```
function loginClick() {
  gotoAndStop("LoginForm");
}
```

```
cancelClick()
```

This function is called whenever a user clicks a Cancel button on any of the forms, and simply jumps the playhead to the StartFrame.

```
function cancelClick() {
  gotoAndStop("StartFrame");
}
```

showError()

This last function is called whenever an error occurs, or an error message needs to be displayed. This function is called, for instance, from within the (childMessagesLoaded) function when the success or status values are not what we expect.

```
function showError(errorMessage) {
  txtStatus = "The following error occurred: " + errorMessage;
}
```

Scripts for ReadMessage (frames 11-20)

Select frame 11 on the Actions layer and attach the following function.

replyClick()

This is called when the user clicks the Reply button below the message they're currently viewing.

```
function replyClick() {
  if (UserID > 0) {
    var nodeData = currentMsgNode.getData();
    if (nodeData["MessageID"] != null) {
      txtNewSubject = "Re: " + nodeData["SubjectText"];
      txtNewMessage = "\n\n--- Previous Post ---\n\n"
        + nodeData["MessageText"];
    } else {
      txtNewSubject = "";
      txtNewMessage = "";
    }

    txtNewMessageStatus = "";

    gotoAndStop("NewMessage");
  } else {
    gotoAndStop("NotLoggedIn");
  }
}
```

If the user is logged in and the MessageID is valid, then the New Message form variables are initialized and we jump to the NewMessage frame. By default, we initialize the subject and message text with the values of the message the user is currently viewing.

Scripts for NewMessage (21-30)

Now select frame 21 on the Actions layer and attach the following function.

addMessage()

When a user completes the New Message form and clicks the Submit button, the (addMessage) function is called.

```
function addMessage() {
  myTree.setEnabled(false);
  var parentID = 0;
  var nodeData = currentMsgNode.getData();
  if (nodeData["MessageID"] != null) {
    parentID = nodeData["MessageID"];
  }

  myDoc = new XML();
  myDoc.ignoreWhite = true;
  var addUrl = "";
  // Uncomment the following line for debugging
  // addUrl += "http://localhost/";
  addUrl += "?parentID=" + parentID;
  addUrl += "&userID=" + UserID;
  addUrl += "&subjectText=" + escape(txtNewSubject);
  addUrl += "&messageText=" + escape(txtNewMessage);

  myDoc.load(addUrl);
  myDoc.onLoad = addMessageLoaded;
}
```

The first step is to disable the Tree component so no other events take place while we attempt to send the new message data to the web service. Our next step is to determine the ParentID of the new message, the default value being 0.

Similar to the (loadMessages) function, we create a new XML object instance and then build a URL to pass to the load method. In this case, we use the (escape) function to properly encode the characters the user has typed in the subject and message text boxes. Finally, the (load) method is called and the (addMessageLoaded) function is declared to handle the response.

```
function addMessageLoaded(success) {
  if (success) {
    if (myDoc.status == 0) {
      txtNewMessageStatus = "The new message was added
                    ➡ successfully. Refreshing the
                    ➡ current list of messages.";

      var currentNode = myDoc.firstChild;
      txtSubject = currentNode.attributes.SubjectText;
      msgDate = currentNode.attributes.MessageDate;
      txtMessage = currentNode.firstChild.nodeValue;
      txtUsername = Username;
      scrMsgText.setScrollTarget("txtMessage");
      scrMsgText.setEnabled(true);

      loadMessages(currentNode.attributes.ParentID);

      gotoAndStop("ReadMessage");
    } else {
      txtNewMessageStatus = "The new message data returned
                    ➡ was not valid. Status code: " + myDoc.status;
          myTree.setEnabled(true);
    }
  } else {
    txtNewMessageStatus = "There was an error adding
                    ➡ the message.";
    myTree.setEnabled(true);
  }
}
```

When the web service response is complete, the (addMessageLoaded) function is called. After checking that the success and status values are correct, we update the status text on the form.

Next, we parse the XML to retrieve the returned Message attributes and message text, and set the variable values on the ReadMessage frame. We then call the (setScrollTarget) and setEnabled methods of the ScrollBar component to ensure that it recognizes that scrolling for the txtMessage text box should be enabled or disabled.

We then call the (loadMessages) function with the ParentID of the message that was just added. This will refresh the list of messages, should there be any sibling nodes.

Finally, we jump to the ReadMessage frame to display the newly added message.

Scripts for NewUser (frames 31-40)

Select frame 31 on the Actions layer and attach the following functions.

addUser()

This function is called when the user completes the Register form and clicks the Submit button.

```
function addUser() {
  txtRegStatus = "";

  if ((txtRegPassword == txtRegPassword2)
    && (txtRegEmail.length > 5) && (txtRegUsername.length > 2)
    && (txtRegPassword.length > 3)) {
    myDoc = new XML();
    myDoc.ignoreWhite = true;
    var addUrl = "";
    // Un-comment the following line for debugging
    // addUrl += "http://localhost/";
    addUrl += "messageService.asmx/addUser";
    addUrl += "?userName=" + escape(txtRegUsername);
    addUrl += "&password=" + escape(txtRegPassword);
    addUrl += "&email=" + escape(txtRegEmail);

    myDoc.load(addUrl);
    myDoc.onLoad = addUserLoaded;
  } else {
    txtRegStatus = "Your registration information is not valid.";
    if (txtRegPassword != txtRegPassword2) {
      txtRegStatus += " The supplied passwords do not match.";
    }
    txtRegStatus += " All fields are required. Your user name
      must be at least 3 characters in length";
    txtRegStatus += ", and your password must be at least 4
      characters in length.";
  }

}
```

Our first step is to validate the form information. We need to verify that the two password fields match, the e-mail text is filled in, the user name is at least three characters, and that the password is at least four characters. If any of the checks fail, we display a message on the form, prompting the user to change their information.

Similar to the `loadMessages` and `addMessage` functions, we create a new XML object instance and then build a URL to pass to the `load` method. In this case, we use the `escape` function to properly encode the characters the user has typed into the user name, password, and e-mail text boxes. Finally, we call the `load` method.

addUserLoaded()

We now declare the `addUserLoaded` function to handle the response.

```
function addUserLoaded(success) {
    if (success) {
        if (myDoc.status == 0) {
            var currentNode = myDoc.firstChild;
            UserID = currentNode.attributes.UserID;
            Username = currentNode.attributes.Username;
            if (UserID > 0) {
                txtRegStatus = "Thank you!  You are now registered.";
                txtLogin = "Logged in as: " + Username;
                btnRegister._visible = false;
                btnLogin._visible = false;
                btnSignOut._visible = true;
            } else {
                txtRegStatus = "Registration failed. The user name or
                    e-mail address you supplied already exists in
                    our database.";
            }
        } else {
            txtRegStatus = "The user data returned from the server was
                not valid. Status code: " + myDoc.status;
        }
    } else {
        txtRegStatus = "There was an error registering your information";
    }
}
```

When the web service response is complete, the (addUserLoaded) function is called. After checking that the `success` and `status` values are correct, we parse the XML to retrieve the returned user attributes, and update our (UserID) and (Username) variables.

If the (UserID) returned is greater than 0, we know that registration was successful. In this case, we need to update the status text, hide the Register and Login buttons (as they're no longer needed), and make the Sign Out button visible.

If the returned UserID is *not* greater than 0, we display a message indicating the user name or e-mail address is already registered.

Scripts for LoginForm (frames 41-50)

Select frame 41 on the Actions layer and attach the following code:

```
function submitLogin() {
   txtLoginStatus = "Validating, please wait...";
   var loginUrl = "";
   // Un-comment the following line for debugging
   // loginUrl += "http://localhost/";
   loginUrl += "messageService.asmx/validateUser?";
   loginUrl += "userName=" + escape(txtLoginUsername);
   loginUrl += "&password=" + escape(txtLoginPassword);
   myDoc = new XML();
   myDoc.ignoreWhite = true;
   myDoc.load(loginUrl);
   myDoc.onLoad = loadUser;
}
```

When the user completes the Login form and clicks the Login button, the (submitLogin) function is called. Similar to the previous functions, we build a URL to pass to the (load) method using the (escape) function to properly encode the user name and password.

Finally, a new XML object instance is created, the load method is called with the created URL, and the (loadUser) function is declared to handle the response.

```
function loadUser(success) {
   if (success) {
     if (myDoc.status == 0) {
       var currentNode = myDoc.firstChild;
       UserID = currentNode.attributes.UserID;
       Username = currentNode.attributes.Username;
       if (UserID > 0) {
         txtLogin = "Logged in as: " + Username;
         btnRegister._visible = false;
         btnLogin._visible = false;
         btnSignOut._visible = true;
         gotoAndStop("StartFrame");
         txtLoginStatus = "";
       } else {
         txtLoginStatus = "Logon Failed.";
       }
```

continues overleaf

```
        } else {
          txtLoginStatus = "The data returned was not valid. ";
          txtLoginStatus += "Status code: " + myDoc.status;
        }
      } else {
        txtLoginStatus = "There was an error validating your ";
        txtLoginStatus += "user name and password.";
      }
    }
```

When the web service response is complete, we call the (loadUser) function. After checking that the success and status values are correct, we parse the XML to retrieve the returned user attributes, and update our UserID and Username variables. If the UserID returned is greater than 0, then we know login was successful. In that case, we need to update the login status text, hide the Register and Login buttons (since they're no longer needed), and make the Sign Out button visible.

Otherwise, we display a message indicating that the login failed.

Our Flash document's now complete, so make sure the FLA is saved somewhere safe, and compile a SWF called messageReader.swf in the wwwroot folder as usual.

Testing the message board application

Now that we have a finished movie, we can take it out for a test run. Point your browser at http://localhost/messageReader.swf, and wait a moment or two while the messages load in. Before long, you should be able to select messages from the list on the left:

Try replying to this message, and you'll see the message reminding you that you're not logged in. Rather than simply logging in as BigDog, let's use the Flash interface to register another new user.

Click on the Register button, and enter some new user details. I've used my own name, and a secret password that I don't intend to share with anyone – go on, make up some details of your own!

Register

User name: David

Password: ******

Confirm: ******

E-mail: big@d.com

Submit   Cancel

Registration failed. The user name or email address you supplied already exists in our database.

Oops! I've used the wrong e-mail address, and user BigDog already registered this one. Still, it's good to know that our system can spot when there's a conflict. Let's try it out again.

This time, everything's gone okay, and the message in the top-right corner confirms that I'm now logged in as David. Your name may be different, but you should be seeing something similar on your own screen.

Now let's try replying to that message again. Select the top message from the list on the left, and hit the Reply button. Add some message text of your own, and hit Submit.

Now wait a moment while the message board refreshes, and you should see the new message added beneath BigDog's original posting in the tree display.

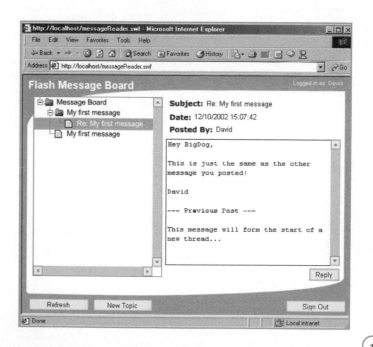

Looks like it's all working okay!

Summary

In this chapter, we've looked at how databases can add a whole new level of sophistication to our data-driven applications. Free from the intrinsic limitations of simple files, we can use databases to store massive quantities of information efficiently, and then access it quickly from our applications whenever we need to.

We've looked at MSDE as a handy, but powerful database engine, and got it installed and configured so that we could experiment with some simple SQL commands and queries. We then went on to develop a fairly sophisticated message board application, which uses a database to keep track of registered users and the messages they've posted.

You may not have absorbed every last detail covered here, but that's understandable. We can't give you a comprehensive introduction to databases in a single chapter, nor would we want to.

However, now that you've seen a few of the things that we can do with just a few lines of code, you should be able to experiment a little for yourself, and will hopefully have gained a better understanding of the intricacies involved in working with these powerful systems.

chapter 5: **Flash Remoting**

In this chapter we're going to take a look at another way to pass Flash data to and from the server. We'll be making use of a technology called Flash Remoting for .NET, which was designed by Macromedia to help take the hard work out of connecting Flash movies up to the .NET Framework.

Now despite whatever rumors you might have heard, there's nothing mystical about this Flash Remoting business – fundamentally, it does very much the same thing as we've already done in the course of the last few chapters: passes data back and forth. The important difference (as far as we're concerned at least) is that once it's plugged in at both ends, we can all but completely forget the fact that we're sending data over the Internet, and treat our ActionScript and C# objects almost as if they were parts of the same program!

> *Flash Remoting MX for .NET requires you to have the .NET Framework SDK installed. If you only have the .NET Redistributable, you won't be able to run the examples in this chapter.*

In this chapter, you'll see how to do the following:

- Install Flash Remoting MX components and service for .NET
- Make a simple Remoting-enabled service function and access it from Flash
- Debug connections
- Pass complex data via Flash Remoting MX
- Bind data
- Make a Remoting-enabled web service and access that from Flash
- Use Flash Remoting to access a third-party web service

Setting up Macromedia Flash Remoting for .NET

Flash Remoting doesn't actually come as part of Flash MX, so you need to download the relevant files from www.macromedia.com. It comes in two parts: **Remoting components** for the Flash movie, and a **Remoting service** for .NET.

Flash Remoting components

These define all the Remoting functionality needed by the Flash MX authoring environment, and therefore need to be installed on whatever machine(s) you use for authoring Flash movies.

At time of writing, you can download an installer for the Flash Remoting components from http://download.macromedia.com/pub/flash/flashremoting/FlashRemotingCmpntsInstall.exe

Run the executable, and you'll get the usual parade of install dialogs. You just need to click through the default settings and, all being well, you should soon find yourself looking at an Installation Completed message.

It's quite easy to check whether the installation's succeeded. The next time you start up Flash MX, you should discover the following new entries listed in the menus:

> Help > Welcome to Flash Remoting
> Window > NetConnection Debugger

If they don't show up immediately, you may need to wait a couple of minutes or (in the worst case) reboot your computer.

Installing the Flash Remoting service for .NET

This is the server-side part of the Flash Remoting system. It provides .NET with all the information and resources it needs to set up and maintain remote connection to a Flash movie. It's therefore responsible for handling client requests, handing them over to the relevant .NET code, picking up the results, and sending results back to the Flash client. For fairly obvious reasons, it needs to be installed on the server machine!

The Remoting service has to integrate very closely with the server technology, so a different version's needed for each of the server systems Macromedia has chosen to support. At time of writing, ColdFusion, WebSphere, and JRUN4 all have their own versions of the Flash Remoting service. You can download the .NET version from http://www.macromedia.com/go/remoting/.

> *If you already have one of the earlier beta releases installed, you'll need to remove it (using* Start > Control Panel > Add/Remove Programs*) before going any further. The Beta 1 uninstaller may not remove all files. After uninstalling Beta 1, if the* `flashservices` *folder still exists in your* `wwwroot`*, delete the folder. For example, if Beta 1 was installed to the default location, delete* `C:\Inetpub\wwwroot\flash services`*.*

Make sure you're logged into the server machine with admin privileges, and run the setup file. Once you've flown by the opening screens of the Install Wizard, you'll be asked for a Serial Number. Don't panic if you don't have one – leave it blank and the trial version will be installed. The trial version will operate full-featured for 30 days, after which you can still use it for simple development purposes (connecting from localhost only).

Now zip through the next few screens, accept the defaults, and finally click on Install to begin the installation proper. If all goes well, you'll soon see Installation Completed.

Now, to check that the Flash Remoting service has installed successfully, take a look at the files inside `C:\inetpub \wwwroot\flashremoting`. This is where we find all the resources needed to develop .NET applications that use Flash Remoting.

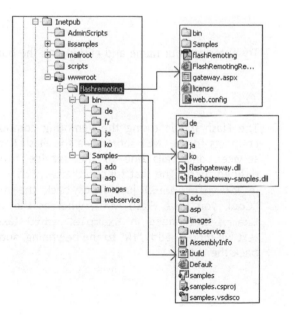

Testing the installation

As you can see, one of the folders here is called Samples, inside which you can find a few sample projects that Macromedia has provided to illustrate the use of Flash Remoting.

Now that we've installed both parts of Flash Remoting, we're all set to take it out for a test drive. So, point your web browser at http://localhost/flashremoting/samples/ and the sample page shown below should appear.

Try entering your name and clicking on the buttons – you should see something like this:

The Flash movie (using the Remoting components) connects to the .NET server (via the Flash Remoting service), and calls one of the **service functions** defined there. The first function, Example1 (defined in Example1.aspx) just sends back the message "Cool, you have Flash MX!", whereas the second, Example2 (defined in Example2.aspx) takes the text we send it, adds "Hi" to the beginning, and sends back the result.

> *Service functions are really just like the web methods we've used in previous chapters: functions that we can call via the Internet. Our movies send data to the server, which processes it, applies any local changes, and sends back the results.*

Okay, it may not be that impressive to look at, but at least we know that Flash Remoting works okay!

Build your first Flash Remoting application

Let's have a go at making our own mini-application, by writing the simplest of all simple ASP.NET service functions and then calling it from a Flash movie.

Writing a service function

We'll start our first remoting example by writing an ASP.NET page that defines a service function called helloworld.

1. Open up your text editor and enter the following code:

   ```
   <%@ Page language="C#"%>
   <%@ Register TagPrefix="MM" Namespace="FlashGateway"
   ➥ Assembly="flashgateway" %>

   <MM:Flash ID="myFlash" runat="server" >
   Hello, you're viewing this page via Flash Remoting!
   </MM:Flash>
   ```

2. Save the file in c:\inetpub\wwwroot\flashRemoting as helloWorld.aspx.

This is quite different to the ASP.NET pages we've looked at before – there's no sign of the page_load function, but instead there's a mysterious markup element called MM:Flash. What's going on? Well, let's walk through it one line at a time, and we'll soon figure it out.

As usual, the first line tells .NET to expect C# code, not that there actually is any yet. The second line is something we haven't seen before: a Register directive telling .NET that the tag prefix "MM" denotes an object that belongs in the FlashGateway namespace, as defined in the flashgateway assembly. Huh?

Okay, this may sound fairly daunting, but all it means is that whenever .NET sees an XML-like element in the page whose name begins with MM: it needs to interpret that element as an object. The namespace helps to uniquely identify the object being requested (more on this later), and the assembly is a block of compiled code (a file in the `bin` folder with a `.dll` extension) that holds a class definition for that object.

More specifically, when .NET now sees this mysterious tag called `MM:Flash`, it knows to look in `flashgateway.dll` for a class called `FlashGateway.Flash`. It makes an object based on this class, and gives it the name `myFlash` (as specified in the `ID` attribute). The element contents are automatically assigned to a property called `result`.

> The `runat="server"` attribute is used by .NET to mark out elements that need to be processed on the server. If it weren't there, the whole element would be sent out verbatim to the client, which wouldn't have a clue what it meant!

So what next? Well, if you call up this page in a browser, you won't see anything at all. The `Flash` object is a reclusive creature; it only ever shows itself when the page is requested by a Flash Remoting connection. That means we need to make a Flash movie before we can go any further!

Building the client

Now we turn to the Flash side of the equation and build a front-end that will request data from the server via a Flash Remoting connection. The movie we're going to build will need to:

- Connect to the `FlashRemoting` service via a gateway
- Call the `helloWorld` service function
- Handle whatever result (or error) it sends back

Let's build the interface.

1. Create a new Flash document and save it as `helloWorld.fla`.

2. Put a dynamic text field on the stage, and give it the instance name `tbMessage`.

3. Now attach the following code to the first frame on the timeline:

    ```
    #include "NetServices.as"

    if (init == null) {
      init = true;

        gateway = "http://localhost/flashRemoting/gateway.aspx";
        myConn = NetServices.createGatewayConnection(gateway);

        service = "flashRemoting";
    ```

continues overleaf

```
      myServiceObject = myConn.getService(service, this);
   }

      myServiceObject.helloWorld();
```

Okay, let's break this down into nice, digestible chunks before we go any further. Our first step on the Flash side is to include a file called `NetServices.as`, which defines all the objects we need to do Flash Remoting in ActionScript:

```
      #include "NetServices.as"
```

Before we start setting up our connection to the server, it's important to make sure we're not already connected. We put all the following connection code inside the body of an `if` statement, using the variable `init` to tell us whether the connection's been initialized:

```
if (init == null) {
  init - true;
  // connection code goes here
}
```

Connecting to the server

Next, we tell Flash where to find a gateway through which it can connect to the server. We then use the granddaddy of all Flash Remoting objects – `NetServices` – to establish a connection through that gateway:

```
gateway = "http://localhost/flashRemoting/gateway.aspx";
myConn = NetServices.createGatewayConnection(gateway);
```

This gives us a `NetConnection` object called `myConn`, which holds the information that we need to start communicating with the server. Before Flash makes the connection though, we must tell it what service we want to use, via `myConn`'s `getService()` method. Note that we specify `this` as the second parameter here, so that any results get sent back to the current timeline.

```
service = "flashRemoting";
myServiceObject = myConn.getService(service, this);
```

Using the service object

We now have a bona fide ActionScript service object, which you can think of as being like a second body for the `flashRemoting` service. That's to say, all the service functions we define under `flashRemoting` are available as functions on this object. Say we want to call the service function `helloWorld` (as defined in `helloworld.aspx`). All we need to do is this:

```
myServiceObject.helloWorld();
```

Try running the movie now, and you'll see the following message appear in the Output window:

```
NetServices info 1: helloWorld_Result was received from server: You
called this page up with Flash Remoting!
```

That's the result we wanted! Still not exactly earth shattering, but it proves all the same that something's gone right. We called the `helloworld` service from ActionScript, and the result we hard-wired into the ASP.NET page has made it back to the movie inside a message called `helloWorld_Result`.

Handling feedback from the server

You'll be glad to hear that we're not limited to reading messages off the Output window. We can act on this message by defining a function called `helloWorld_Result`.

```
// Invoked when helloworld function returns a result
function helloworld_Result(result) {
   tbMessage.htmltext = result;
}
```

Likewise, we'll get a message called `helloWorld_Status` whenever an error occurs, so we can deal with that too.

```
// Invoked when helloworld function returns an error
function helloworld_Status(status) {
   tbMessage.htmltext = status.description;
}
```

A more flexible way to use the MM:Flash control

Because the Flash control is actually generated as an object in .NET (in this case, with the instance name `myFlash`), we can just as effectively set its `result` property like this:

```
<%@ Page language="C#"%>
<%@ Register TagPrefix="MM" Namespace="FlashGateway"
➥ Assembly="flashgateway" %>
<script>
   void Page_Load(Object source, EventArgs e) {
     myFlash.Result = "This result's been set from ";
     myFlash.Result += " inside the Page_Load function."
   }
</script>
<MM:Flash ID="myFlash" runat="server" />
```

In fact, this is a much more flexible way to use it, as we're no longer limited to storing plain text. As we're about to see, there's nothing to stop us assigning complex structures like arrays or objects to the `result` property. What's more, they come out unscathed at the other end!

The Flash Remoting control exposes some other properties that we can make good use of:

- `Flash.params` contains a list of all the parameters sent from the Flash movie. The first value passed is in `Flash.Params(0)`, the next in `Flash.Params(1)`, and so on...

- `Flash.DataSource` lets us **bind** our control to a .NET dataset, and pass the whole dataset back to the Flash movie.

Configuring ASP.NET applications

In our examples so far, we've defined both the service function (`helloWorld.aspx`) and the SWF file in the folder `FlashRemoting`. This folder comes pre-configured to run Flash Remoting applications. However, if you want to work with Flash Remoting in your own web applications (that is, keeping all your server resources in another folder, inside or outside `wwwroot`, with all their own specialized settings), you need to configure that folder first.

To create a new application, create a new folder with the name you want to give to your application. For example, if you want an app called `flashDotNet`, you might start by creating `C:\flashDotNet\`. Right-click on it, select **Properties**, and then select the tab marked **Web Sharing** Select the radio button labeled **Share this folder**, and OK the next couple of dialogs.

You've now set up this folder as a virtual directory under the IIS web server. This means you can point your browser at http://localhost/flashDotNet/ to find any of the server files in this folder, despite the fact that it's outside `wwwroot`.

The next step is to mark this folder out as a web application, so that ASP.NET will allocate resources and assign special configuration settings to all the pages we run from this folder.

Select Start > Program Files > Administrative Tools > Internet Services Manager to run the Internet Services Manager, expand the Default Web Site item in the left panel, and look for the entry that corresponds to the folder you just created.

Once you've found it, RIGHT-CLICK and select Properties. Now press the Create button in the lower half of the Properties dialog.

You'll see the Application name and Starting Point change, and with that, we're done! We now have an ASP.NET application called flashDotNet. Now let's configure it to use Flash Remoting MX.

First, we must copy a couple of files across from C:/inetpub/wwwroot/FlashRemoting to our new application folder: gateway.aspx is a blank file that gives Flash a way to refer to the application without putting any extra load on the server, while web.config contains configuration settings, telling the server how it should deal with Remoting requests from Flash.

Next, create a folder called bin inside C:/flashDotNet, find flashgateway.dll inside C:/inetpub/wwwroot/flashremoting/bin, and copy it across to the new bin folder. This file defines all the functionality that lets us hook up Flash to the service functions so easily.

> *In technical terms, this is a .NET **assembly** (compiled code with a common purpose) that acts as a proxy for the Flash client. All the assemblies placed in an application's* `bin` *directory are loaded automatically when that application starts.*
>
> *When we use Flash Remoting to pass data back and forth between a movie and a service function, that data will pass through this file. That's why we need to refer to this assembly when creating our service functions.*

We're now ready to run Remoting-enabled service functions from our `flashDotNet` application. From now on, we'll use it to hold all our remoting-enabled examples. Let's go see what we can do with it!

Different data types

When we use Flash Remoting to transfer application data between the Flash client and the server, the messages that actually get passed over the Internet are in a format called **AMF**, which stands for Action Message Format.

When a Flash client sends data to a server, the client's Remoting components will convert that data into AMF and send it to the relevant gateway. Over on the server, the AMF data is translated back into a form that can be sent to whichever service we're interested in using, whether that's part of a local application, or a Flash Remoting-enabled service function (or even a full-blown XML web service) accessed via the Web.

Once the server's done its stuff, the whole process is reversed. Results from the server are converted into AMF, which is sent back to the client and translated back into ActionScript.

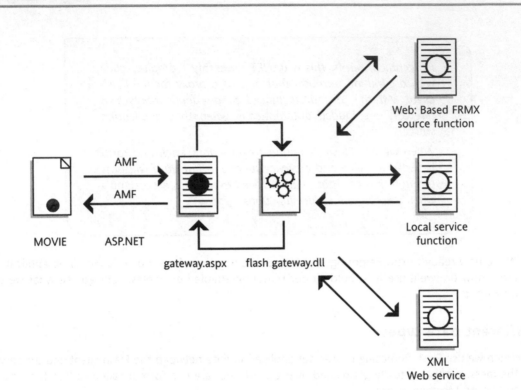

Web: Based FRMX
source function

Local service
function

XML
Web service

MOVIE   ASP.NET

gateway.aspx   flash gateway.dll

Flash Remoting does all the data conversions automatically and transparently. So, your Flash movie will deal exclusively with ActionScript data, while your remote service never deals with anything other than .NET data. Most of the time, you simply won't notice the conversion process.

AMF is a very compact format, which means it's very fast and efficient. What's more, it was designed specifically for Flash Remoting, so it doesn't limit us to using name-value pairs or XML documents in the way that our HTTP messages did in previous chapters. We can use almost any data type in our Remoting function calls, whether we're sending it from Flash to the server or vice versa.

Here are the server data types into which the Flash gateway converts ActionScript data types:

ActionScript Data Type	C# Data Type
Null	Null
undefined	Null
Boolean	System.Boolean
Number	System.Double
String	System.String
Date	System.DateTime
Array	System.Collections.ArrayList or System.Collections.HashTable
RecordSet	Cannot be sent to server
Object	FlashGateway.IO.ASObject
XML	System.XMLDocument

As you can see, every ActionScript data type apart from RecordSet has a counterpart in C#.

Flash Remoting also converts from .NET data types back into ActionScript. The following table shows which types correspond to each other on the return journey:

C# Data Type	ActionScript Data Type
Null	Null
Bool – System.Boolean	Boolean
any number type	Number
System.Char, System.String	String
System.DateTime	Date
System.Collections.ICollection Object []	Array
System.Collections.Hashtable or System.Collections.IDictionary	Associative array
System.Data.DataSet	Associative array of RecordSets

Let's now work upon some examples to demonstrate the data mapping concepts. We'll first build a prototype Flash application to send an array from Flash to an ASP.NET page.

Passing data back and forth

In this section, we'll build a sample application to show how we can pass data (in this case an array) from Flash to the .NET application server via Flash Remoting, and manipulate it so as to generate the result we display.

1. Firstly, create a new movie, save it as passArray.fla, and create an interface as shown here:

2.   Now, bring up the Actions panel, and attach the following ActionScript to the first frame:

```
#include "NetServices.as"
if (init == null) {
  init = true;

  gateway = "http://localhost/flashDotNet/gateway.aspx";
  myConn = NetServices.createGatewayConnection(gateway);

  service = "flashDotNet";
  myServiceObject = myConn.getService(service, this);
}
```

As before, we include our basic Remoting functionality (as defined in `NetServices.as`), set up a connection to the gateway, and use it to call the service we want. We're going to define our service function (the ASP.NET page) inside the `flashDotNet` application, so we specify `flashDotNet` as the name of the service we want to use.

3.   Next, add in the following function, which will be invoked whenever the user releases the Go button:

```
//*** Handlers for user interaction ***
btnGo.onRelease = function() {
  var movies = new Array(5);
  movies[0] = "Speed";
  movies[1] = "Minority Report";
  movies[2] = "Panic Room";
  movies[3] = "Men in Black II";
  movies[4] = "Star Wars";
  myServiceObject.passArray(movies);
  tbResult.text = "Please wait...";
};
```

We initialize an array, called `movies`, and store a few dummy values in it. We then call a service function called `passArray()`, which we'll define in just a moment, passing in the array. Finally, we set a loading message in the textbox `tbResult`.

4.   Now we define the same old functions for handling result and error messages received from the service function:

```
function passArray_result(result) {
  tbResult.htmltext = result;
}

function passArray_status(status) {
  tbResult.htmltext = status.description;
}
```

That's it for the Flash movie. We'll publish it once we've set up our service function in the ASP.NET page `passArray.aspx`. This page will be responsible for requesting the array from the Flash movie and then processing it to generate some suitable output.

5.   Open up Notepad and add the following code:

```
<%@ Page language="C#"%>
<%@ Register TagPrefix="MM" Namespace="FlashGateway"
➥ Assembly= "flashgateway" %>
```

Once again, we begin by rendering the `Page` directive and registering the `MM` prefix for our custom Flash control.

6.   Next, we add the main code for the page:

```
<script runat="server">
  void Page_Load(Object source, EventArgs e) {

    ArrayList myList = new ArrayList();
    string strResult = "";
    int count = 0;
```

We now declare some variables. Our Flash movie's going to send over an array, which we know will be interpreted by .NET as an `ArrayList` object, so we set one up ready, along with a couple of other variables that'll help us manipulate its values.

7.   Next, we check if any values have been passed to this page from the Flash client.

```
if(myFlash.Params.Count>0) {
  myList = (ArrayList) myFlash.Params[0];
  foreach (string item in myList) {
    count = count + 1;
    strResult += "Item "+count+"="+item+"<BR>";
  }
  myFlash.Result = strResult;
}
```

If yes, we request the array (using `Flash.Params(0)`) and store it in `myList`. We use a `foreach` loop to loop through the items present in this `ArrayList` and store each of the values (along with some additional text) in the string variable `strResult`. `Count` is a counter variable to keep a track of the current array index. Finally, we output this to the Flash client using the `Result` property of the Flash custom control.

8. Now, we just have to close the `page_load` function and the script block, and add the Flash control to the page.

```
    }
</script>
<MM:Flash ID="myFlash" runat="server" />
```

All that's left now is to publish the SWF and test it. You should obtain output like this:

Since we're still just getting started, we've simply returned the array's contents to the Flash client. Don't worry – we'll get onto some more elaborate applications soon enough.

Debugging with Flash Remoting

As is the case with any code, you'll inevitably encounter the odd problem with your Flash Remoting applications sooner or later. Because it does so much work hiding away the hard work involved in connecting the client to the server, it's a fair bit harder than normal to spot what's gone wrong with Flash Remoting. On its own, good old `trace()` isn't always that much help in figuring out why a movie can't connect, and we can't even test out our service functions the usual way in a browser, since the Remoting-specific data won't show up.

In order to make life easier for us, the Remoting components ship with some rather handy tools: an ActionScript file called `NetDebug.as` and an authoring environment utility called the **NetConnection Debugger (NCD)**. Believe me, both have done a great deal to help me stay sane during late-night debugging sessions on my own Flash Remoting apps!

They're specifically designed to work alongside Flash Remoting to help us keep a track of events occurring, errors thrown, results returned and lots more. You can use them to track down many potentially havoc-inflicting problems in a matter of seconds.

> *Using the NCD in association with methods on the* NetDebug
> *object (as defined in* NetDebug.as*) provides us with a great
> technique for tracing events that span the creation of
> ActionScript* NetConnection *objects to dispatch, execute,
> and respond to remote Flash services and applications.*

The NCD gives us a comprehensive list of the events used to connect client and server, and pass data back and forth between them. With its help, you can quite easily track down the smallest connection error in your application.

We can therefore get some very good clues as to what our movie is trying to do, where it's actually successful, and where things are going wrong (if they're going wrong, that is!).

So what are waiting for? Let's get this tool started to work for us.

Using the NetConnection Debugger

To make use of the NCD, you first need to add the NetDebug.as file to your Flash movie. Let's see it in action by adding it into our last example, arrayHandler.fla..

```
#include "NetServices.as"
#include "NetDebug.as"
if (init == null) {
  init = true;

  gateway = "http://localhost/flashDotNet/gateway.aspx";
  myConn = NetServices.createGatewayConnection(gateway);
```

Now, fire up the NCD by going to Window > NetConnection Debugger. You should get a screen like the one below:

Hit CTRL + ENTER to test the movie, and the NCD should soon list a single Connect event (in the left pane) like the one shown below. Click on it, make sure that you've selected the Details tab in the right pane, and you'll see a corresponding list of details.

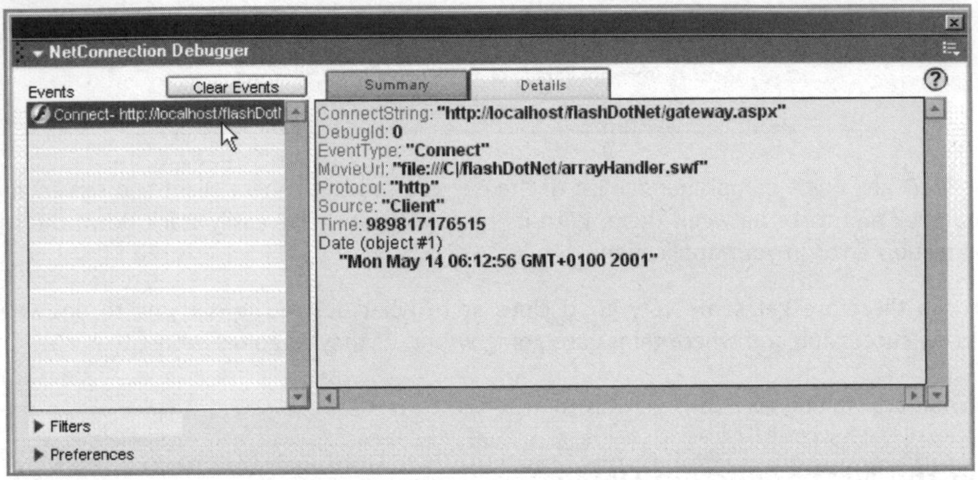

We can see that our Flash client has triggered a Connect event, defining a connection to the server gateway. We can even see how it's done so, with a variety of event parameters – they're all fairly self-explanatory.

Note that it hasn't actually connected yet. That'll only happen when we make a service function call, so hit the Go button and you'll see a new Call event triggered off, complete with a details list of its own. As you can see below, the details include all the data sent with the movie's call on the service function:

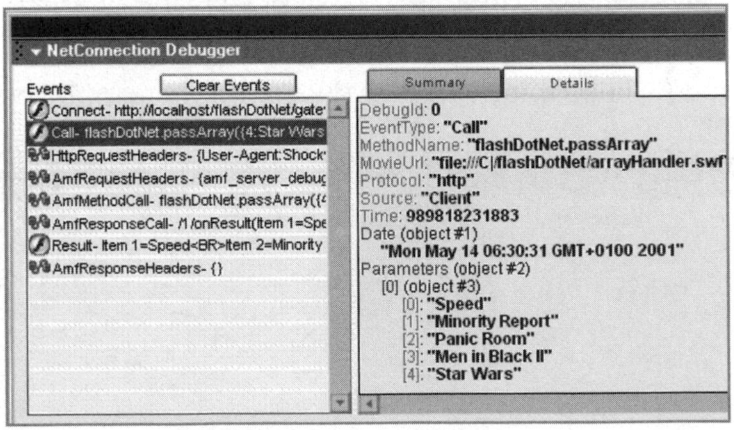

If everything's working okay, the Call event will quickly be joined by six more, as shown. Most of these describe the low-level details of HTTP and AMF used to send the messages across the network, and won't usually be of much interest (unless you're doing something fairly sophisticated). In this case, the important event to look at is the Result.

This shows us what the server function has sent back, and looks just like we expect it to. Fair enough, since the app's working okay – but what if it's broken?

Here's what happens when I put a deliberate typo into the code:

As you can see, we now get a Status event in place of the Result, and we can read all the information associated with it, including a description that tells us "No Such Service FlashDoNet with function passArray". Okay, I confess – that's where I put the typo. In fact, this is exactly the same information that our original example would've shown in the event of an error: the description property of the status object.

```
tbMessage.htmltext = status.description;
```

Don't forget to fix the typo before you move on!

Custom event tracing

Flash also offers you the ability to create and trace your own events from ActionScript. For example, if you wanted the NCD to notify you each time the user clicked on a button, you could use the `NetDebug` object's `trace` method to output the event to NCD.

The following modifications in the user interaction event handler function ActionScript of `BondCalc.fla` illustrate the use of this method:

```
btnGo.onRelease = function() {
  NetDebug.trace({level:"testing", Event:"ButtonClick",
  ➥ message:"Test msg to NCD on the event of a button click."});
  myServiceObject.passArray(movies);
};
```

Now, when you test publish the movie, enter the data and click the Go button, the events shown in the NCD should look more like this:

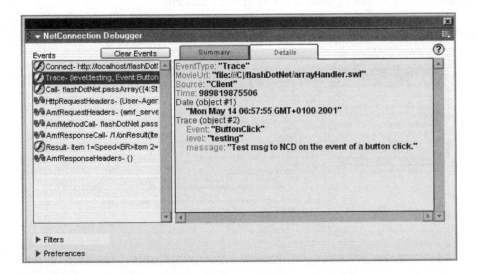

As you can see, the event we just created in ActionScript finally got a place in the NCD. This is particularly useful when debugging large code files. Now that we've seen how to make use of the NCD, let's look at some more challenging applications of Flash Remoting.

So far, we've seen how to pass simple Flash data types to the server and retrieve a simple string response. What about accessing more complex data types from the server, such as we might get in response to a database query?

Flash Remoting and databases

Flash Remoting MX makes it easy to integrate database content with our Flash movies. When we started using databases in the last chapter, we didn't have Remoting to fall back on, so we had to spend time encoding the data we sent in our query, and then interpret the data we retrieved. Fortunately, ASP.NET web services took a lot of the hard work out of things, by generating XML documents for us, but we still spent quite a while trying to parse it into useful data, and all that tedious `firstChild/nextSibling` business isn't exactly the most intuitive way to find the information you want.

Once we bring Flash Remoting into the picture, we don't even need to worry about this. It gives us a brand new ActionScript object called a `RecordSet`, which in many ways is just like a database table: a grid of rows and columns, with each row containing a record, and each column corresponding to one of the fields that can be stored for each record.

As you may have spotted from the data mapping tables earlier on, if we have a Flash Remoting service function that returns a `DataSet` object (that's the equivalent object in ADO.NET for representing data tables), it'll be automatically converted into an ActionScript `RecordSet` object by the time it reaches the movie.

> As you may recall from the last chapter, ADO.NET is simply the group of .NET object classes responsible for handling database connections and data.

So big deal! How does this actually make our lives any easier? As ever, the best way to demonstrate is with an example. Let's build a simple address book application, using a database to store our data, an ASP.NET page (using ADO.NET objects) to talk to the database, and Flash Remoting to help us pass data back and forth between Flash and the server.

Address book application

In this application, we're going to use Flash to provide us with a user-friendly interface for viewing contacts in a database of contact details. Each contact in the address book will represent a person with a unique contact ID, a first and last name, an e-mail address, a snail mail address and a phone number.

The interface will show a list of contacts, and let users view full details for each one. They can also sort the contacts' last names in ascending or descending order.

Here's what we'll be working towards:

Creating the database

Once again, we're going to use MSDE to manipulate a brand new database called `Contacts`. Let's kick things off by creating that database, assigning the permissions we'll need, and storing some data inside it.

1.   Press WINDOWS+R to call up the Run dialog, enter `cmd` in the input box, and hit OK to call up the command prompt. Type in the following command to create the database:

```
C:/>osql -E -S (local)\NetSDK -Q "CREATE DATABASE Contacts"
```

As before (back in Chapter 4) you should now see messages, confirming that you've created a pair of new databases, one for our contact details, and another to help MSDE keep track of all the changes we make to it.

```
The CREATE DATABASE process is allocating 0.63 MB on disk 'Contacts'.
The  CREATE  DATABASE  process  is  allocating  0.49  MB  on  disk
'Contacts_log'.
```

If this doesn't work for you as expected, just pop back to Chapter 4 and make sure you've set up MSDE as described there.

2.   The next step is to CREATE a table in the database, giving us somewhere to store each of our contacts' records. We'll call it `tblContacts` and define the following fields:

- `ContactId` will be our auto-numbered Primary Key field, which we can use to uniquely identify records.

- `FirstName` will be a `varchar` field of up to 20 characters, storing the first name for each contact.

- `LastName` will be `varchar` field of up to 20 characters, storing the last name for each contact.

- `Email` will be `varchar` field of up to 50 characters, storing the e-mail address for each contact.

- Address will be varchar field of up to 250 characters, storing the address for each contact.

- PhoneNo will be varchar field of up to 25 characters, storing the telephone number for each contact.

> Of course, there's nothing to stop you adding in extra fields of your own. For example, you might have a varchar field called Comment, and use it to store a brief description of each person listed. That way, next time you drop them a line, you won't have to rack your brain trying to remember whether you're talking to the one guy with a mole on his nose or the other who has three broken teeth.

We'll also use some INSERT INTO commands to add in a few sample records.

3. Open up Notepad and enter the following code.

```
CREATE TABLE [dbo].[tblContacts] (
    [ContactId] [int] PRIMARY KEY  IDENTITY (1, 1),
    [FirstName] [varchar] (20) NOT NULL,
    [LastName] [varchar] (20) NOT NULL,
    [Email] [varchar] (50) NOT NULL,
    [Address] [varchar] (250) NOT NULL,
    [PhoneNo] [varchar] (25) NOT NULL,
)
GO

INSERT INTO tblContacts VALUES('Pallav', 'Nadhani',
➥ 'pallav@nadhani.com', '123 Bangur Avenue, Kolkata - 700055', ➥ '91-
33-5552515');

INSERT INTO tblContacts VALUES('Vinay', 'Ranka',
➥ 'vinay_r@yahoo.com', '40-A Lake Town, Kolkata - 700055',
➥ '91-33-5554872');

INSERT INTO tblContacts VALUES('Sabya', 'Sachin',
➥ 'sabyasachin@hotmail.com', 'Sector 1, Tank 2, Salt Lake,
➥ Kolkata - 700032','91-33-5553575');
```

continues overleaf

```
INSERT INTO tblContacts VALUES('Mrinal', 'Somani',
➥ 'mrinalsomani@yahoo.com','P-20, Bangur Avenue, Kolkata -
700055','91-33-5552376');

INSERT INTO tblContacts VALUES('Asok', 'Nadhani', 'akn@nadhani.com',
➥ '567/1, P-10, Bangur Avenue, Block B, Kolkata - 700055','91-33-
➥ 5550651');

INSERT INTO tblContacts VALUES('Kisor', 'Nadhani', 'kkn@nadhani.com',
➥ '51/8, Bangur Avenue, Block D, Kolkata - 700055','9831060176');

INSERT INTO tblContacts VALUES('Nihit', 'Shah', 'nihitshah@vsnl.com',
➥ '11B, 4A, Shovabazar, Kolkata - 700019','91-33-5301266');

GO
```

4. Save it in C:/ as setupContactsTable.sql, and run the following from the command prompt:

    C:/>osql -E -S (local)\NetSDK -d Contacts -i C:\setupContactsTable.sql

    You should see the following, confirming that the table's now been set up and populated.

5. Now that's all in place, we just need to create a new login that we can use to access and control the Contacts database from the ASP.NET page. Run the following commands:

    C:/>osql -E -S (local)\NetSDK -Q "sp_addLogin 'abuser','abpass'"
    C:/>osql -E -S (local)\NetSDK -d Contacts
    ➥ **-Q "sp_grantdbaccess 'mbuser'"**
    C:/>osql -E -S (local)\NetSDK -d Contacts
    ➥ **-Q "sp_addrolemember 'db_owner', 'abuser'"**

Now let's build the service function that'll call up the data we want.

Writing the service function

The address book application is backed by an ASP.NET page `contacts.aspx`, which is responsible for the following deeds:

- Connecting to the database
- Getting a `DataSet` containing the list of contacts from the database
- And finally, passing the `DataTable` to Flash

A `DataTable` represents a single database table. The `Dataset` maintains a collection of these tables in the `TablesCollection` object. The `DataTable` completely represents the corresponding table, including its relationships and key constraints.

1. The following code in `contacts.aspx` does the work for us:

```
<%@ Page language="C#"%>
<%@ Import Namespace="System.Data" %>
<%@ Import Namespace="System.Data.SqlClient" %>
<%@ Register TagPrefix="MM" Namespace="FlashGateway"
➥ Assembly="flashgateway" %>
```

First of all, we set out the `Page` directive, import all the namespaces we'll need for working with databases, and register the `FlashGateway` assembly, so that we can make use of the Flash control.

2. Now we add the main code to run when the page loads.

```
<script runat=server>
  void Page_Load(Object sender, EventArgs e){
    //Build a connect string.
    string cnnString = "server=(local)\\NetSDK;";
    cnnString += "database=Contacts;";
    cnnString += "uid=abuser;pwd=abpass;";

    //Connect to the server.
    SqlConnection sqlCnn = new SqlConnection(cnnString);

    string sqlQuery="SELECT * FROM tblContacts";
    SqlDataAdapter sqlData = new SqlDataAdapter(sqlQuery,sqlCnn);

    DataSet myDataSet = new DataSet();
    sqlData.Fill(myDataSet,"contacts");
```

Once we've connected to the database, we use a new object called `SqlDataAdapter` to run our `SELECT` command, and then call its `fill` method to store the results in a `DataSet` object. Don't worry too much about the details here – the upshot is that we now have a `DataSet` object, called `myDataSet`, which contains the table of records sent back to us from MSDE.

The great thing about having this `DataSet` object is that it makes it extremely easy to attach the table of data to our Flash control, using the `DataSource` property we mentioned earlier on in the chapter:

```
myFlash.DataSource = myDataSet.Tables["contacts"];
```

3. Now we just have to finish off the `page_load` function, close the script block, and place our Flash control on the page itself.

```
    }
</script>

<MM:Flash id='myFlash' runat=server/>
```

4. Just before you save the file, add a couple of extra lines to help us check that everything's working okay:

```
    myFlash.DataSource = myDataSet;

    myDG.DataSource = myDataSet;
    myDG.DataBind();

    }
</script>

<MM:Flash id='myFlash' runat=server/>
<ASP:DataGrid id='myDG' runat=server/>
```

This is an ASP.NET server control, which does almost exactly the same thing as the `MM:Flash` control, and sends out a table of information. The difference is this: the Flash control will only show up if we call it via Flash Remoting, whereas the ASP control will only show up if we call up the page via a browser. Let's do that now.

5. Save the file in `C:/flashDotNet` as `contacts.aspx`, and point your browser to http://localhost/flashDotNet/contacts.aspx. You should see the following:

It won't win any prizes for looks, but it proves that we're accessing the data okay. Now let's turn to the final piece in our jigsaw, the Flash interface.

The Flash movie

The Flash front-end for this application will need to call the contacts service function, and pick up the `RecordSet` object that gets sent back. This will contain all the contact details obtained by the ASP.NET page (as shown above), which it then needs to display inside a scrollable list box.

When a user selects one of the listed contacts, Flash will need to display full details of the contact in the text fields below. We also want to provide a sort option, so that contacts can be ordered in ascending or descending order of last name.

1. Create a new Flash document called `address.fla`, create a few background elements and lock down the relevant layers so that they don't interfere with the interface we're about to build.

2. Now add a new layer called Contact Info, and add the elements shown below:

Apart from the static labels, we're looking here at a ListBox component (instance name `lbContacts`), two buttons (`sortAsc_btn` and `sortDesc_btn`), and four dynamic text fields (with Var set to `tbName`, `tbEmail`, `tbPhone`, and `tbAddress` respectively). Make sure you set up the ListBox parameters as shown below.

3. Hide this layer, add another called User Feedback, and add in the following elements:

The top one is just a text field that I've placed inside a movie clip called `error_mc`; we'll make it appear if there's an error. The lower one is another instance of my loading clock, which I've named as `clock_mc`. As usual, this will appear while Flash is waiting for data from the server.

4. Now it's time to bind up our Flash components using ActionScript, so add a third new layer called Actions. Select frame 1 and attach all the following code to it:

```
#include "NetServices.as"
#include "NetDebug.as"
#include "DataGlue.as"

error_mc._visible = false;

// Set up connection to the service
if (init == null) {
  init = true;

  gateway = "http://localhost/flashDotNet/gateway.aspx"
  myConnnection = NetServices.createGatewayConnection(gateway);

  service = "flashDotNet";
  myServiceObject = myConnnection.getService(service, this);
}

myServiceObject.contacts();
```

Our first block of code is responsible for setting up Flash Remoting, requesting data from the ASP.NET page and dealing with whatever's sent back.

We begin by including the Flash Remoting header files. As well as `NetServices.as` and `NetDebug.as`, which we've seen before, we list a new file called `DataGlue.as`. This helps us 'glue' the data stored in `RecordSet` objects to components like the ListBox, and believe me this will come in very useful!

We then go through the usual setup process, establishing a gateway connection, getting a reference to the service, and calling the service function `contacts`.

Next, we need to define handler functions for whatever the service function sends us back, whether it's a result or an error:

```
function contacts_Result(result) {
  _global.rsContacts - result;
  clock_mc._visible = false;
  setupListBox();
}
```

If we get a result, we store it in a global `RecordSet` called `rsContacts`. We hide the clock, and call a function that'll set up the main ListBox with all the contact details. More on that in a moment.

If the server sends back an error, we hide the clock and show the error message.

```
function contacts_Status(status) {
  clock_mc._visible = false;
  error_mc._visible = true;
}
```

5. Now we have to set up the ListBox, and this is where our 'data glue' comes into play.

```
function setupListBox() {
  lbLabelFormat = "#LastName#, #FirstName#      ";
  lbLabelFormat += #PhoneNo#     #Email#";
  lbDataFormat = "#ContactId#"

  DataGlue.bindFormatStrings(lbContacts, _global.rsContacts,
  ➡ lbLabelFormat, lbDataFormat);
  lbContacts.setSelectedIndex(0);
}
```

We're using an object called `DataGlue` (defined in `DataGlue.as`) here to bind the rows of data in `rsContacts` to the list entries `lbContacts`. Rather than simply copying values across from one to the other, this literally glues the ListBox entries to the values of records in `rsContacts`. Add a record to `rsContacts`, and `lbContacts` will show a new entry; change the ordering and the ListBox will reflect the change automatically. Powerful stuff!

> The `DataGlue` object provides functions that help up **bind** `RecordSet` objects (data providers) to User Interface components such as `ListBox` and `ComboBox` (data consumers).

We use format strings (the ones with all the pound signs # in them) to tell the ListBox how it should use the various fields to create each new list item. In this case, we want the label on each item to show the contact's names, number, and e-mail address (formatted with a few commas and spaces), while the corresponding data should just be the `ContactID`.

Once the ListBox has been forcibly attached to our data, we use the component method `setSelectedIndex()` to select the first entry in the list (index number 0).

> In many ways, `RecordSets` are similar to two-dimensional arrays, so the first record always has an index of 0, and not 1.

6. Next, we set up a function called `lbContacts_Change()`, which will be invoked whenever the user changes the selected item in `lbContacts`.

```
function lbContacts_change() {
   itemData = lbContacts.getSelectedItem().data
   ShowDetails(itemData);
}
```

All we do here is call up the data for the selected item (remember, this will just be the `ContactID` value) and pass it to another function called `ShowDetails`. Here's what that function looks like:

```
function ShowDetails(myId) {
   for (i=0; i<_global.rsContacts.getLength(); i++) {
      recordId = _global.rsContacts.getItemAt(i).ContactId
      if (recordId == myId) {
         // Set values for the text fields
         tbName = _global.rsContacts.getItemAt(i).FirstName;
         tbName += " "
         tbName += _global.rsContacts.getItemAt(i).LastName;
         tbEmail = _global.rsContacts.getItemAt(i).Email;
         tbAddress = _global.rsContacts.getItemAt(i).Address;
         tbPhone = _global.rsContacts.getItemAt(i).PhoneNo;
      }
   }
}
```

We loop through each item in `rsContacts`, looking for one whose `ContactId` matches the value specified in `myId`. On finding the right record, we use its properties to fill up the textboxes with the relevant contact details.

7. Now all that's left is to create the `onRelease` event handlers for both our sorting buttons.

```
sortAsc_btn.onRelease = function() {
   _global.rsContacts.sortItemsBy("LastName", "ASC");
};

sortDesc_btn.onRelease = function() {
   _global.rsContacts.sortItemsBy("LastName", "DESC");
};
```

Here we see another handy method of the `RecordSet` object in action – no prizes for guessing what it does! Best of all, once we've re-ordered all the records in `rsContacts`, we don't even need to update the ListBox – thanks to `DataGlue`, it'll update itself!

8. We're now ready for action, so open the NetConnection Debugger and test run the SWF. If everything's gone to plan, you should see the following:

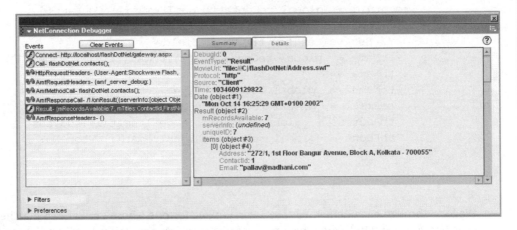

Flash Remoting and web services

So far, all our Flash Remoting examples have used simple remoting-enabled ASP.NET pages to define individual service functions for our movies to call up. In fact, we can just as easily connect to web services, both local and external, seamlessly connecting Flash clients to global applications.

We've already built a couple of ASP.NET web services in the course of this book, one of which we used to drive a dynamic image gallery back in Chapter 3. That example simply listed all the files in a specified folder, and we then used that information inside Flash to call up all the JPEG images present.

Let's see how we might update that example to use Flash Remoting, and interact with the web service in a new (and simpler) way.

Remoting-enabled picture gallery

1. First, you'll need to copy your source files for the gallery example (`picBrowser.fla`, `picList.asmx`, and the `images` folder complete with JPEGs) across to `C:/flashDotNet`. Open up the FLA, and change the lines that I've highlighted below:

```
#include "NetServices.as"
#include "NetDebug.as"
if (init == null) {
  init = true;
  gateway = "http://localhost/flashDotNet/gateway.aspx";
  myConn = NetServices.createGatewayConnection(gateway);
  service = "http://localhost/flashDotNet/picList.asmx?WSDL";
  myServiceObject = myConn.getService(service, this);
}
myServiceObject.getPicList();

var currImg = 1;
btnPrev.enabled = false;
txtMessage = "Loading image list...";

function getPicList_Result(result) {
  _global.picList = result;
  txtMessage = "";
  showImage(currImg);
}

function getPicList_Status(status) {
  txtMessage = "An error occurred: "+status.description;
}

function showImage(imgIndex) {
  txtMessage = imgIndex + ". " + picList[imgIndex];
  path = "http://localhost/images/";
  loadMovie(path+picList[imgIndex], "container");
};

btnNext.onRelease = function() {
  if (currImg<picList.length-1) {
    ...
  }
};

btnPrev.onRelease = function() {
  ...
};
```

Believe it or not, that's all the code we need to change in order to use Flash Remoting in this example. Apart from the initial setup code, we've simply rearranged the functions (so the old `readList` is now replaced by `getPicList_result` and `getPicList_status`), and replaced all the XML references with simple use of `picList` – no more mucking about with loops and nodes, just a plain old array.

What's more, there are no changes needed to the web service; all that Flash Remoting needs is a link to the WSDL document that describes it.

```
service = "http://localhost/flashDotNet/picList.asmx?WSDL";
```

ASP.NET will use this information to create a brand new assembly (in a DLL file) in the `bin` folder, and use that to communicate with the web service directly. So, no more code needed from us – hurrah!

2.   Before ASP.NET can create this new DLL though, we'll need to give it write permissions on the `bin` folder. Just right-click on the folder to call up its Properties dialog, and select the Security tab. Now use the Add button to an entry for `GOON\ASPNET` (not forgetting to replace `GOON` with the name of your own machine!), and check the bottom left box in the lower pane to allow this new 'user' write access to the `bin` folder.

3. Now open up the NetConnection Debugger, and test run the movie:

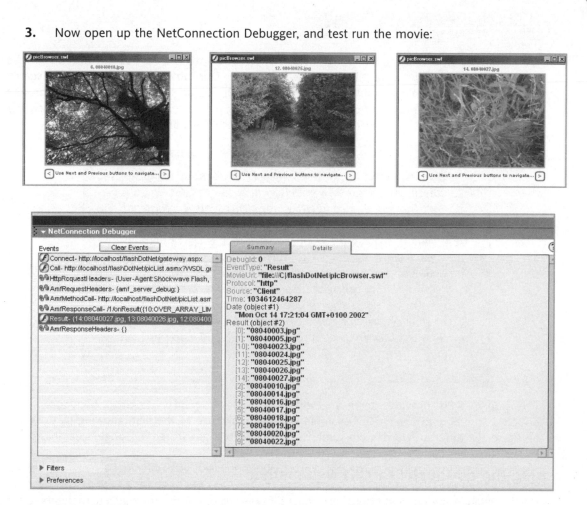

Hopefully you'll find it's working just as effectively as it did before, and this time letting us sneak a peek at what's actually going on under the hood.

Hang on a minute though. If it's so easy to tap into the picList web service, then what about using a third-party web service in the same way? ASP.NET doesn't have all those awkward security restrictions that stop us calling them up from Flash, so surely we can call them up via Flash Remoting.

Indeed we can, and it's not that hard to do either! Let's finish off the chapter with a look at how we can use Flash Remoting to tap straight into external web services from Flash. Remoting tells .NET how to do all the hard work, so we've not even any ASP.NET pages to write here – just plain old-fashioned ActionScript!

Flash Google

We're now going to build a Remoting-enabled Flash movie that can act as a front-end for the popular (and extremely powerful) Google search engine. Our movie will simply collect a search string from the user and submit it to the Google web API's service, which will then hunt through an enormous database for a list of web pages containing the search term. When Flash receives a list of results from the web service, it simply has to display them all.

> *Before you can access the Google API, you'll need to register yourself at* https://www.google.com/accounts/NewAccount. *Don't worry — it's completely free! Once you've registered, you'll be sent a license key that you'll need to use in your code. At time of writing, the Google web service is a free beta, for which queries are limited to 1000 per user per day, with a maximum number of ten results per query. By giving you a unique key, they can keep track of your usage, and make you sure you're not some unscrupulous type selling on their valuable services for your own financial advantage! You can check out their FAQs at* http://www.google. com/apis/api_faq .html.

The Google APIs provides three methods: `doGoogleSearch()`, `doGetCachedPage()` and `doSpellingSuggestion()`. Our example will only make use of the first, allowing us to search on up to ten different words from some two billion web pages stored in Google's database.

Using the doGoogleSearch() web method

We can change the queried results, providing different values in the method's parameters. Once we have created an object from the Google API's web service we can execute the `doGoogleSearch()` method.

This method accepts ten arguments that help us to narrow down our search, specifying and refining search terms, filtering results for similar pages, adult content, language, and so on. Here's what a call to this method might look like:

```
doGoogleSearch(Key, Q, start, maxResults, filter,
➥ restrict, safeSearch, Lr, Ie, Oe)
```

`Key` is a string that specifies your personal license ID.

`Q` is a string that specifies the query string on which you want to search. You can specify up to ten words, remembering that some 'stop' words, such as 'what', 'who', and 'the' will be excluded from the searched words. You can use double quotes to search for an exact phrase ('stop' words included) or use a preceding hyphen to exclude a word from the query string.

`start` is an integer that specifies the zero-based index of the first result we want. For example, if we set the start index as 0, Google will returns the matches numbered 1-10.

`maxResults` is an integer specifying the maximum number of results you want to retrieve from your search. In the beta stage, its maximum allowed value is 10.

`filter` is a Boolean value, specifying whether or not you wish to enable a filter to remove similar results and pages that come from the same website.

`restrict` is a string that lets you restrict the search to a specific topic such as 'friends of Ed' or a specific country.

`safeSearch` is a Boolean value that specifies whether or not you want to enable a filter to remove all results that contain adult content.

`Lr` is string that lets you retrieve results in the specified language only. You have to specify a valid string value such as `lang_en` for English language, or more than one value separated by a pipe | character.

`Ie` is a string that lets you specify the character encoding used in the string you send to Google.

`Oe` is a string that lets you specify the character encoding used in the string you receive from Google's search engine.

> *You can find more information on all of these as part of the Google API's kit, which is available for download after you register at the Google site.*

Creating the Flash interface

Now let's get to the creation of our Flash front-end, which will interact with this web service and display the results.

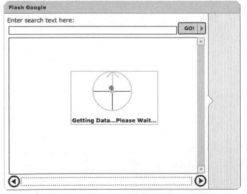

1. Create a new movie and save it as `Google.fla`. Once you've popped in a few background graphics and locked down the relevant layers, create a new layer called Controls, and add the following elements to the stage:

    At the very top, we have an input text field (with Var set to `tbQuery`) and button (instance name `go_btn`), which we'll use to submit queries to the search engine.

    Just below those are a dynamic text field (instance name `results_txt`) and a ScrollBar component (whose Target TextField is also set to `result_txt`), which will display the results returned by Google.

    At the bottom, we have a dynamic text field (instance name `resultCount_txt`) that we'll use to show which ten results are currently displayed, and a couple of buttons (`back_btn` and `next_btn` respectively), which let us call up the last ten or next ten results.

2. Add another level called User Feedback, and add a looping movie clip that we can show while Flash is waiting for data. As you can see, I've used my old clock clip, and given it the instance name `clock_mc`.

3.   Add one more level, and call it Actions. Select frame 1, open up the Actions panel, and get your keyboard ready. We begin by adding the familiar lines of code that open all our Remoting examples.

```
#include "NetServices.as"
#include "NetDebug.as"

if (init == null) {
  init = true;
  gateway = "http://localhost/flashDotNet/gateway.aspx";
  myConn = NetServices.createGatewayConnection(gateway);
  service = "http://api.google.com/GoogleSearch.wsdl";
  myServiceObject = myConn.getService(service, this);
}
```

Once again, we specify the service by linking to the WSDL file that describes the Google API web service. The only difference between this and the last example is that the WSDL file (and the service itself) is accessed via the Web.

4.   Now we hide the clock movie clip, and disable the buttons.

```
clock_mc._visible = false;
back_btn.enabled = false;
next_btn.enabled = false;
```

5.   Next, we write a function to handle the Go! button's onRelease event, and call a function named doSearch, passing it the query and an index of 0 (specifying that we want to view the first ten records).

```
go_btn.onRelease = function() {
  doSearch(tbQuery, 0);
};
```

6.   Here's where we define that function. Once we've shown the clock and ensured that the results text field is empty, we call the doGoogleSearch() method on our service object, passing it various arguments.

```
function doSearch(query, startIndex) {

  results_txt.text="";
  clock_mc._visible=true;

  licenseKey = "???" // add your own key value here
  myServiceObject.doGoogleSearch(licenseKey, strQuery,
  ➥ startIndex, 10, false, "", false, "lang_en", "", "");
};
```

The crucial arguments here are the license key value (which I'm afraid you'll have to fill in for yourself), the query itself, the index of the first result we want to view, and the number of results we want to view, which in this case is the maximum 10.

7. Now it's time to define the functions that'll deal with responses from the Remoting method call. First, we have the `result` function, which will be called if the method call is successful.

```
function doGoogleSearch_result(result) {
  _global.searchString = result.searchQuery;
  _global.maxIndex = result.estimatedTotalResultsCount;
  _global.currentIndex = result.startIndex-1;

  clock_mc._visible = false;
  back_btn.enabled = true;
  next_btn.enabled = true;

  displayResults(result);
};
```

We start by storing several pieces of information about the search in global variables. We need the string that was last searched on, the estimated total number of results, and the index of the first result. We subtract 1 from the index to account for that fact that the `startIndex` property counts results from one, whereas the value we use in the method call needs to start counting from zero.

Once we've done that, we hide the clock, enable the buttons, and call a function that will display the specified results.

8. We also have to account for the Remoting call being unsuccessful, so we define the following function, which will display error text and hide the clock.

```
function doGoogleSearch_status(status) {
  tbResult=status.description;
  clock_mc._visible = false;
};
```

9. Now onto the function that's responsible for displaying all the data we've managed to pull into Flash. We do this by building up a couple of long strings of HTML and assigning them to the `htmlText` property of our two dynamic text fields.

```
function displayResults(data) {
  //Display the results
  strResult = "Your search for <b>"+data.searchQuery+"</b>";
  strResult += " took "+data.searchTime+" seconds.";
  strResult += "<br><br>";

  //Generate HTML to display results
```

continues overleaf

```
        for (i=0; i<10; i++) {
            // 'item' will contain each result in turn
            item = data.resultElements[i];

            strResult += "<u><font color='#0000FF'>";
            strResult += "<a target='_blank' href='"+item.URL+"'>"
            strResult += item.title+"</a>";
            strResult += "</font></u>";
            strResult += "<BR>";

            strResult += "<font color='#000000'>"
            strResult += item.snippet+"</font><BR>";
            strResult += "<font color='#009900'>"
            strResult += item.URL+"</font>";
            strResult += "<font color='#000000'><B> - "
            strResult += item.cachedSize+"</B></font>";
            strResult += "<BR><BR>";
        }
    results_txt.htmlText = strResult;

        strInfo = "Showing results "+data.startIndex;
        strInfo += " to "+data.endIndex+" from ";
        strInfo += data.estimatedTotalResultsCount+" matches";

        resultCount_txt.htmlText = strInfo
    };
```

10. Finally, we wire up the two buttons that let us summon up the last ten or next ten results, by calling the doSearch() function again.

```
back_btn.onRelease = function() {
    gotoIndex = currentIndex-10;
    if (gotoIndex<0) { gotoIndex=0 }

    doSearch(searchString, gotoIndex);
};

next_btn.onRelease = function() {
    gotoIndex = currentIndex+10;
    if (gotoIndex>maxIndex-10) { gotoIndex=maxIndex-10; }
    if (gotoIndex<0) { gotoIndex=0 }

    doSearch(searchString, gotoIndex);
};
```

This is where we use the global variables that were set aside earlier on. These buttons should only ever let us navigate between sets of results from the same search, so the string that they trigger a search on needs to be based on the original term `searchString` (rather than the text box value). Likewise, we use `currentIndex` and `maxIndex` to figure out where to jump to and when to stop.

We're now ready to test the movie, so save the document in `C:\flashDotNet\` as `google.fla` and press CTRL+ENTER to run it in the projector. Since we've hard-wired all our URLs, it should work okay from there. Of course, you'll need to make sure you have an active connection to the Internet, but all being well, you should find that you're able to run your own web searches on Flash Google.

Summary

In the course of this chapter we've looked at how Flash Remoting MX gives us a whole new approach to passing data back and forth between our Flash movies and the .NET Framework.

Once we'd seen how to install the Flash Remoting components (to make the Flash end of the equation work) and service (to let .NET handle Flash Remoting requests), we built a simple service function, using the Flash server control <MM:Flash/> to send .NET data back to Flash, in whatever form it happened to be.

We looked at configuring new ASP.NET applications so that you can use Flash Remoting service functions from wherever you want on the server, and considered the different types of data that it can send in either direction.

We then went on to look at NetDebug.as and the NetConnection Debugger, which help us to see what data Flash Remoting MX is actually sending back and forth, and (if necessary) track down any problems at source.

After that, we spent a while looking at some techniques for data binding. We saw how Flash Remoting MX can help us to integrate with databases on the server side, and how DataGlue.as lets us wire up data-consumers in Flash (such as the ListBox component) to data sources, saving us the trouble of copying and updating data from one to the other.

Finally, we saw a brand new way to access web services, both on and beyond the local server. With Flash Remoting MX to automate all the .NET functionality, we simply needed a few lines of ActionScript to call up arrays and objects full of data from (theoretically) just about anywhere on the Web.

In the next chapter, we're going to see a Case Study that uses the same approach to an even more elaborate end. Hopefully though, you've already got a feel for the possibilities this Flash Remoting business opens up – there's a whole world out there waiting to see what you can come up with for yourself!

case study 1: **Airport weather**

Given the fact that I spend all day developing applications in Flash, you might think the last thing I'd want to do when I get home each night is boot up a computer, load in Flash, and start all over again, creating full Flash applications just for fun. But on any given day, that's me. Okay, I admit it – I'm a Flash junkie!

Of course, when Macromedia opened up the Flash Remoting beta to the public, I jumped at the opportunity. I'd recently started working with web services, and the chance to link up my favorite front-end tool with all this newfound web-based functionality got me all gooey inside. Junkie hardcore!

In this chapter, I'm going to take you through the development process of one of the test applications I built exploring these brand new horizons. With the new skills you learned back in Chapter 5, you should be all set to follow this, and even use it as a jumping off point for your own ideas.

What I'm going to do here is try and explain the reason behind *how* and *why* I did what I did, as well as provide a few details for those of you who want to have a go at replicating my results. I've therefore tried to approach this chapter from the angle of discussing the major points of the application, how and why I wrote the app the way I did, and to provide some insight into some cool coding practices that you, as a reader, may not be aware of.

Starting out

I began my foray into uncharted territory as so many others did: by looking at existing web services, picking one, and creating a nice Flash interface for it.

Most of the folks I talked to had done this, and most of them had followed exactly the same path: Flashifying the Google search web service (http://www.google.com/apis). Sure, it was one of the first big-name commercial web services available, but I simply wasn't interested. I realized that, before long, there would probably be a million different Flash interfaces for searching the Web, and I wanted to tread a different path.

I spent a lot of time looking through lists of public web services – in particular, the one at www.xmethods.com. For each web service that piqued my curiosity, I tried to envisage what sort of app it might lend itself to, and how an animated, interactive Flash interface might raise the bar on its practical value and all-round usefulness.

At that time though, options were limited – only two dozen or so services were listed, and of those only a handful seemed to be more than just "Hello World" type web services. Since then, however, the numbers have grown steadily as more and more people release their services to the public.

I quickly noticed several different weather reporting services, which immediately got me thinking how useful a graphical interface would be for helping users find out about local weather conditions. It's the sort of thing you might find on a web portal: small, generic, very to the point, very utilitarian.

But plenty of those apps exist already. I wanted something just a little different, something a little more focused. I wanted something that would make use of all the things that make Flash so cool, but not just gratuitously for effect.

Just at that point, I noticed that one of the weather services reported the conditions at any given airport in the world. Right then, bells started going off.

Right away, I started dreaming up ideas for in-terminal airport waiting area kiosks: "Select your destination and see what the weather will be like when you land! Uh, hello? It's just a beta test. All day I'm used to thinking in complete application terms, so I tend to go to extremes; besides, what better way to test than to build a plausible, real-world-type application?

What are the goals of the project?

Once I had I decided that I was going to create this application, I determined that I would keep with my original idea of a kiosk installation, and not a web application. I knew that there would be subtle implementation differences between a kiosk app and a web app, but I would deal with those as I met them. Now that I had my base platform decided upon, I could begin to put together my goals and feature set.

My goals for this project were simple:

- Let users select from a pre-defined list of cities.

- Gather weather information for the selected city's main airport.

- Display the returned weather information to the user.

- Make the whole thing incredibly simple to use.

The feature set seems equally trivial:

- Present a method to let the user pick a city with a fun, "Look what Flash can do" interface; so no drop-down lists or static links.

- Display a "Please wait" message to keep the user occupied while we query the web service.

- On retrieving information, display the relevant weather: sky conditions (clear? overcast? raining? hurricane?), temperature, and wind conditions (speed and direction).

- Display the selected city's name, along with the name of the airport.

- If there was a problem with the web service, report an error to the user.

In any case, the user should be able to select as many cities as they need, even if just to pass the time. The weather information I chose to present could help an airline passenger approach such upfront concerns like there could will be delays with their flight, if they should get their jacket out of their luggage before boarding, or even just to satisfy their curiosity.

One of the features of a kiosk-based application is that normally there is no such thing as a mouse. Using a touch-screen facilitates most user interaction. With this in mind, I had to make sure that my final user interface didn't rely on dragging elements around or any sort of hovering effects, and base everything on a single click.

Choosing a suitable web service

Having my application goals and feature set laid out, I now needed to see if I could find a web service that would match my needs in one fell swoop, if I needed to use several different services, or if I needed to write my own custom service. I also had to take into account whether any of the possible web services were free, public access, or whether there were licensing issues to deal with.

At the time of my initial testing, www.xmethods.com had the option of four different weather web services. Let's look at the services that were available and how they fit into my plans.

- www.xmethods.net – Weather, Temperature

Web Service homepage: http://www.xmethods.com/ve2/ViewListing.po?serviceid=8
First up was this free web service from the same site as the repository I was browsing. A quick look at the service information page, and I see that all it returns is the current temperature for a given zip code. Certainly nowhere near the amount of information I'm looking for, but perhaps a good backup.

- www.vbws.com – Weather Conditions

Web Service homepage: http://www.vbws.com/services/weatherretriever.asmx

This is a nice web service, certainly providing more information that the first – temperature, sky conditions, humidity, and barometric information. It even provides a link to a GIF of the conditions. However, it doesn't provide wind conditions (which I think for my app is more applicable than barometric pressure) and a GIF is nice, but I can only load JPEGs dynamically into Flash.

The kicker for me not using this service is that the information page states that this is for educational purposes only, and it obtains its information from The Weather Channel. Since it doesn't seem to be officially sponsored by The Weather Channel, and it's not meant for production use, I could infer that the web service uses a screen-scrape type method for information gathering, and one change from The Weather Channel could possibly shut down this web service.

- www.capeclear.com – Airport Weather

Web Service homepage: http://capescience.capeclear.com/webservices/airportweather/

This web service takes the International Civil Aviation Organization's registration code for any airport in the world and returns a nice collection of common information – temperature, sky conditions, wind, and more. A quick look at the site, and it appears to be free to use for testing and educational purposes.

This certainly looked like it could be the perfect web service for my app. But (and there's always a but) testing out the service through the company's web site showed one of the problems with third-party web services: it was terribly slow and there was nothing I could do about it. For this amount of information, I can live with slowness; however, there's I still have one more web service to investigate.

- www.unisysfsp.com – Weather

Web Service homepage: http://www.unisysfsp.com

The last third-party web service available was a nice service from Unisys. However, the information returned goes well beyond the information I was looking for. Instead of current weather conditions, this service provides a seven-day forecast for a given zip code. Nice – but not what I need.

Once I'd gone through the services that were pre-built and already available, my remaining option was to write my own. I scoured the Web and found several official sources where I could obtain just the information I required. But then I thought, "Hey – this is a Flash test – not a test of my amateur web service writing skills." Whew – that revelation just made life a lot easier.

I think it's fairly obvious from the four services shown that the web service from Cape Clear is the preferred choice, albeit a slow one. I'll just have to take the slowness into account in my front-end so the user doesn't get too annoyed at how long it's taking to view the weather.

The nitty-gritty

It may seem strange to put so much forethought into a simple test application, but I think this process is important for projects of any size. Earlier in my coding career, I used to just jump into programming projects with reckless abandon. As I started to work with more and more clients at once, I learned the hard way that if you don't have solid foundations behind every project you take on, you can not only get yourself tied up in knots, but possibly lose customers and future work. The more projects I work on with this in mind, the more I see that I become much more productive and reach the final end-point much more rapidly than if I had kept to my earlier ways of coding without care.

Nevertheless, with our goals and feature set all laid out, we can finally get into the details. The first thing to determine is the method or methods needed to utilize the web service in our app.

Getting to know the web service

Most public web services provide either a web interface to their method list, or, at the very least, a viewable WSDL file (more on these in a moment). Cape Clear provides a very nice, custom interface to their methods, allowing for web-based testing of all functionality.

Go to:

http://www.capescience.com/webservices/airportweather/index.shtml

and select the Web interface option from the table at the bottom.

The methods available in this web service are:

- getHumidity()
- getLocation()
- getOb()
- getPressure()
- getSkyConditions()
- getSummary()
- getTemperature()
- getVisibility()
- getWind()

I started by looking at the methods available for each of the desired information sections in my app: getLocation(), getTemperature(), getSkyConditions(), and getWind().

The input parameter for each of these methods is a string representing the registration "number" for any airport in the world. Using a link from the Cape Science web site, I found the string for the airport here in New Orleans – KMSY – and started testing each required method.

getLocation()

I first tried out the getLocation(), method, passing in my airport code, "KMSY", as the only argument. This call returned fine results:

StationBinding: getLocation Response

> return *string*   New Orleans, New Orleans International Airport, LA, United States

Perfect! This method accepted my airport code and returned a very descriptive string containing the city, the airport name, the state, *and* the country, all in a nice readable format.

getTemperature()

I then tested the getTemperature() method, again passing in my airport code. The results from this call looked very similar to the last result:

StationBinding: getTemperature Response

> return *string*   The Temperature at New Orleans, New Orleans International Airport, LA, United States is 80.1 F (26.7 C)

However, I soon realized that this format was going to be tricky to parse. Certainly in the results shown, I could split the string into sections based on several different characters: space, open parenthesis, commas, but I can't guarantee that these will be the same from one airport to the next. Okay – first problem.

getSkyConditions()

StationBinding: getSkyConditions Response

> return *string*   The Sky conditions at New Orleans, New Orleans International Airport, LA, United States is overcast

Let's look at the results from our next method – getSkyConditions():
Again, we see a lengthy string that's informative, but hard to use as it is. Certainly, we could split this into individual words, searching for the word 'is' and using the remaining words as the sky conditions. But that, too, could be messed up should an airport have the single word 'is' in its name.

Well, this is beginning to be a little less perfect than I first thought. What to do?

Not wanting to give up so soon, I decided to look at two other methods of the web service that were not individual items – getOb() and getSummary().

The first method, getOb(), returns a string representation of... well, actually I'm not exactly sure what it is. Perhaps it's some kind of technical specification, perhaps it's a special encoding of the information useful to those in the airport or weather industries. Since there's no clear way to tell what this information is, I decided to ignore it.

getSummary()

Next I tried the getSummary() method with my KMSY airport code. The results were exciting:

StationBinding: getSummary Response

return	WeatherSummary		
	location	string	New Orleans, New Orleans International Airport, LA, United States
	wind	string	Calm
	sky	string	overcast
	temp	string	80.1 F (26.7 C)
	humidity	string	76%
	pressure	string	29.94 in. Hg (1013 hPa)
	visibility	string	10 mile(s)

This method outputs all parameters as individual, very succinct strings (or at least easily parse-able strings). A single element named WeatherSummary wraps all the response output elements. I think this is the way to go.

Service description

Before we get into Flash code (yes, I know you're anxious), let's talk a little about reading a WSDL file. The great majority of web services don't have such convenient web interfaces to test their functionality. If you're lucky, the web service was created with Microsoft's .NET platform, which provides a built-in web access method (though not quite as 'pretty' as this weather service's front-end). The rest of the time, you'll be presented with nothing but a WSDL file as an interface to the web service.

A WSDL file is a Web Service Description Language file – which does exactly as its name implies – it **describes** the functionality of a web service via a readable "language". In this case, the language is good-old XML. This chapter isn't about the ins-and-outs of WSDL so I'm just going to show you a portion of the WSDL file for this web service and show how we can use this information inside Flash. The AirportWeather WSDL file can be found online at http://live.capescience.com/wsdl/AirportWeather.wsdl.

Among the information contained in a WSDL file, two things are required: public method invocation names (messages), and input and output parameter variable types. Here we see the messages sections for two methods – getSkyConditions and getSummary:

```
- <message name="getSkyConditions">
    <part name="arg0" type="xsd:string" />
  </message>
- <message name="getSkyConditionsResponse">
    <part name="return" type="xsd:string" />
  </message>
- <message name="getSummary">
    <part name="arg0" type="xsd:string" />
  </message>
- <message name="getSummaryResponse">
    <part name="return" type="xsd1:WeatherSummary" />
  </message>
```

From this snippet of XML, you can see that the getSkyConditions() method takes one argument of type string (our airport identifier) and returns a string via the getSkyConditionsResponse message.

The getSummary() method also requires a string parameter when being called, and it shows a return type of WeatherSummary. This is the same information we were presented with in the web interface.

> *If you don't have access to a web interface to test methods, knowing how to read a WSDL file is a must for working with third-party web services.*

The next step is to figure out exactly what a variable of type WeatherSummary consists of.

WeatherSummary

If we look back at the web response for this method, we see that 'inside' the WeatherSummary listing are seven properties of type string. This is what's known as a **complex element type.**

Let's take a look at the section for this complex type from the WSDL file:

```
- <xsd:complexType name="WeatherSummary">
  - <xsd:sequence>
      <xsd:element maxOccurs="1" minOccurs="1" name="location" nillable="true" type="xsd:string" />
      <xsd:element maxOccurs="1" minOccurs="1" name="wind" nillable="true" type="xsd:string" />
      <xsd:element maxOccurs="1" minOccurs="1" name="sky" nillable="true" type="xsd:string" />
      <xsd:element maxOccurs="1" minOccurs="1" name="temp" nillable="true" type="xsd:string" />
      <xsd:element maxOccurs="1" minOccurs="1" name="humidity" nillable="true" type="xsd:string" />
      <xsd:element maxOccurs="1" minOccurs="1" name="pressure" nillable="true" type="xsd:string" />
      <xsd:element maxOccurs="1" minOccurs="1" name="visibility" nillable="true" type="xsd:string" />
  </xsd:sequence>
</xsd:complexType>
```

There's quite a bit of information here, and luckily we can ignore most of it. The parts of this snippet that are relevant to us are the type of each element and the name. Each element in a complex type can be thought of as a property of the wrapper type – which can in turn be thought of as an object. As we'll see shortly, this is very important to us inside Flash and Flash Remoting.

Setup

Before we jump into testing code and so on, we need to think about sorting things out so that our project is arranged tidily. I set up individual folders for each of my Flash Remoting projects, rather than getting everything into a mess in the default installation folder. To do this, there are a few settings to tweak...

1. Create a folder in the root of your local drive, and call it `airportweather`.

2. Your project folder now needs to be created as a .NET Application folder. In IIS terms, this is also known as a Virtual Site. Right-click on your new folder, select the Web Sharing tab from the properties dialog, and click the Share this folder radio button option.

3. In the Edit Alias dialog that follows, you can give your .NET application a name that you will use in a URL request to access this site. In this case, give it an alias of `airportweather`.

4. Now create a subfolder inside your new folder, and call this `bin`.

> This folder **must** be named `bin` – there's no two ways around it. The `bin` folder holds the .NET DLLs, also known as **assemblies**, that make a .NET web application work.

Since the Flash Remoting gateway automatically creates proxy DLL's for any web service used in a Remoting app, the `bin` folder has to allow the gateway permission to write to this folder. The gateway runs under the default ASPNET user account, so we need to give this user both READ and WRITE permissions.

5. Right-click on the `bin` folder, and select the Security tab from the properties dialog. Click on the placeholder text in the bottom pane, and – just as we have done before – replace it with *your computer name*\aspnet.

6. OK this, and back in the main panel, turn on both Read and Write in the list of permissions. OK this as well.

7. Inside the Flash Remoting installation folder (the default path is `C:\inetpub\wwwroot\flashremoting`) select and copy `web.config` and `gateway.aspx` into our `airportweather`.

8. Return to the Remoting installation directory, and copy the `gateway.dll` file from the `bin` directory into `airportweather\bin`. All three of these files combined are under 100k, so having several copies on one server shouldn't break any system.

> *If you already have a* `web.config` *file you need to use, there is only one section from the* Macromedia *supplied web.config that you need to include in yours – the* `<httpModule>` *settings. Add this section into your* `web.config` *file and you'll be good to go.*

Look out Flash – here I come!

As I have taken the time to lay out my goals and feature set, and to understand ahead of time what the data I'll be working with looks like, I can start writing code. However, I also want to apply the same methodical, step-by-step approach to my Flash movie creation. I don't want to get bogged down with interface or usability issues before I even see if I can work with the data I'm querying.

Therefore, I always start off by creating a dull, empty movie, with my code focused on communication and data parsing, making heavy use of the `trace()` method inside Flash for output. I used to jump straight into the graphics, but would spend way too much time on artwork only to find out later (normally in a rush) that the data side of things wasn't working and wasn't ever going to work – leaving me with a pretty app that didn't do anything!

1. Open up Flash MX, create a new Flash movie, and save it to your project folder as `AirportWeather.fla`. At this point, the default stage size is fine; we won't actually be placing anything on stage just yet.

2. We can now jump straight into code and call the web service via Flash Remoting to see what we get back. Select frame 1 on the main timeline, and add the following standard Flash Remoting code:

```
// standard Flash Remoting include files
#include "NetServices.as"
#include "NetDebug.as"

if (inited == null)
{
  // do this code only once
  inited = true;
  // set the default gateway URL
  NetServices.setDefaultGatewayUrl
("http://localhost/airportweather/gateway.aspx")

  // connect to the gateway
  gatewayConnection = NetServices.createGatewayConnection();

  // create a reference object that points to the
  // web service we are calling
  weatherws = gatewayConnection.getService
("http://live.capescience.com/wsdl/AirportWeather.wsdl",this);

  // call the getSummary method of the web service
  weatherws.getSummary("KMSY");
}

function getSummary_Result(result)
{
  // report that everything worked okay
  trace("We have a result");
}

function getSummary_Status(result)
{
  // report the details should an error be encountered
  trace("There was an error: " + result.details);
}
```

3. Re-save the file. Before I run any Remoting applications during development, I always make sure to save the project - I never want unsaved work to be at the mercy of the network connection demons.

4. Make sure the NetConnection Debugger window is open (if it's not already open, call it up from the Windows menu), and hit CTRL+ENTER to test run the app. Providing there were no typos in the code, it will start running and you'll begin to see trace output in the debugger window.

> *The first time you run a Remoting application that uses a web service, the Flash Remoting gateway needs to work its magic and create a proxy DLL for the service. This step takes a few extra seconds that you won't notice on subsequent runs of the app.*

If all went well, you should receive trace output information that "We have a result". You should also see information appearing in the NetConnection Debugger window. As our application runs, you should see something that looks like the following:

In this case, on the left panel you can see the initial connection to our gateway, the call to the web service, and the result information that was returned. In the right-side panel, you can see the particulars of our call to the web service – the method name we are calling, the protocol we are using to make the call, and any parameters we are passing. In this case we are passing the airport code for New Orleans KMSY.

Remember, the Debugger window is your friend. Learn to read what it reports to you, and you'll find your life will be much easier. Without it, we'd have no way of knowing what was happening behind the scenes, short of using a TCP/IP packet sniffer – not a pretty thing!

Should you encounter any errors, check your code and try again. Once you get familiar with calling one web service, you will be able to work with just about any web service with ease – usually getting your code right the first time around.

Have some class

Now we can start looking at how to work with a `WeatherSummary` complex type inside Flash. Working with Flash, you are already used to working with objects and classes. Whether you realize it or not, every item you can place on stage or create via code is an object, each with it's own properties. For instance, a `Movie clip` has properties of `_x`, `_y`, `_alpha`, and so on. Each of these properties can be accessed directly by using dot syntax – like `myMovieclip._alpha` or `myMovieclip._rotation`.

Defining WeatherSummary in Flash

Wouldn't it be cool if we could access the information in this `WeatherSummary` complex type the same way? This is where a new feature in Flash MX comes into play - the `Object.registerClass()` method. This function allows us to associate our own class name with a custom ActionScript object. In our case, we can create a version of the `WeatherSummary` complex type in ActionScript, and register it as an object inside our Flash movie.

Thanks to the magic of Flash Remoting, when we then receive an object of a type we have registered, the incoming data will automatically have the properties and methods we created. We'll add functions to return just the information we need, though we will modify these functions later on as we determine exactly how we want the information to look.

To begin with, we'll insert some new code into our existing app.

```
// standard Flash Remoting include files
#include "NetServices.as"
#include "NetDebug.as"

// create a new class named "WeatherSummary"
WeatherSummary = function() { };
```

continues overleaf

```
      // custom methods to return elements inside the
      // WeatherSummary complex type

      WeatherSummary.prototype.getCityLocation = function() {
        return this.location;
      }
      WeatherSummary.prototype.getSkyConditions = function() {
        return this.sky;
      }
      WeatherSummary.prototype.getWind = function() {
        return this.wind;
      }
      WeatherSummary.prototype.getTemperature = function() {
        return this.temp;
      }

      // register the class name with an ActionScript object
      Object.registerClass("WeatherSummary",WeatherSummary);

      if (inited == null)
      ...
```

Let's go through this code line-by-line. First, we start creating our new class by creating a new, empty function:

```
      WeatherSummary = function() { };
```

Of course, this isn't really a class just yet – right now it's just an empty function. Now we have to add methods to the function, using the prototype chain that is part of every object. By using the prototype chain to add methods and variables to an object, we create classes, and are able to pass those custom capabilities to all objects that inherit from our new class.

```
      WeatherSummary.prototype.getCityLocation = function() {
        return this.location;
      }
      WeatherSummary.prototype.getSkyConditions = function() {
        return this.sky;
      }
      WeatherSummary.prototype.getWind = function() {
        return this.wind;
      }
      WeatherSummary.prototype.getTemperature = function() {
        return this.temp;
      }
```

You'll remember that the WeatherSummary complex type from our web service contains seven elements. Since our methods will be applied to an object of type WeatherSummary, we use the this keyword to say, "Hey, I'm my own WeatherSummary object, and here's my information". So, we could have ten different WeatherSummary objects in our movie, and each one would return their own information. Beautiful.

Finally, we register our new class with an ActionScript object name:

```
Object.registerClass("WeatherSummary",WeatherSummary);
```

We can now begin to put this functionality into our app. Since we have methods that return specific elements, we can use these functions to trace out information and make sure that we receive what we expected. Let's give our getSummary_Result() method a facelift – replacing the simple confirmation text with some detailed information from our result data:

```
function getSummary_Result(result) {
        // report that everything worked out okay
   trace("Airport Location : " + result.getCityLocation());
   trace("Sky Conditions   : " + result.getSkyConditions());
   trace("Wind Speed       : " + result.getWind());
   trace("Temperature      : " + result.getTemperature());
       }
```

Since we created the WeatherSummary class in ActionScript, any time we receive a Remoting result object of type WeatherSummary, the result will automatically inherit the methods we've defined for the class.

If you haven't added the code already, add it, save the app, and run it. You should get a trace output that looks like the following:

```
Airport Location : New Orleans, New Orleans International
                        ➥ Airport, LA, United States
Sky Conditions   : partly cloudy
Wind Speed       : from the N (0 degrees) at 5 MPH (4 KT)
Temperature      : 80.1 F (26.7 C)
```

Since we created the methods that return the data inside the WeatherSummary class, when we call these methods via the trace commands in our getSummary_Result() function, the proper details are automatically returned. No fuss, no mess, and no cryptic code needed every time we want to use the data from a WeatherSummary object.

Sticky GUI

Now that all of our information is working, we can focus on putting together the final application. Reviewing the feature set, I remember that I want a user interface that is both fun to use and makes good use of Flash. I want it to be bright, colorful, and "sticky" – that is, I want the users to feel like they want to use it repeatedly. I quickly sketched out an idea of what I wanted the final design to look like: In a kiosk situation, I would normally

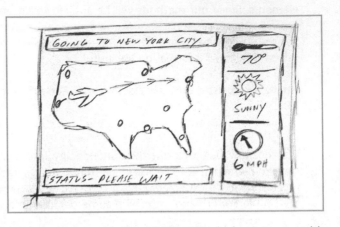

go full-screen with my application, anticipating a base resolution of 800x600 pixels. However, with an application that could be used in a public area by a private company (an airline in this case), there's a good probability that the client will want space on screen for advertising, so I need to consider this with my final stage size. I opt to make my stage 800x400 pixels – leaving an area of 200 pixels at the bottom of the screen for advertisements or other information that might be required.

Our full screen area can be broken down as shown:

This should allow plenty of room for extras at the bottom of the screen: ads, on-screen keyboard, text information, or anything else the client might want.

800 x 400 - Flash Movie Area
800 x 200 - Advertising and Information

To split up the Flash application area, I looked to my local television stations' nightly news broadcasts and their weather segments for inspiration. I found that each of them displayed the weather information in the same manner: area map on the left of the screen, and specific information on the right.

I figured that if this is what TV viewers are used to, I should use this as a guideline to make an interface that will be immediately familiar to the user.

Since I'm working with a larger scope than a local area, I need room to display the name of the destination location. I also need to consider that, since I'm working with network transmissions, I need room to display status information to the user, in case of web service errors, network outages, etc. The final breakdown of the applications stage looks like this:

With the display of selected city location, and status information, I've covered two of the requirements set in the app's feature set. What remains is a method to select a destination city, graphical representations of temperature, sky and wind conditions, and a way to keep the user occupied during web service communications.

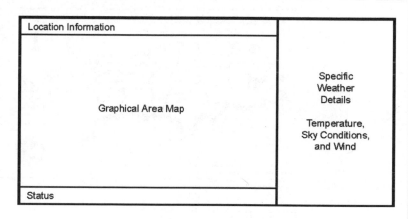

I like the thought of having a map on screen as a method to let the user select a city. As I'm working on the premise that this application would be used for an airline, I decide that the airline will be a domestic airline, so instead of trying to fit a world map into the allotted screen space, I'll stick with a map of just the United States. Now, I'm certainly not one to try to actually draw the entire outline of the US, as well as each individual state, when I know full well I can find all the graphics I could ever need free on the Internet.

I set out online, and within minutes find many versions of the image I'm looking for. I settle on a plain black and white graphic with a slight perspective to it – simple and nice looking.

Again, referring to my local television news broadcasts for specific information graphic inspiration, I find that they all use common metaphors for each type of information – a thermometer for temperature, a compass for wind direction, and different states of clouds and sun icons for sky conditions. These are simple enough for my design skills, so I decide to create these all inside Flash.

Taking a look

Let's jump into the future of my app and see how it ended up looking – so you'll have a better idea where I'm heading. As you can see, it's fairly close to my original sketch, and uncluttered and usable as a result of the careful thinking we've done.

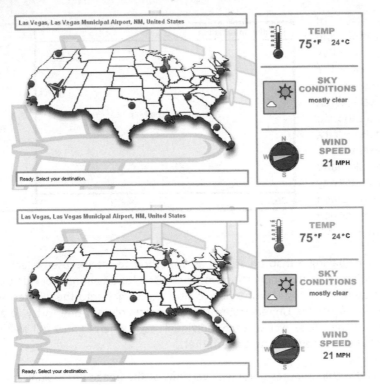

From this, you should be able to see that there are a number of elements that make up the application:

- The map
- The thermometer you can see at the top right-hand corner
- The Sky Conditions window on the middle right
- The Wind Speed compass display at the bottom right
- The text boxes for the three windows on the right, and at the top and bottom of the screen
- The locations on the map
- The 'plane' animation
- Some code to wire everything up

We're going to go through each of these now, but – as always – check back with the finished item if you've got any questions; this is as much about the way this application was built as how to duplicate it.

The map

1. Open up your existing movie, and change the stage size to the new dimensions of 800x400.

2. Drag in some guides to roughly match the layout template on the previous page.

3. Place a US map on screen and quickly draw in some outlines of each main area. Very quickly, the app should start to take shape:

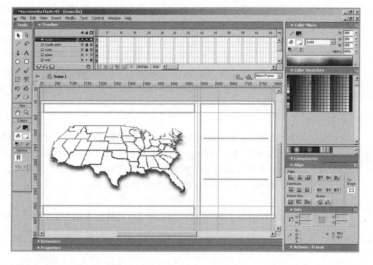

4. Add two dynamic text fields to the stage, one in the top area, and one at the bottom. These will hold our location and status information. Keeping with the touch-screen kiosk scenario, make each text field non-selectable - this keeps the mouse cursor from turning into the normal text field 't-bar' cursor, should the user touch the screen over either of these areas.

The thermometer

The first graphic information section to tackle is the temperature area. Since the common iconography for this information is a thermometer, that's what we'll use.

1. Create a new movie clip and draw a basic thermometer outline.

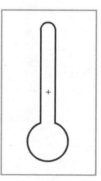

2.   To make the 'mercury' inside the thermometer, create a second layer and draw a red-filled rectangle covering the outline of the thermometer.

3.   Duplicate the outline layer to a new layer, and create a mask layer of the mercury layer – thus making the red mercury only inside the outlines.

To make the mercury rise and fall based upon the temperature, there are several options. I could have turned the mercury rectangle into its own movie clip, and created a function that scales the mercury clip to the correct size, but that involves math, and well, I prefer not to go there.

4.   Instead, create a shape-tween 110 frames long on the mask layer between the mercury at 0 degrees (just above the bottom 'pool' of mercury), and 110 degrees (the very top of the outline).

5.   To make the mercury level meaningful, add temperature lines at 10-degree intervals, and text labels at 20-degree intervals. To determine the correct position for the lines and labels, move the timeline playhead to the desired frame number – which now correlates to the temperature – and draw the line at the top of the mercury level.

Add some highlights and shading to taste, and your thermometer should look a little like this:

Sky conditions

Next up is the sky conditions movie clip. Regardless of region or season of the year, there are only a finite number of descriptions used for sky conditions – clear, cloudy, snow, and thunderstorms, just to name a few. Again, as this is the middle of summer, I can count out snow, hail, blizzard and icy, and focus on good ole' summer-time weather conditions – sunny, overcast, rain, and so on.

1. Start by creating a single rectangle graphic clip to use as the outline for each sky condition image.

2. Now create several graphic clips of standard sky icons – clouds, the sun, raindrops, and a lightning bolt.

    After all the pieces are done, it's time to determine exactly which conditions we need separate graphics for, and which ones we can re-use for multiple conditions. To assist in narrowing the list, I ran my application several times, replacing the airport code with a different airport code each time. After trying out the application on roughly twenty different airports, I settled on a simple list of nine different graphic frames:

- Sunny or clear
- Mostly Clear
- Partly Cloudy
- Cloudy
- Mostly Cloudy
- Overcast
- Rain or drizzle
- Lightening, stormy, or thunderstorms
- Unknown (in case of no report or a condition I could not anticipate)

3. Create a single frame with the empty outline graphic clip, then create nine additional keyframes, leaving the first as an empty, outline square only frame.

4. Using the graphic elements we've just created, and the handy 'Tint' color effect to vary the background box color from sky-blue to rainy gray, lay out each individual sky condition from the list above onto a frame.

5.   Label each keyframe with the condition it represents - I replaced spaces with underscores to keep to my normal naming conventions – and add a `stop()` action to each frame.

The final sky condition movie clip should look something like this:

The compass

The last weather condition we need a movie clip for is wind conditions. Based on television news icons, we will use a compass graphic with a needle that points in the direction the wind is blowing.

1.   Create a simple compass graphic, as shown.

2.   Create a movie clip to represent the pointer, and give it an instance name of `pointer` so we can rotate it as needed with ActionScript.

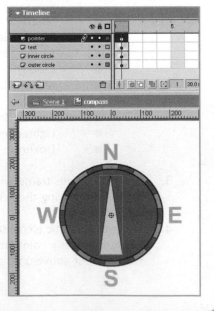

Luckily, the wind direction in degrees coming from the web service happens to be the same coordinate system as that used by Flash: 0 = North, 90 = East, and so on around the compass. This means that we'll be able to rotate the pointer to the correct orientation simply by using the information provided from the web service.

Text

Now that all the movie clips are created, we can put them on stage, along with static text explaining what each movie represents. Displaying the information through use of just the graphics doesn't work very well, though - we need to include text fields that turn our graphics from being somewhat ambiguous to truly iconic metaphors.

1. Add dynamic text fields to hold the temperature in Fahrenheit *and* Celsius, the sky conditions, and the speed in Miles Per Hour (MPH) of the wind (the directional compass pointer is sufficient to know which way the wind is blowing).

2. Give the text boxes instance names of `tempF`, `tempC`, `sky_text`, and `wind_speed`.

3. Our stage should look almost complete:

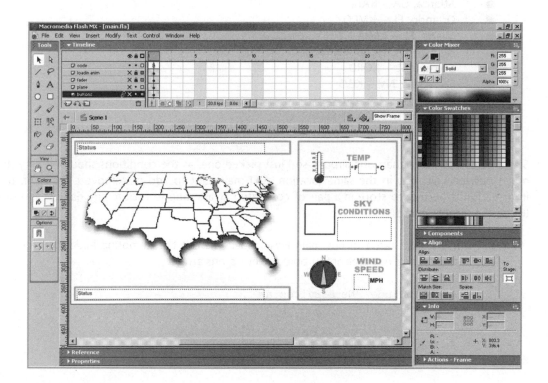

Adding the locations

Our stage looks nice, and we know we can get data, so now we can focus on the user interaction with our application. Anticipating that the user will only have a touch-screen to work with, we need a method to select a city for which to display the weather information. Having a map already on screen lends itself to having touchable buttons for each city, in their respective locations on the map.

As I decide which cities to add as clickable locations, I also need to determine their respective airport identifier codes. Once again using the convenient link on the Cape Clear web site, I pick my cities and search for their codes:

- New Orleans, LA – KMSY
- Dallas, TX – KDFW
- Atlanta, GA – KATL
- Orlando, FL – KMCO
- Miami, FL – KMIA
- New York City, NY – KJFK
- Chicago, IL – KORD
- Las Vegas, NV – KLVS
- Los Angeles, CA – KLAX
- San Francisco, CA – KSFO
- Seattle, WA – KSEA

Some cities had more than one airport, so I just picked one, as the conditions shouldn't vary too much between airports in the same location. As I may want to add or remove cities later, this information is perfect to store in a pair of correlated arrays: one to list the city names, and one listing the airport codes.

1. Back in the first frame of our main Flash movie, before the Remoting initialization code, add the following ActionScript in bold to set up our arrays:

```
#include "NetServices.as"
#include "NetDebug.as"

// total numbers of cities in our arrays
var numCities = 11;

// the names of each city on our map
var cityNames = new Array("New Orleans","New York",
    ➥ "Seattle","Dallas","Chicago","Miami","Los Angeles",
    ➥ "San Francisco", "Las Vegas","Atlanta","Orlando");

// the airport codes for each city on the map
```

continues overleaf

```
var cityCodes = new Array("KMSY","KJFK","KSEA","KDFW",
    ➥ "KORD","KMIA","KLAX","KSFO","KLVS","KATL","KMCO");

if(inited == null)
{
```

Now that we have the cities selected and the arrays built, we can add buttons to the map. The buttons I used are a simple blue circle with some shading to make them appear more 3D-button-like.

2. Place one button on stage for each city, in the relevant location.

> *Remember that a kiosk normally doesn't have a mouse, so there never is a rollover state to buttons – there's only clicked or not clicked.*

3. Give the buttons instance names to correlate to the array index of that city. So, for the New Orleans button, the button's instance name is `city_0`, for New York City the button's instance name is `city_1`, and so on.

4. The chosen naming convention also allows several nice coding practices to come into play. First, we can programmatically add functionality to each button using a single loop, instead of lots of repetitious code. Add this underneath the last lot of code:

```
// setup buttons to correspond with arrays
for (var p=0;p<numCities;p++)
{
    _level0["city_"+p].onPress = getAirportWeather;
}
```

5. Add the following function to the script:

```
function setStatus(inMsg) {
    status_msg.text = inMsg;
}
```

6. In the `getAirportWeather()` function we assign to each button press, we can determine which city was selected by stripping the number off the `_name` property of the clicked button. This number is the index of the selected city in our arrays. Neat, huh?

```
function getAirportWeather() {
```

continues overleaf

```
    // get the number from the end of the button name
    city_array_element = this._name.split("_")[1];

        setStatus("One Moment... Querying Web Service.");
    weatherws.getSummary(cityCodes[city_array_element]);
    }
```

After we parse out the number in the `city_array_element` variable, we inform the user that the data is loading by calling a custom function, `setStatus()`, which changes the text in the status text field, and then call the web service's `getSummary()` method, passing in the proper code for the selected city's airport.

The plane

The one thing lacking in our interface is some graphic indicator as to which city we are currently looking at. Sure, we have the location text field at the top - which will hold the city name and airport name - but we need an icon to go with our text field.

The obvious graphic icon is, well, an airplane. A user will immediately be able to identify the current selection. We can utilize this same graphic as a way to keep the user occupied during network transmissions by programmatically moving the airplane from the city to the selected city, as if it were flying there.

1.   Create a single-frame movie clip with a colorful graphic of a jet plane. The map is black and white, so the more colors we can add onto the screen, the better.

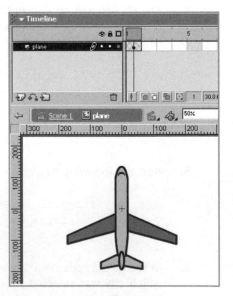

2.   Since we're starting the application by loading the weather information for New Orleans, place the plane on-screen over the New Orleans button.

We need a way to move the plane from one location to another. We could simply jump the plane from point to point, but that's... well... boring! As I mentioned, we can use the plane movement to our advantage by distracting the user from the time it's taking to gather the information. Therefore, the plane should smoothly 'fly' from one city to the next. A real plane doesn't have a steady speed from takeoff to landing, and neither should ours. We will add an easing equation into our flying code to make the plane speed up until it reaches halfway, and then slow down until it 'lands'.

3. Add a few function calls to the button handler `getAirportWeather()` method that we added in the last section. Find this code:

```
function getAirportWeather() {
    city_array_element = this._name.split("_")[1];
    setStatus("One Moment... Querying Web Service.");
```

Underneath, add these two lines:

```
flyPlane(this._x,this._y);
disableAllButtons();
```

Here, we call our function to move the plane, passing in the x and y location of the button clicked (this). Then we disable all the other city buttons so the user can't select a different city before we've arrived at our destination and retrieved the weather information.

4. Now, we've got another function to add underneath `function getAirportWeather()`:

First, add three global variables at the start of the script:

```
_global.startX = thePlane._x;
_global.startY = thePlane._y;
_global.flying = false;
```

Now, return to your previous location, and add:

```
function flyPlane(inEndX,inEndY) {

    _global.startX = thePlane._x;
    _global.startY = thePlane._y;
```

The first line calls a function `flyPlane()`, and we then set the global variables to store the plane's current location on screen. The next section calculates the distance between the end location that was passed into this function, and the current location:

```
            _global.endX = inEndX-_global.startX;
            _global.endY = inEndY-_global.startY;
```

Finally, we rotate the plane to face the end point, and set a global variable to state that we should be moving:

```
        thePlane._rotation = rotatePlane
                ➥ (_global.startX,_global.startY,inEndX,inEndY);


    _global.flying = true;
}
```

This function doesn't seem to actually make the plane do anything, other than rotate to face the city selected. Actually, this is correct. By itself, this function isn't very special. The important line to note is the line:

```
        _global.flying = true;
```

In the background, we have a separate function attached to our plane movie clip that is constantly looking at the value of _global.flying. When this variable is set to true, the magic happens.

5.   To make the magic happen, add the following:

```
    thePlane.onEnterFrame = function() {
      if (_global.flying) {
        _global.t++;
        if (_global.t <= _global.duration) {
          this._x = Math.easeInOutSine(_global.t, _global.startX,
                    ➥ global.endX, _global.duration);
          this._y = Math.easeInOutSine(_global.t, _global.startY,
                    ➥ global.endY, _global.duration);
        }
        else {
          _global.t = 0;
          _global.flying = false;
        }
      }
    }
```

When our global variable flying says we should be flying, this function will trigger off a counter, which counts from zero to a global time duration (measured in seconds). It passes this counter value (along with the global variables set in flyPlane() and the duration) to a function called easeInOutSine().

> This wonderful easing function is provided by a godsend to all Flash developers: Mr. Robert Penner (http://www .robertpenner.com). It helps to produce smooth changes in speed as objects move from one point to another.

Adding this `easeInOutSine()` function to our application means that calling the function twice (once for the_x position, once for the_y position), we get a smooth acceleration and deceleration, while 'flying' from start city to end city. When we reach our destination, we reset our counter and set our global variable to state that we should no longer be flying.

6. Of course, we need to add `easeInOutSine` to the beginning of our code, so add this (somewhere at the beginning of the script, after our initial variable declarations)

```
Math.easeInOutSine = function (t, b, c, d) {
    return c/2 * (1 - Math.cos(t/d * Math.PI)) + b;
};
```

7. We also need to set up the two variables the function uses: `global.t`, and `global.variation`. Just above the previous lines, add:

```
_global.t = 0;
_global.duration = 190;
```

8. The rotation of the plane is a straightforward function that takes into account the start location, and the end location, and returns the correct rotation angle for our plane movie clip:

```
function rotatePlane(x1,y1,x2,y2) {
    x = (x2 - x1);
    y = (y2 - y1);
    hyp = Math.sqrt(Math.pow(x,2) + Math.pow(y,2));
    cos = x / hyp;
    rad = Math.acos(cos);
    deg = Math.floor(180/(Math.PI / rad));
    if(y <0){
        deg = -deg;
    }else if((Math.floor(y) == 0) && (x <0)){
        deg = 180;
    }
```

continues overleaf

```
        return deg + 90;
    }
```

The code

The major pieces of the app are in place and all we have to do is tie everything together. You'll notice we use our button handler function, `getAirportWeather()`, to call the web service. However, our `getSummary_Result()` function still simply traces out the information coming in, and doesn't have any effect on the graphics.

1. Let's revisit the weather summary function, and make some radical changes to our `WeatherSummary` class. Add the code in bold:

    ```
    function getSummary_Result(result) {
        if (result.getCityLocation() != "null") {

        setWind(result.getWindSpeed(), result.getWindDirection());
        setTemperature(result.getTemperatureF(),
        result.getTemperatureC());
        setCitylocation(result.getCityLocation());
        setSkyConditions(result.getSkyConditions());
    ```

2. This makes sure we have a valid result from the web service. You need to add

    ```
    setTemperature(1)
    ```

    at the beginning of the script to provide a default value, and the following function later on:

    ```
    function setCityLocation(inCity) {
        city_location.text = inCity;
    }
    ```

3. Once we have the data, we can enable all the buttons so the user can select another city. First, add these two functions:

    ```
    function disableAllButtons() {
        for (var p=0;p<numCities;p++)
        {
            _level0["city_"+p].enabled = false;
            _level0["city_"+p].useHandCursor = false;
        }
    }
    function enableAllButtons() {
    ```

continues overleaf

```
            for (var p=0;p<numCities;p++)
            {
                    _level0["city_"+p].enabled = true;
                    _level0["city_"+p].useHandCursor = true;
            }
        }
```

4. Now, we can use these, so add:

```
        enableAllButtons();

        setStatus("Ready. Select your destination.");
    }
    else {
      // problem loading the selected information
      setCityLocation("");

      // enable all the buttons so user can select another city
      enableAllButtons();

      setStatus("Error loading airport data. Please try
                ➡ another destination.");
    }
  }
```

Wow. That's a serious overhaul to not only the getSummary_Result() function, but you'll also notice a lot of new methods applied to our WeatherSummary class.

We'll go step by step and see how we tie this all together. We see that we call a custom function to display the wind information, but the parameters we are passing are something new:

```
        setWind(result.getWindSpeed(), result.getWindDirection());
```

If you recall, our wind movie clip needs a direction in degrees to rotate the pointer in the correct direction, and we have a text field that holds the wind speed in MPH. Therefore, we need to split the incoming wind data into two distinct sections – direction and speed. We do this by adding two methods to our WeatherSummary class – getWindSpeed() and getWindDirection():

```
        WeatherSummary.prototype.getWindSpeed = function() {
          return Number(this.wind.split(")")[1].split(" ")[2]);
        }
        WeatherSummary.prototype.getWindDirection = function() {
          return Number(this.wind.split("(")[1].split(" ")[0]);
```

continues overleaf

```
    }
```

The wind speed data we get looks like this: *from the N (0 degrees) at 5 MPH (4 KT)*. The first method splits the wind data on closing parenthesis (`")"`), grabs the second element from split (`[1]`), and splits that element on spaces (`" "`). The third element is the wind speed value and we return the result as a `Number`.

The wind direction data we get looks exactly the same: *from the N (0 degrees) at 5 MPH (4 KT)*. We split this data on opening parenthesis (`"("`), grab the second element from split (`[1]`), and split that element on spaces (`" "`). The first element is the wind direction in degrees, and we return the result as a `Number`.

We add this sort of functionality to our base class so we don't have parsing functions all over the place – each `WeatherSummary` object knows how to give us the data we need from wherever it may reside. Plus, by adding the parsing to the class, the functions that utilize this data become less complex. In fact, the `setWind()` function that we call is really quite mundane:

```
function setWind(inSpeed, inDirection) {
    // set the text field to the speed in MPH
    wind_speed.text = inSpeed;
    // rotate the pointer sub-movie clip to correct angle
    compass.pointer._rotation = inDirection;
}
```

Along the same lines, our thermometer movie clip requires a number representing the degrees in Fahrenheit, and we have two text fields that display the temperature as a number in Fahrenheit and Celsius.

```
setTemperature(result.getTemperatureF(),
result.getTemperatureC());
```

Just like the new wind functions, we add two new functions dealing with temperature to our `WeatherSummary` class – `getTemperatureF()` and `getTemperatureC()`:

```
WeatherSummary.prototype.getTemperatureF = function() {
    return Math.round(Number(this.temp.split(" ")[0]));
}

WeatherSummary.prototype.getTemperatureC = function() {
    return Math.round(Number(this.temp.split("(")[1].split
        ➥ (" ")[0]));
}
```

The temperature data we get looks like: *80.1 F (26.7 C)*. We split the temp data on spaces (`" "`), so that the first element is the temp in Fahrenheit. We return a rounded version of the temperature since we need a round number to use in `gotoAndStop()`.

For the temperature data for Celsius, we want the second element. We split the data on opening parenthesis (`"("`), and split the `this` element on spaces (`" "`). Now, the first element is the temperature in Celsius, and we return the rounded version to use in `gotoAndStop()`.

Once again, the web service returns data that we need to split into separate sections to use in our application. And once again, we add the parsing to the class for ease of use. As with our `setWind()` function, our `setTemperature()` function is quite to-the-point:

```
function setTemperature(inTempF, inTempC) {
   thermometer.gotoAndStop(inTempF);
   tempF.text = inTempF;
   tempC.text = inTempC;
}
```

The next informational section we set is the airport city location. This section of our custom class is the same as it has been. However, we are simply passing the location string to a function that places the string in the text field at the top of the screen. There's nothing special here – just some simple string handling.

The last informational section we set is the sky condition. In this case, the web service returns a string that doesn't need parsing, so we don't have to modify our custom class. However, we do need to do more than simply report the conditions.

As we have previously determined that we will be using sky graphic icons for multiple conditions, we can build our `setSkyConditions()` function around a big `switch()` ActionScript conditional statement:

```
function setSkyConditions(inSky) {
   sky_text.text = inSky;
   switch (inSky.toLowerCase()) {
     case "sunny":
     case "clear":
       sky_icons.gotoAndStop("clear");
       break;
     case "mostly clear":
       sky_icons.gotoAndStop("mostly_clear");
       break;
     case "partly cloudy":
       sky_icons.gotoAndStop("partly_cloudy");
       break;
     case "cloudy":
```

continues overleaf

```
            sky_icons.gotoAndStop("cloudy");
            break;
        case "mostly cloudy":
            sky_icons.gotoAndStop("mostly_cloudy");
            break;
        case "overcast":
            sky_icons.gotoAndStop("overcast");
            break;
        case "rain":
        case "drizzle":
            sky_icons.gotoAndStop("rain");
            break;
        case "thunderstorms":
        case "lightening":
        case "stormy":
            sky_icons.gotoAndStop("lightening");
            break;
        case "unknown":
        default:
            sky_icons.gotoAndStop("unknown");
            break;
    }
}
```

Remember that we named our sky condition movie clip's keyframes to be the same as the possible results from our web service, only replacing spaces (" ") with underscores ("_").

The switch statement in our setSkyConditions() function is based on the verbiage coming from the web service, all converted into lower case (just to be on the safe side).

As switch statements allow for multiple cases to result in the same code being applied, we can group sky condition strings with our movie clip's keyframe names. Using this method, we can add or remove cases as need be – or, if we want to actually create separate frames for each specific condition, we have one central location for all code required.

Final touches

I made two final touches to the app. These are fairly generic, and not terribly interesting code-wise but still contribute to the look and feel of the finished application, so I'll leave you to take a look at the FLA to see the details if you're interested.

The first of these was a movie clip with a single, solid white rectangle sized to cover the weather information graphics. This movie clip has a 60-frame animation of the white rectangle fading to transparent. While gathering information, I made this 'fader' movie clip visible and stopped on the opening, solid white frame.

When I received the information, and *after* I had set my graphic icons to their new values, I played this movie clip, starting the fading animation so the information graphics would appear to fade into view. Here we can see the plane just about to 'land' in Orlando, Florida, and the graphics of our weather conditions starting to fade into view:

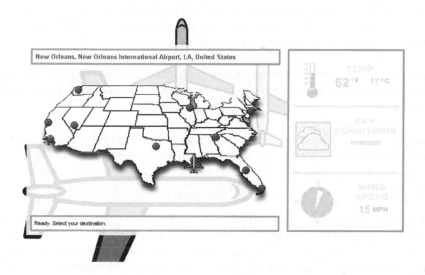

The second of the extras is a secondary 'Loading Data' animation. This would be used if the web service took longer than the six seconds of flying airplane animation. On retrieval of the information, and immediately before running the fading white rectangle animation, I hid this loading animation.The application with the loading animation looks like this:

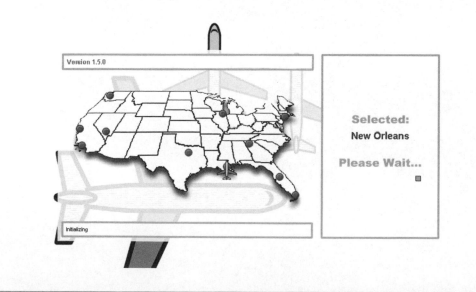

The overall effect was a smooth flow between user interaction, web service data retrieval, and display of final information.

Future steps

Certainly, there's room to expand this application. Animated sky condition icons could be added, as could audio for when the plane is flying, not to mention the entire bottom section of our screen. We could tie it into multiple web services to retrieve extended weather forecast information (remember - we did find a web service that provided this information).

You could also use the selected city name and search Google through their web service for information pertinent to the user's selection – hotel websites, tourist information, restaurant guides, and so on.

The biggest thing to remember is that Flash is your friend, and to have fun with it. This project gave me all sorts of new insight into how to approach my everyday work. As each step started to work, I gained the confidence to keep going with this project – turning it into a fairly realistic real-world application.

I hope that by seeing how I approached this test application, you've discovered a new angle on not only how to go about starting a new project, but on experimenting with new technologies. Don't be afraid to try working ideas out – you never know where they will lead you. The more you play, the more you learn, and the more you're able to make better decisions in your work – and your life.

case study 2: **PenPad**

One of the great new features introduced with Flash MX is the **drawing API** (Application Programming Interface), which allows developers to dynamically draw shapes within their movies at run-time. Using a little creativity and ingenuity, you can now create effects such as scalable interfaces that resize and redraw with the browser, charts that can graphically represent dynamic data, and solid 3D objects that can respond according to user input. But what about an interface that gives the user control over these drawing methods?

This could be accomplished to some extent in Flash 5, but drawing interfaces were then limited to using hairline strokes or duplicated movie clips. Now we can provide a much more robust illustration interface with Flash MX, but still we must consider the value for the user. Why not incorporate some server-side code to save a user's drawing creations in an editable format so they can come back and edit it (or simply admire it!) at a later time?

Then, with an interface that allows for the creation of graphic shapes and the ability to save and load them to and from the server, we'll have what could be an extremely useful application.

Methods of drawing

When I began this project, I considered creating a freehand drawing application that simply recorded the user's mouse position when the mouse button was pressed. You could alter the width, color, and alpha of the stroke and allow the user to toggle a fill on and off (giving them choice of color and alpha), and that would be a fine little doodle pad.

However, editing such a creation would be difficult at best, and I knew we could do so much more than that! I chose instead to use an interface that I'd already been working on for a few months, originally designed for a component that (at time of writing) is still in the works. The component in question is designed to let Flash designers place and animate dynamic text on paths, a feature I've always felt that Flash itself was lacking.

> *You can find out its current status (you never know, it might just be finished by the time you're reading this!) at www.27Bobs.com.*

Of course, to accomplish this I needed to let users define paths on which to place the text. Since it's not yet possible to extract path information directly from shapes created in the Flash authoring environment, I created an interface for the component where users could draw their paths using the drawing API. Here's a shot of the work in progress:

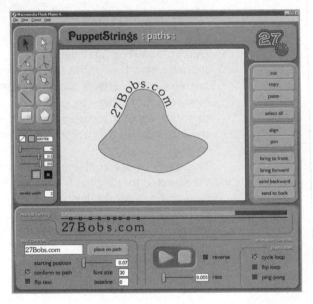

This interface features many of the standard Bezier tools provided in most vector drawing programs (such as Illustrator, Freehand or even Flash – simplified, of course!). This was the interface I chose to enhance for our case study project, since the shapes themselves are simply defined by anchor points and control points, making it easy to go back and edit them at a later date, rather than trying to edit a mammoth list of mouse coordinates!

Code, code, and more code

There's a lot of code involved. There, I've said it. Because of this, it isn't possible to go through the code line by line and explain how it works. Otherwise, this chapter would be a book in itself!

Instead, I felt it would be more useful to focus on certain specific tasks in the interface that might interest you, talk about how I accomplished, and clue you into *why* I chose to code them as I did. I'll give you an overview as well, looking at where everything's located in the movie. By the end of the chapter, you should know the movie well enough to feel comfortable about going in and adapting it for your own purposes.

Since the focus for this book is server-side integration using ASP.NET, I'd be remiss if I didn't spend some time discussing how the shape data is packaged up, sent and processed on the server, then how it is loaded back into the interface and used to redraw your graphic creations.

There's a lot to explore, so we need to get right to it!

Of course, exploring is a bit easier once you are familiar with the general terrain, so if you haven't yet opened penPad.swf and played with the application, I'd encourage you to get right in there and spend a while having some fun with it!

To make use of the loading and saving functionality, you'll need to run the SWF from a folder under wwwroot *(or wherever else you have a virtual directory), with the accompanying ASP.NET page (*saveDrawing.aspx*) and a sub-folder called* PenPadDrawings *in the same place. This chapter's code download includes a sample drawing called* phoenix.ppx *(shown above), which you might like to experiment with. Copy it into the* PenPadDrawings *folder, and you can load it into the application as* phoenix.*

The plan was to create a simple and intuitive environment in which the user could draw. The canvas takes up most of the interface, while the tools (which sport large, friendly icons) are off to the side, but still close at hand.

The rounded corners of the interface and its buttons help to soften the experience, with plenty of open space (in addition to the canvas) leaving an uncluttered feeling. Finally, I've provided tooltips to help users learn the tools' functions, as well as showing them keyboard shortcuts.

The idea is that users should be able to access these tools, figure out what they do, and start using them as quickly as possible.

PenPad.fla

If you open up PenPad.fla from the download bundle, you'll see that the entire interface exists on the main timeline, just as you see it in the published movie. We don't initially attach anything through code, and apart from the grouped color sliders and multiple states for each of the buttons (which are actually movie clips), there are no nested timelines. What you see is what you get!

What's more, there is no code located on any of the interface items. All the ActionScript is either in frame 1 of the root timeline or inside exported symbols in the library. This makes it extremely easy to track things down, and really made my life bliss while I was building and debugging the movie!

Exploring the main timeline

The layers you'll find on the main timeline are all tucked away inside a couple of layer folders, just to help keep things tidy. If you expand the code folder, you'll see it contains many layers of separated code and another sub-folder named canvas code. Expanding canvas code reveals two more layers and another sub-folder named tools, which also expands into many layers.

Don't panic though! This isn't because every layer contains an exorbitant amount of code, but because I find it extremely helpful to separate off even the smallest amount of code if it's unrelated to any other code. Then it's nice and easy to find it for editing, instead of having to hunt through hundreds and hundreds of unrelated lines to locate the one I want to change.

We'll discuss some of this code in a bit, but let's first finish our tour.

Expanding the interface folder on the main timeline reveals all of the graphics layers. There's not too much to explain here, as each layer just contains a few simple elements.

All the toolbox buttons on the left-hand side of the stage are located on the toolbox layer, while the interface buttons on the right-hand side are all on the buttons layer. They're all named instances, but none of them have any code attached – not *directly* at least. All the code for both sets of buttons is located on the buttons code layer (in the code folder).

> For those of us who've previously worked in Flash 5, hunting through a crowded, nested interface in order to find where we had placed a certain clipEvent was a common, often frustrating task. No more! Now we can assign functions to event handlers in a centralized location (like the main timeline), and that's exactly what I've done in this movie.

Also of interest, the mask layer masks the two movie clips on the noFills layer. These two movie clips are used to show when 'no fill' or 'no stroke' are selected for a shape. The mask is especially helpful for the stroke swatch, which needs a nice rectangular hole in the middle of it.

The movie clip buttons

All the buttons used in this interface are actually movie clips masquerading as buttons. Flash MX movie clips can respond to button events, and I find there's really very little point in using button symbols anymore, especially considering how easy it is to configure your movie clips to do anything a button can do, plus so much more!

Open the Library panel, and double-click on wideButton to take a look at its timeline.

As you can see, we have two layers for the button's graphics (though we could easily settle for one), a single layer of labels to define each button state, and a single layer of code with a solitary stop() action to halt the timeline's playhead. Nothing else is needed.

If we then assign some function to a button event handler for this movie clip instance, whether on the movie clip itself or elsewhere (in this case, on the buttons code layer), we can make it act just like a button:

```
mcInstance.onRelease = function() { trace("hi") };
```

The movie clip *automatically* knows to use the states that you have defined just as a normal button would. Pretty easy, isn't it? In fact, you can go way further with this, by creating additional states such as _Inactive, or even animating *between* states with simple gotoAndPlay() actions.

Note that we keep the toolbox buttons on their _Down state whenever they're toggled down, an action not possible with actual button symbols. All in all, it's an extremely useful feature and one to take advantage of.

While we've got the Library panel open, let's take a look at some of the other symbols defined for this interface.

The library

You should see three folders that contain all the assets of the interface. The sounds folder has a single MP3 that will play whenever an error pop-up window opens. The interface assets folder contains all of the graphical aspects of the interface, including the buttons, the tool icons, and all the elements that make up the color palette.

The topmost folder in the library is exported symbols, and is easily the most important one of the bunch. Each of these items in here is a movie clip that creates a new Class (all extensions of the MovieClip object). They're all graphically blank, but contain code that defines their functionality. We'll take a more detailed look at them all soon, but first let's discuss extending a movie clip so that you can see how easily it's done.

Extending movie clips

When I speak of extending a movie clip, I'm not referring to the practice of adding methods to the current movie clip prototype, but rather to creating a new class that inherits all of the functionality of a movie clip instance, but then *adds* to it as well. It's actually very easy to do, and once you've picked it up I believe you'll find yourself using it all the time – and wondering how you ever got along without it!

All you need to do to create a new class of movie clips is to export a movie clip from your library with a unique identifier, and associate this symbol with a class definition in your code. This code can be located anywhere in your movie, but it's common practice to put it in the symbol itself. Let's take a look at one of the exported symbols for PenPad, so you can see how we've done it.

Marquee

Double-click on the Marquee symbol in your library to enter symbol-editing mode. You will see that it's an empty movie clip with a single layer of code. Call up the Actions panel and select the frame to take a look at this code. The first several lines are the most important:

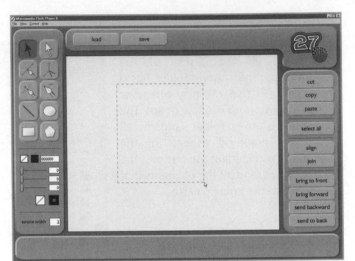

```
#initclip

Marquee = function() {
   this.init();
}

Marquee.prototype = new MovieClip();
```

`#initclip` is used to let Flash know that the following code defines a class. This is done for two reasons:

- Firstly, it lets Flash know that although this code is contained inside a movie clip symbol, it needs to be run *before* the first frame. Otherwise, it wouldn't be run until an instance of the symbol was placed on the stage. This way, the class will be defined and ready to go well before it might be needed. If you were defining this class on the main timeline, you wouldn't need to use this.

- Secondly, it tells Flash that this code only needs to be run *once*, no matter how many instances exist on stage. Otherwise, it would be run for each instance.

In the next couple of lines, we create a constructor function for creating (and initializing) instances of the new class. Within the function, we call a method `init`, which we'll define later on.

The final line in the code above sets the prototype of the new class as a new MovieClip object. This may sound technical and jargony, but what it really means is that our Marquee class (and all instances of it) can now use all of the methods and properties you'd expect to find on any movie clip. What's more, we can add in extra functionality of our own; that's what we do in the remaining lines.

This is a fairly simple class, and contains only two methods.

- `init()` sets up a function to occur as the mouse moves. Basically, it draws a box between the marquee's origin position and the current mouse position.

- `lineDash()` draws a dashed line between a given pair of points. This function can be used for diagonal lines as well, so there's a bit of trigonometry in there, though we won't use that functionality in this particular application.

After these methods are defined, we end with two final lines of code:

```
Object.registerClass("Marquee", Marquee);

#endinitclip
```

The first registers an instance of our new Class as a symbol in the library. If you right/command click on the Marquee symbol in the library and select Linkage, you'll see that we've also exported the symbol as Marquee. The registerClass line just says:

The symbol exported as Marquee is an instance of the class called 'Marquee'.

Now, whenever any instance of this symbol is placed on stage, it's automatically an instance of the Marquee class.

The last line of this code is a partner for the `#initclip` we used at the beginning of the code. It tells Flash that we've finished the class definition.

Not so hard, is it? What's nice about this is now we can attach this symbol to the stage whenever we need a marquee (with our Move and Direct Selection tools) and it will act just as we need it to without us have to worry about it.

Each of the other exported symbols follows a very similar structure, so we won't bother going through them all in detail. Feel free to open them up and have a look at what's going on inside. It might give you some ideas for your own interfaces.

Interface communication

The next step in understanding how this Flash interface works is to look at the different objects it uses, and see how they all talk to each other.

Shape

At the heart of everything in PenPad is the Shape object, which you'll find in the exported symbols folder in the library. This object holds all the information on a single shape drawn on the canvas, including its fill, stroke, position, anchor points and control points. If the user draws multiple shapes, then multiple Shape instances are placed on the stage. When the time comes to package up the shape data (so that we can save it on the server), it's the Shape instances that will provide us with that information.

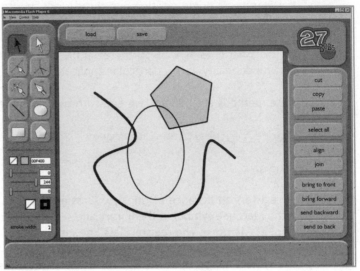

Of course, it should be noted that in addition to holding the shape information, the Shape instances also take care of graphically drawing themselves onto the screen.

Canvas

All communication with shapes is done through the canvas, the large white rectangle in the middle of the stage. This is just a regular movie clip with the instance name canvas. It houses the vast majority of the interface code, including what to do when each tool is active, and what Shape instances currently exist. Essentially, the canvas serves as a middleman between the user and the individual Shape instances.

Tools

The toolbox buttons at the left of the interface only do one thing: change the active tool. All the functionality for each tool is actually contained in the canvas movie clip.

ScaleGizmo and Marquee

These two exported clips are added to the stage by canvas, but all their functionality lies within the symbols themselves. A marquee instance, as you've already seen, takes care of drawing a dashed-line box while the mouse button is depressed. Once it's released, canvas runs through a series of actions (which includes performing a test to see if the marquee area overlaps any shapes. The marquee instance itself has nothing to do with this – it simply draws a box and is then removed when it's no longer needed.

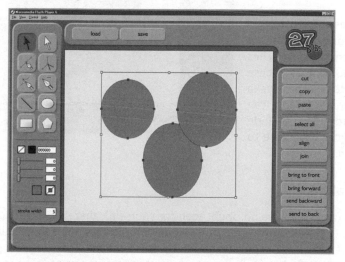

The ScaleGizmo object is bit more complex. It's added to the stage to surround a shape whenever a shape is selected with the Move tool. Dragging the handles of the ScaleGizmo instance then lets users resize the selected shape(s). Again, the ScaleGizmo itself has no knowledge or control of this – all the shape manipulation is controlled by canvas.

We'll see more on this in a few pages' time, but the basic premise is this: a ScaleGizmo instance is added to the stage; the user drags its handles; the instance sends out a custom event that says, "I'm rescaling now!"; canvas hears this event and scales the selected shapes accordingly. The left hand doesn't know what the right hand's doing, as they say!

Clipboard

The clipboard is a virtual object created in the clipboard layer in the code folder. When the user cuts, copies or pastes shapes, canvas sends the shape data to or retrieves it from the clipboard. It makes a nice container for data out of the way of canvas, and includes three straightforward methods: clear(), save(), and retrieve().

Pop-up windows

The final exported symbols in this movie help to communicate information back to the user when necessary. We're all used to windows popping up in applications with messages or options, so I've incorporated them into this interface for a few specific purposes.

Whenever a pop-up window is needed (usually by canvas), an instance of PopUpClass is placed on stage – but only after it's been given the parameters it needs, including a message, options, and a callback function.

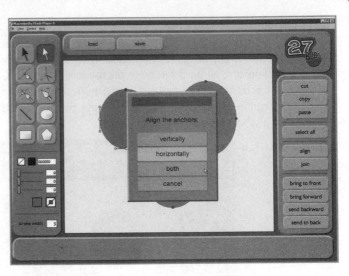

If there are buttons to be placed in the pop-up (OK, for example), then the PopUpClass instance attaches instances of the ButtonClass. These pop-ups and buttons can serve a multitude of purposes, and can easily be expanded to include more, so we'll take a little time to step through them.

The code not taken

As I stated earlier (and as you've no doubt seen for yourself!), there's a lot of code flying around here. We're going to break down some of the more interesting and useful sections over the rest of the chapter, but I think it's important to briefly point out the code we'll be passing over, and give a brief description of what you'll find there – just in case you want to go in and tweak things for your own purposes.

I've broken it down into individual layers on the main timeline:

variables

Here we record the stage dimensions and create a text format for the pop-up windows.

button code

This is where we assign functions for event handlers on all the buttons. We also set up tooltips (code we'll discuss in more detail shortly) and all the keyboard shortcuts.

This is done by making a new object called keystrokeListener, and adding it as a listener to the Key object. Whenever a key is pressed, it runs through a long switch statement and calls the corresponding function.

It's nice containing all the code for keystrokes in one place, so that they can be added to or changed fairly easily. You'll also notice that, to make things easier, we've assigned new constants to the Key object to make the keys more readable. For example:

```
Key.V = 86;
```

Now, instead of checking to see whether the current KeyCode equals 86 inside the `switch` statement, we can simply see if it equals `Key.V`, which is much clearer.

```
switch (Key.getCode()) {
  case Key.V:
    moveButton.onRelease();
    break;
```

colors

The colors code layer contains all the code for the color palette at the bottom of the toolbox. It controls color sliders for the three channels, the text fields next to each one, the fill and stroke focus-setters (beneath the sliders), the hexadecimal field, color swatch, and null fill swatch.

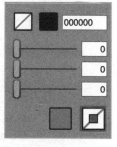

There's nothing out of the ordinary with this code, except perhaps that you can alter the colors in one of three ways: dragging the sliders, altering a single color's text value, or changing the hex value of the color.

clipboard

As already discussed, this object records the data sent by `canvas` to save, then returns it upon request. If you look closely, you'll notice that currently the clipboard is only prepared to save the "shapes" infoType, which translates to mean entire shapes. If you wanted to extend this to include segments or partial shapes, or perhaps text (if you chose to incorporate it into the interface), then you could add that functionality here.

bezier

This is a one-line function – which I picked up from lifaros at the were-here forums – that allows the ScaleGizmo to work correctly:

```
MovieClip.prototype.bezierQuadratic = function(t, a, b, c) {
  return (1-t)*(1-t)*a+2*(1-t)*t*b+t*t*c;
}
```

Let me first explain how frustrated I was when I found that I couldn't get an accurate size returned by a movie clip filled with drawing objects. This made it impossible for me to fit the ScaleGizmo instance tightly around a shape.

The reason for this was that even though *graphically* a curve only went a certain distance on the screen, Flash considers the invisible control point the line is curving *towards* to be part of the clip's area. So _width, _height and getBounds() often returned sizes that were much larger than the movie clip appeared on the screen.

This function lets you find coordinates for *any point* on the curve, where a, b, and c are control point coordinates, and t specifies how far along the line we want to look (t=0 gives us one end, t=1 gives us the other, t=0.5 gives us a point in the middle, and so on).

By running through values of t for every curve in a shape, we can get a makeshift boundary around the shape and so fit the ScaleGizmo instance snugly about it. There are times when this doesn't give a totally accurate result, but they're few and far between, and won't affect the functionality of the ScaleGizmo.

canvas

I know what you're thinking: "How can we not be going over the canvas code, when you've said it basically runs everything else?" Well, I've already mentioned that the canvas code works as middleman between the user and the shapes. canvas does a lot of checking to see which tool is active, checking to see what's currently selected, and telling the selected shapes to do something based on the active tool – but it's the Shape object itself that takes care of *doing* what needs to be done, that's where we'll find the really interesting code.

In addition, canvas includes a lot of if statements that check for errors and conditions (such as whether SHIFT or ALT keys are being held down), plus plenty of for loops that will run through all the shapes, or all the currently selected shapes, and add to or replace the selection. All in all, it's a whole lot of tedious, nitpicky code that wouldn't serve you well to go through line by line. At the heart of it all are the shapes that canvas is talking to, and that is what we will focus on.

So have a glance at some of the code (we will be running through a few lines a little bit later, such as those dealing with ScaleGizmo and PopUpClass) and notice that each tool function of the canvas has its own layer in the tools sub-folder. Know that the purpose of the canvas is to take the user's mouse commands and translate them into a form that a Shape instance can understand, such as addAnchor() whenever the mouse clicks the canvas while the pen tool is active. Does canvas know what addAnchor() is? Of course not! But *you* will before we're through!

Interface Enhancements

There are three small areas of the code I'd like to explore before we get into the shapes themselves. Each offers a kind of feedback for the user during a session in the interface, and each offers some concepts or code you might find useful in future applications.

tooltips

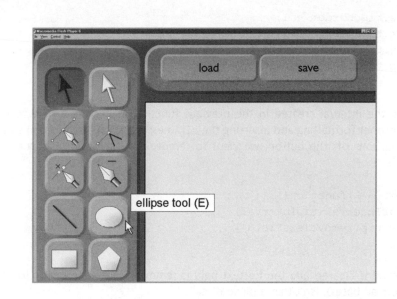

All of the code for the tooltips is contained in the tooltips layer in the code folder. It's actually extremely easy to implement tooltips in your applications, and there are several ways to accomplish it. In PenPad, we have each button send a tooltip message to a single function in the button's onRollOver event handler. The function call looks like:

```
button.onRollOver = function() { timeTip(this.toolTip) };
```

The function it calls, timeTip, is almost as simple:

```
timeTip = function(tip) {
  tipInterval = setInterval(this, "toolTip",
                            ➥ waitTime, tip);
}
```

All that this function does is set up a new interval that calls the function toolTip() after one second (as specified in waitTime) has elapsed, sending it the single argument tip. The upshot of all this is that one second after the user moves their pointer over the button, Flash calls the following function:

```
toolTip = function(tip) {
  clearInterval(tipInterval);
  this.createTextField("tip", 100, this._xmouse + 10,
                               ➥ this._ymouse - 15,
                                   ➥ 0, 0);
  this.tip.autoSize = "left";
  this.tip.selectable = 0;
```

continues overleaf

```
        this.tip.border = 1;
        this.tip.background = 1;
        this.tip.text = tip;
        this.tip.setTextFormat(toolTipFormat);
    }
```

After clearing the interval created in the previous function, it creates a new text field object, applying the proper formatting and inserting the `tip` message as an argument. It's as easy as that. When the user rolls off the button, we want to remove the tip, so we call the `removeTip()` function:

```
    removeTip = function() {
        clearInterval(tipInterval);
        this.tip.removeTextField();
    }
```

Here the interval is cleared and the tip text field is removed (only one needs to occur, but this function covers all bases). Isn't that a piece of cake?

pop-up windows

There are several instances when a pop-up window is attached to the interface in order to offer feedback or options to the user. To handle these occasions, I decided to create a new class named PopUpClass. You will find the code in the popUpSymbol symbol in the library in the exported symbols folder.

If you go into symbol editing mode for this symbol, you will find, just as with Marquee, an empty movie clip with a single layer of code. We won't go through this line by line, but I will explain the important points to you and show you how it's implemented.

The class only contains three methods, two of which (drawDragger() and drawBox()) are strictly drawing methods, which draw the graphic elements of the pop-up. Most of the code is contained in the init() method. It's here that a text field is created and formatted to contain the message (an element in every pop-up). All the pop-up's content, meaning its text and buttons, is created inside a new content movie clip.

```
var content = this.createEmptyMovieClip ("content", 0);
content.createTextField("messageTF", 0, 0, 0, 0, 0);
content.messageTF.setNewTextFormat(this.textFormatting);
content.messageTF.autoSize = "center";
content.messageTF.selectable = 0;
content.messageTF.text = this.message;
```

A long switch statement then checks to see what type of pop-up is needed, and adds the appropriate elements. For instance, the type options needs buttons for all of the options offered, so a for loop runs through each one and attaches an instance of buttonSymbol (which are instances of the special ButtonClass) to the stage:

```
for (var i = 0; i < this.options.length; i++) {
  var props = {};
  props.label = this.options[i];
  props.parameter = this.parameters[i];
  props.height = 30;
  props.width = 150;
  props.textFormatting = this.textFormatting;
  props.clickHandler = function() {
    this._parent._parent.callBackHandler(this.label,
    ➥ this.parameter)
  };
  var option = content.attachMovie("buttonSymbol",
  ➥ "option" + i, i+1, props);
  option._y = startY + option._height/2;
  startY += option._height;
}
```

props is a local object that we use to send a list of properties to the new button in the attachMovie method. Each button needs a label, a parameter (what to return when the button's clicked), a size, a text format for the label and a function to be called when clicked. Once we've set these properties, we attach the button.

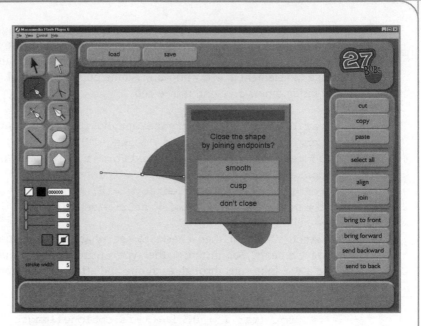

There's not much more to PopUpClass, and it's fairly easy to add to if you need additional types of pop-up. Now let's quickly take a look at how to implement this code.

To create an instance of a pop-up, a number of properties have to be sent in order for the pop-up to know what type it is. Back on the main timeline, take a look in the canvas layer in the canvas code folder, and you'll find three methods that call special pop-up windows: openCloseShapePopUp(), openErrorPopUp(), and openAlignPopUp(). They're all fairly similar, so let's break one down so you can see how it works:

```
canvas.openCloseShapePopUp = function(shape) {
  var props = {};
  props._x = stageWidth/2;
  props._y = stageHeight/2;
  props.type = "options";
  props.padding = 40;
  props.message = "Close the shape\nby joining endpoints?";
  props.options = ["smooth", "cusp", "don't close"];
  props.parameters = [shape, shape, shape];
  props.callBackHandler = setClosingAnchorPoint;
  props.textFormatting = popUpTF;
  props.draggable = 1;
  props.playSound = "warning";
  this._parent.attachMovie("popUpSymbol", "popUp", 578, props);
}
```

First, we create a new local object to hold the pop-up's properties, and then set its coordinates to the center of the stage. We then specify the following:

- A type (in this case "options")
- A pixel-padding value, specifying the number of pixels between the message text field and the pop-up's border (in this case 40)
- A message ("Close the shape...")
- An array of option labels ("smooth", "cusp", "don't close")
- A corresponding array of parameters ("shape", "shape", "shape")
- A function to be called when a button is clicked (`setClosingAnchorPoint`)
- A TextFormat object for the text (as defined in `popUpTF`)
- A value for the Boolean flag draggable (`true`)
- The linkage identifier for a sound to play when the pop-up opens ("warning")

Once all of these parameters have been set, we attach the `popUpSymbol` instance.

ScaleGizmo

The last interface enhancement is directly related to the shapes themselves, so it's probably not something you're likely to want to drop into other movies. However, it does demonstrate an interface communication technique that you might find very useful indeed.

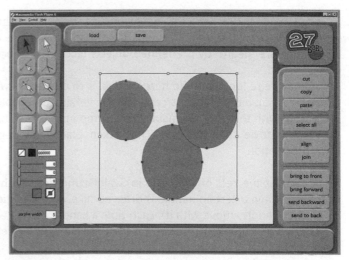

As you'll recall, ScaleGizmo is the box with tiny square handles that forms around selected shapes in the interface, allowing you to rescale them. All the functionality to control the ScaleGizmo instance itself is located in the ScaleGizmo class, but the instance knows nothing about the shapes it manipulates, nor what it's doing to them. So how *does* it work?

Let's start by taking a look at how a ScaleGizmo instance is added to the stage. When a shape (or group of shapes) is clicked on with the Move tool, `canvas` calls its `addScaleGizmo()` method (found in the `canvas` layer in the `canvas code` folder). This runs through each shape on the stage, finding its boundaries and saving the coordinates of its anchors and control points. It then attaches a ScaleGizmo instance to the stage, sending it appropriate center coordinates and the proper dimensions:

```
        this.scaleGizmo =
➡ this._parent.attachMovie("ScaleGizmo", "sg", 1010,
        ➡ {_x:centerX, _y:centerY, w:right-left, h:bottom-top}
        ➡                        );
```

The final two lines in the method are the most interesting:

```
    this.scaleGizmo.addListener(this);
    this.onRescale = this.rescaleShape;
```

Here we add `canvas` (specified with `this`) as a listener to the instance `scaleGizmo`. This allows `canvas` to hear any custom events sent out by `scaleGizmo`. We'll set up a custom event called Rescale to fire whenever `scaleGizmo` is rescaled. In fact, on the very next line, we tell canvas to run its `rescaleShape()` method whenever it hears this custom event.

Double-click on ScaleGizmo in your library (under exported symbols) to enter symbol-editing mode. Once again we have an empty movie clip with a single layer of code. The most important line for us is right at the beginning of the `init()` method:

```
    ScaleGizmo.prototype.init = function() {
        ASBroadcaster.initialize(this);
```

`ASBroadcaster` lets us give new objects the ability to broadcast custom events. You're probably familiar with the default events in a Flash movie, like Key's `KeyDown` or Mouse's `MouseDown`, which are 'heard' by predefined objects (such as instances of MovieClip).

What we're looking to do here though, is to create a new event – Rescale – that will fire whenever a ScaleGizmo instance is rescaled. We've already enabled `canvas` to hear the event when it is fired. With this line, we enable ScaleGizmo instances to broadcast the event, telling the rest of the Flash movie that the event has taken place. Any registered listeners can then act on that information.

Much of the rest of the code in ScaleGizmo deals with drawing the instance itself, and how to react when a certain handle is dragged (like what direction the handle can be dragged and which other handles move with it). Each time a handle is dragged, though, a number of interesting things occur. It is all taken care of in a MouseMove handler defined in the `startScaling()` method:

```
    this.onMouseMove = function() {
        this._parent.rescale(this);
        this._parent.getProportions();
        this._parent.broadcastRescale();
    };
```

_parent is used since the nested handle is actually calling the function. You can see that the rescale() method is first called, which takes care of moving all of the handles to their correct positions based on the handle being dragged. Then getProportions() is called to find the ScaleGizmo instance's current height and width. Finally, broadcastRescale() is called, which is defined as follows:

```
ScaleGizmo.prototype.broadcastRescale = function() {
  var centerX = this.handles[0]._x + this.w/2;
  var centerY = this.handles[0]._y + this.h/2;
  var centerPoint = {x:centerX, y:centerY};
  this.localToGlobal(centerPoint);
  this.broadcastMessage("onRescale", this.w, this.h, centerPoint);
}
```

Here we broadcast the message that the Rescale event has fired, sending along additional parameters that registered listeners (in this case, canvas) might need. These parameters include the width and height of the ScaleGizmo instance, as well as its center point.

Now head back to the canvas layer in the canvas code folder on the main timeline, and find the rescaleShape() method that's called by the onRescale handler we saw earlier. This code runs through all of the saved coordinates of the anchor and control points and places them according to the current size and position of the ScaleGizmo instance:

```
canvas.rescaleShape = function(w, h, centerPt) {
  var percentX = w/this.selectionSize.w;
  var percentY = h/this.selectionSize.h;
  for (var i in this.selectedShapes) {
    var shape = this.selectedShapes[i];
    var anchors = shape.anchors;
    for (var j in anchors) {
      var anchorNum = anchors[j];
      var cp1 = anchorNum.control1;
      var cp2 = anchorNum.control2;
      var savedCoor = this.savedCoordinates[i][j];
      shape.placeAnchor(anchorNum,
➥          savedCoor.anchor.x*percentX + centerPt.x,
➥          savedCoor.anchor.y*percentY + centerPt.y);
      shape.placeControlPoint(cp1,
➥          savedCoor.control1.x*percentX + centerPt.x,
➥          savedCoor.control1.y*percentY + centerPt.y);
      shape.placeControlPoint(cp2,
➥          savedCoor.control2.x*percentX + centerPt.x,
➥          savedCoor.control2.y*percentY + centerPt.y);
    }
  }
}
```

It's nice to have the functionality separated in this way and communicated by custom events so that `scaleGizmo` and `canvas` can each take care of their own tasks without having to worry about the functionality of the other's.

The Shape Class

And now we come to it! The backbone of the interface: Shape. The Shape instances hold information for the shapes drawn by the user and actually draw them to the screen. All of the code used to manipulate the shapes is included in the Shape class, so we'll step through it in a moment so you understand how it is all set up.

First, however, let's discuss how we handle the curves that make up our shapes.

cubic vs. quadratic Bezier curves

In most vector drawing applications, lines are represented by cubic Bezier curves. We're not going to get too much into theory here, as it really isn't too much a part of this application, but it is enough for us to know that a cubic Bezier curve is defined by four points: two anchor points and two control points.

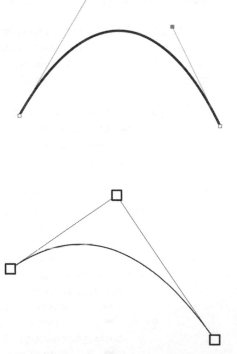

If you have worked at all with the drawing methods in Flash MX, you'll know that lines are actually defined using quadratic Bezier curves, with two anchor points and a single control point.

The `curveTo()` command for the drawing API actually draws a line from the current drawing position (the first anchor) to the second anchor coordinates *towards* the control point coordinates using the quadratic method. The command looks like this:

```
mcInstance.curveTo(cp.x, cp.y, a2.x, a2.y);
```

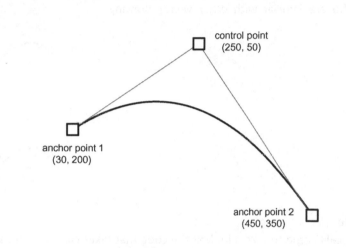

control point
(250, 50)

anchor point 1
(30, 200)

anchor point 2
(450, 350)

mcInstance.moveTo(30, 200);
mcInstance.curveTo(250, 50, 450, 350);

It would be fine to use this method of drawing curves in our application, but for two things:

- Firstly, most users familiar with vector drawing programs and their Bezier toolsets will be used to defining the lines using cubic Bezier curves, not Flash's quadratic Bezier curves.

- Secondly, it's difficult to easily create smooth, continuous curves using the quadratic method.

I finally decided that the best solution would be to provide users with a *simulation* of the cubic method of drawing curves – and it's a lot easier than you might think.

Basically, we just split each curve in two, putting the join at the midpoint in the curve, exactly halfway between the two control points. This midpoint acts as sort of an *invisible* anchor point between the two visible anchor points, and will guarantee you a smooth curve.

The following illustration demonstrates what a curve drawn in this fashion looks like on the screen, then with its anchor and control points visible, and finally with its invisible anchor points drawn as well. It's not a true cubic Bezier curve, but it is any easy approximation that should satisfy users who are familiar with other vector drawing programs.

The Shape code

The time has finally come to take a look at the code that takes care of these shapes! We're going to look at how Shape stores information about itself and how it uses that information to draw itself to the screen. These will be two important points to know when we develop the loading and saving methods in the interface.

Double-click on the Shape symbol in your library and enter symbol-editing mode. Just as you saw with the Marquee symbol, Shape is an empty movie clip containing a single layer filled with code. Call up the Actions panel and look at how we've set it up:

```
#initclip

Shape = function() {
  this.init()
}

Shape.prototype = new MovieClip();

Shape.prototype.init = function() {
  this.anchors = [];
  this.anchorDepth = 0;
  this.selectedAnchors = [];
  this.cpDepth = 0;
  this.fill = {color:null, alpha:100};
  this.createEmptyMovieClip ("fillMC", 1);
  this.stroke = {thickness:2, color:0x0000, alpha:100};
```

continues overleaf

```
            this.lineStyle(this.stroke.thickness,
    ➥            this.stroke.color, this.stroke.alpha);
            this.selectedColor = 255;
            this.moveTo(x, y);
        }
```

The `#initclip` once again informs Flash that a class definition follows. The class is named Shape, and its constructor simply calls the method `init()`, which is found only a few lines below. We also set the prototype of Shape to equal a new MovieClip instance so that we can use all of the methods and properties of a movie clip. This is necessary for many reasons, not least of which is that we wish to utilize all the MovieClip drawing methods.

The `init()` method initializes a number of properties that we'll use throughout the rest of the code. As you can see, we set the fill and stroke properties to a standard default upon the shape's creation, and create a couple of empty arrays that will hold references to the shape's anchors. We also create an empty movie clip to house the fill of the shape and keep it separate from the stroke. You'll see why this is necessary when we look at the `redraw()` method.

So, that's how we set everything up inside Shape. Whenever a new instance is placed on stage, the `init()` method is run and the empty shape waits for any additional information. As yet, there's nothing for us to draw – it's merely a movie clip with a special extra set of commands that help us to represent and modify shapes.

Let's take a look at some of these commands so you can understand better how Shape holds its information.

Anchors

Every time the Pen tool in the interface touches the canvas, a new anchor is added to the currently selected shape. This is performed with the aptly named `addAnchor()` method:

```
Shape.prototype.addAnchor = function(x, y) {
    var a = this.createEmptyMovieClip("a" + this.anchorDepth, 5000 +
this.anchorDepth++);
    a._x = x;
    a._y = y;
    var newAnchor = {};
    newAnchor.anchor = {x:x, y:y};
    newAnchor.control1 = {x:x, y:y};
    newAnchor.control2 = {x:x, y:y};
    newAnchor.clip = a;
    newAnchor.type = "symmetrical";
    newAnchor.selected = 2;
    this.anchors.push(newAnchor);
    for (var i = 0; i < this.anchors.length-1; i++) {
```

```
            this.deselectAnchor(this.anchors[i])
        }
        this.selectAnchor(newAnchor);
        if (this.anchors.length < 2) {
          this.select();
          this.moveTo(x, y);
        }
        this.redraw();
        return newAnchor;
      }
```

The only parameters sent to the method are the x and y position of the new anchor on the stage (relative to the registration point of the main timeline).

The first thing to do is create an empty movie clip that will graphically represent the anchor, which we place at the position specified. We create a new object to hold all of the new anchor's information, such as:

- The x and y placement of the actual anchor and its two control points
- A reference to the physical clip (a)
- The anchor's type ("symmetrical" by default, meaning that its two control points are always equidistant from the anchor point)
- The currently selected control point (this defaults to the second control point)

This newAnchor object is then stored in the Shape instance's anchors array. All other anchors are deselected, and the shape is redrawn.

So now you can see a few things about how Shape holds its information. Its fill and stroke are object properties in the Shape instance (initialized in the init() method), with anchors being an array property that stores references to all the individual anchor objects.

Each anchor object holds information on the x and y coordinates of the anchor point itself and the corresponding control points, as well as the anchor point's type (symmetrical, smooth or cusp). Using just this information, we can work out how to store everything for our shapes in a tidy XML file that we can transfer easily to the server. But we'll get that in a moment!

Methods of manipulation

If you look through the rest of the Shape code, you will see it is broken down into methods to perform fairly specific actions on the elements of the shape – for example:

- setFill() and setStroke() change the stroke and fill properties of the shape.
- moveControlPoint() and moveAnchor() move their respective elements according to the x and y values sent.
- convertAnchor() changes the type of the specified anchor.
- breakAnchor() breaks a single anchor in two, opening the shape.

Take a few minutes to cast your eye over the full list of methods in the FLA provided in the code download. All the code is fully commented, and is also split into helpful sections that should make it relatively easy to find what you're looking for.

These methods all work to change the information stored in the shape, by adding, moving, and removing elements, or by setting different parameters on them. However, the basic structure of the shape never changes, which is helpful when it comes to translating this information into XML. Each Shape object will have exactly the same structure, so we don't need to worry about handling differences in the format of the data.

But how is that structure then translated into a graphical drawing on the stage? That's what our special drawing methods are for!

Drawing the curves

The `redraw()` method is where we go through the shape, look at the position of the anchors and control points, and call the standard MovieClip drawing methods. Let's step through it slowly to see how this is done. The method begins:

```
Shape.prototype.redraw = function() {
  this.clear();
  this.moveTo(this.anchors[0].anchor.x,
           this.anchors[0].anchor.y);
  for (var i = 1; i < this.anchors.length+1; i++) {
```

We first clear any drawing made previously and move the virtual 'pen' to the first anchor's position, since this is where the shape begins. That first anchor will be stored in the first index of the anchors array. To then step through all successive anchors, we run a `for` loop for the length of the anchors array (plus 1, since it is possible that we have a closed shape and need to draw back to the first anchor again). Let's take a look at what we then need to perform for each anchor. The code continues:

```
        if (i == this.anchors.length) {
          if (this.closed) {
            var nextAnchor = this.anchors[0];
            var lastAnchor =
                     this.anchors[this.anchors.length-1];
          } else {
            break;
          }
        } else {
          var nextAnchor = this.anchors[i];
          var lastAnchor = this.anchors[i-1];
        }
```

We need to set two variables at the beginning of this loop for each anchor. `lastAnchor` is the anchor we drew to in the previous iteration of the loop, while `nextAnchor` is the one we're drawing to for this iteration.

To set these variables, we check to see if this is the final iteration of the loop. If it is, and the shape is a closed shape, we need to draw back to the first anchor. If we're in the middle of the shape, then the next anchor is simply the current index in the anchors array.

Once we know which anchors we're drawing a curve between, we need to calculate our invisible middle anchor, which is the midpoint between the two control points at either end of the curve segment (`lastAnchor.control2` and `firstAnchor.control1`):

```
var x = lastAnchor.control2.x - nextAnchor.control1.x;
var y = lastAnchor.control2.y - nextAnchor.control1.y;
var hyp = Math.sqrt(x*x+y*y);
var theta = Math.atan2(y, x);
var middle = {x:lastAnchor.control2.x -
➥               (Math.cos(theta)*(hyp/2)),
➥           y:lastAnchor.control2.y -
➥               (Math.sin(theta)*(hyp/2))
➥       };
```

Okay, I'm not going to try and explain all that in detail, but for the mathematically inclined amongst you, here's a diagram that illustrates what each of these variables represents:

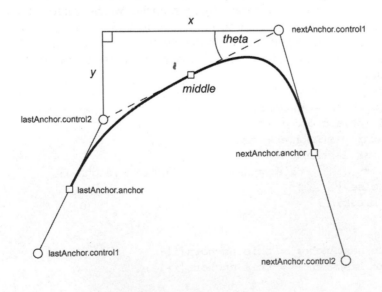

The practical upshot of this is that we now have coordinates for two end anchors and the middle anchor – this means we can draw the curve segment.

```
var startPos = {x:lastAnchor.anchor.x,
    ➥           y:lastAnchor.anchor.y};

this.lineStyle(7, 0, 0);

this.curveTo(lastAnchor.control2.x,
            ➥ lastAnchor.control2.y,
            ➥ middle.x,
            ➥ middle.y);

this.curveTo(nextAnchor.control1.x,
            ➥ nextAnchor.control1.y,
            ➥ nextAnchor.anchor.x,
            ➥ nextAnchor.anchor.y);
```

First, we record the starting position of the curve. This is, for simplicity's sake, when we redraw the curve (as you'll see in a moment). This first curve segment that we draw is actually invisible (`alpha` of 0 in the call to `lineStyle()`) with a thickness of 7. This particular curve is drawn to make selecting the shape easier for the user. By having a stroke thickness of at least 7 pixels (though invisible), the user should be able to select the shape by clicking on the path, even if the path has no actual stroke assigned to it.

The next two `curveTo()` lines draw from the `lastAnchor` to the `middle` anchor, then from the `middle` anchor to the `nextAnchor`, curving towards the two control points.

The next two conditional statements check to see if the segment should be redrawn with a solid, visible stroke, then whether the segment should be drawn a third time to show a thin blue selection line. The `curveTo()` methods are actually exactly the same each time, with only the `lineStyle()` parameters changing.

```
if (this.stroke.thickness > 0 &&
        ➥ this.stroke.color != null) {

    this.moveTo(startPos.x, startPos.y);

    this.lineStyle(this.stroke.thickness,
            ➥ this.stroke.color,
            ➥ this.stroke.alpha);

    this.curveTo(lastAnchor.control2.x,
            ➥ lastAnchor.control2.y,
```

continues overleaf

```
                               ➥ middle.x, middle.y)

        this.curveTo(nextAnchor.control1.x,
                       ➥ nextAnchor.control1.y,
                       ➥ nextAnchor.anchor.x, nextAnchor.anchor.y);
     }

     if (this.selected) {

        this.lineStyle(1, this.selectedColor, 100);

        this.moveTo(startPos.x, startPos.y);

        this.curveTo(lastAnchor.control2.x,
                       ➥ lastAnchor.control2.y, middle.x, middle.y);

        this.curveTo(nextAnchor.control1.x,
                       ➥ nextAnchor.control1.y,
                       ➥ nextAnchor.anchor.x, nextAnchor.anchor.y);
     }
```

There are two final lines in our code to finish up the redraw method:

```
        lastAnchor.middle = middle;
     }
     this.drawFill();
  }
```

Here we store the invisible middle anchor's coordinates in the `middle` property for each anchor so that we can easily access it at later times without having to recalculate. The final line calls the `drawFill()` method of Shape. Let's take a look at that now.

Filling it in
Directly following the `redraw()` method is the method used to fill in the shape if it has a solid fill selected:

```
Shape.prototype.drawFill = function() {
   this.fillMC.clear();
   if (this.fill.color == null || this.fill.alpha == 0) {
      return false
   };
   this.fillMC.moveTo(this.anchors[0].anchor.x,
                   ➥ this.anchors[0].anchor.y);

   this.fillMC.beginFill(this.fill.color, this.fill.alpha);
```

After clearing any previous drawing from inside the `fillMC` movie clip (which we created in the `init()` method), we check to see if we *should* draw a fill. If a color is assigned and the `alpha` property of the fill isn't 0, then we move to the first anchor and set the fill color. The next lines, which finish off the method, should look very familiar to you:

```
for (var i = 1; i <= this.anchors.length; i++) {
  if (i == this.anchors.length) {
    if (this.closed) {
      var nextAnchor = this.anchors[0];
      var lastAnchor =
               ➡ this.anchors[this.anchors.length-1];
    } else {
      break;
    }
  } else {
    var nextAnchor = this.anchors[i];
    var lastAnchor = this.anchors[i-1];
  }
  this.fillMC.curveTo(lastAnchor.control2.x,
                     ➡ lastAnchor.control2.y,
                     ➡ lastAnchor.middle.x,
                     ➡ lastAnchor.middle.y);

  this.fillMC.curveTo(nextAnchor.control1.x,
                     ➡ nextAnchor.control1.y,
                     ➡ nextAnchor.anchor.x,
                     ➡ nextAnchor.anchor.y);
}
this.fillMC.endFill();
}
```

Just as in the `redraw()` method, we run through each anchor and draw the necessary curves. Notice we don't have to recalculate the middle anchor since we saved its value in the `redraw()` method. Once we have run through each anchor, we end the fill. Short and sweet!

Now that you know how each shape stores its data and draws itself to the screen, we can look at how we can package this data as XML to save drawings on the server, and load up previously saved files into the interface.

Saving drawings to the server

Saving a drawing may seem a trivial task, but surprisingly, there are more little steps involved than you might imagine. Once a user's created a drawing and clicked the Save button, the process goes a little like this:

In Flash:

- Ask the user to specify a file in which to save the data.
- Make sure the user enters a filename.
- Validate the filename to make sure it fits our server's requirements.
- Package all the current drawing data into one XML object to send to the server.
- Send the data to an ASP.NET page on the server.

In the ASP.NET page:

- If the filename exists, report that this is the case and stop.
- If the filename does not exist, save the data to the specified file.
- Report the status of the save attempt.

Back in Flash:

- Display a message reflecting the server's status report.

As you can see, there's more to it then meets the eye!

Shapes XML

Before we begin translating the shape data into XML, perhaps it would help to see how we've chosen to store the data. The following simple XML shows how a single blue ellipse on the canvas would be represented in XML:

```xml
<?xml version="1.0" ?>
<illustration>
  <shape closed="1">
    <fill color="202" alpha="100" />
    <stroke thickness="10" color="106" alpha="100" />
    <anchors>
      <anchor type="smooth">
        <a x="286.95" y="241.475" />
        <c1 x="286.95" y="269.837345" />
        <c2 x="286.95" y="213.112655" />
      </anchor>
      <anchor type="smooth">
        <a x="339.45" y="173" />
        <c1 x="317.7045" y="173" />
        <c2 x="361.1955" y="173" />
      </anchor>
      <anchor type="smooth">
        <a x="391.95" y="241.475" />
        <c1 x="391.95" y="213.1195025" />
        <c2 x="391.95" y="269.8304975" />
```

continues overleaf

```
        </anchor>
        <anchor type="smooth">
          <a x="339.45" y="309.95" />
          <c1 x="361.1955" y="309.95" />
          <c2 x="317.7045" y="309.95" />
        </anchor>
      </anchors>
    </shape>
  </illustration>
```

Not too hard to understand, is it? Now let's look at how to write it.

Packaging the shapes

Head back to the main timeline and select the save & load layer in the code folder. All the code that's responsible for packaging, sending and loading the shape data to and from the server is defined in this layer.

Before Flash can save the file to the server, it needs several important variables set up.

File extension

Since this is a full-featured application, its files should have their own special extension. This makes it easier to distinguish PenPad drawing files from those created by (and for) other apps. I've chosen to use an extension of .ppx (short for **PenP**ad **X**ML):

```
// application filename extension
fileExtension = ".ppx";
```

Flash isn't fussy when it comes to loading in data, and will happily accept files with any extension you like. So long as the data is properly formatted XML, Flash will happily parse whatever's thrown at it.

File location

Next, a variable that holds the name of the server folder where these PPX files should be stored:

```
// default server folder
fileFolder = "PenPadDrawings";
```

File path separators

To save a file on the server, we need to use a Windows naming convention that specifies an absolute physical path. As such, we need to use the backslash character to separate the folder name from the file name. Since the backslash character is an escape character in Flash strings, we need to use two in a row for Flash to know we want a single backslash character.

```
// saving filename requires Windows path
saveSeperator = "\\";
```

When the time comes to load our files back in, we'll use a relative HTTP page to load the data. We'll therefore need to use a forward slash to separate folder names:

```
// loading filename requires URL path (forward slash)
loadSeperator = "/";
```

Illegal characters

Again, as we're using a Windows naming convention to save the file, we need to make sure any filename the user enters is a legal Windows filename. Subsequently, we create an array of all the illegal characters that would cause a filename to fail under Windows. We also add an extra character – a period – as we don't want our users to get confused should they enter extra extensions.

```
// illegal filename characters
var badchars = new Array("<", ">", "|", ":", "?",
                     ➥   "/", "\\", "\"", "*", ".");
```

Now that we've seen all the required variables, we can move on to the actual process of saving a drawing to the server.

Sending picture data to the server

The first thing to do here is set up the Save button. Carrying straight on from the previous code, we start with the following:

```
saveButton.useHandCursor = 0;
```

This line disables the hand cursor when the mouse is moved over the button. Instead, the mouse cursor remains a pointer cursor.

When the Save button (instance name saveButton) on the interface is released, a pop-up window opens with an input field for the user to type a filename. This is all taken care of in the following code:

```
saveButton.onRelease = function() {
  var props = {};
  props._x = stageWidth/2;
  props._y = stageHeight/2;
  props.type = "type-in";
  props.padding = 20;
  props.inputWidth = 250;
```

continues overleaf

```
    props.message = "Type in name of file to save:";
    props.callBackHandler = saveXML;
    props.textFormatting = popUpTF;
    props.draggable = 1;
    this._parent.attachMovie("popUpSymbol", "popUp", 1500, props);
}
```

The entirety of this code formats a special pop-up input window of type `type-in`. The `callBackHandler` for this pop-up window (called when its OK button is pressed) is the function `saveXML()`. Let's take a look at that code, since it's there that we translate all our shape data into XML and send it to the server. It begins like this:

```
saveXML = function(option, filename) {
  popUp.removeMovieClip ();
  if (option == "OK") {
    if (filename == undefined || filename == "") {
      canvas.openErrorPopUp("A filename must be
                    ➡ provided in order to save.");
      return;
    }
    var shapesXML = '<illustration>';
```

This function is called with two parameters: the option of the button pressed in the pop-up window ("OK" or "cancel") and a string specifying the filename. After removing the pop-up window instance and making sure OK is pressed, we ensure that the filename is defined properly.

If it isn't, we open an error pop-up window (a method of `canvas`) and exit the function. However, if everything is in order, we begin writing the XML, which is simply a variable holding a string. The root node of our XML will be `<illustration>`.

Now we just need to go through all the shapes on the canvas and store the information.

```
for (var i = 0; i < canvas.shapes.length; i++) {
  var shape = canvas.shapes[i];
  var closed = shape.closed == undefined ? 0 : 1;
  shapesXML += '<shape closed="' + closed + '">';
  shapesXML += '<fill color="' + shape.fill.color;
  shapesXML += '" alpha="' + shape.fill.alpha +
'"/>';
  shapesXML += '<stroke thickness="';
  shapesXML += shape.stroke.thickness
  shapesXML += '" color="' + shape.stroke.color;
  shapesXML += '" alpha="' + shape.stroke.alpha;
  shapesXML += '"/>';
```

`canvas.shapes` is the array that holds a reference to all of the shapes currently on the canvas, so we run through this in a for loop. For each shape, we begin a new XML element `<shape>`, which has a single attribute: `closed`. This attribute's value will either be 1 or 0, depending on whether the Shape we're describing is closed or not (as specified by the object's closed property).

`<fill>` and `<stroke>` are elements inside `<shape>`. Each of these has a color and an alpha attribute, and `<stroke>` also has a thickness attribute. All this information is taken from the fill and stroke properties of the current Shape object.

Believe it or not, the only remaining property of the shape that needs to be explored and stored is the `anchors` property. Another for loop is needed to run through this array:

```
shapesXML += '<anchors>';
for (var j = 0; j < shape.anchors.length; j++) {
   var anchor = shape.anchors[j];
   shapesXML += '<anchor type="'+anchor.type+'">';
   shapesXML += '<a x="'+anchor.anchor.x+'" y="';
   shapesXML += anchor.anchor.y + '"/>';

   shapesXML += '<c1 x="' + anchor.control1.x;
   shapesXML += '" y="' + anchor.control1.y + '"/>';

   shapesXML += '<c2 x="' + anchor.control2.x;
   shapesXML += '" y="' + anchor.control2.y + '"/>';

   shapesXML += '</anchor>';
}
shapesXML += '</anchors>';
shapesXML += '</shape>';
}
```

After creating an `<anchors>` element inside `<shape>` to hold all of an individual shape's anchors, we loop through each anchor in that shape and create an `<anchor>` element with a single attribute of `type`. Each anchor tag is then given three child elements: `<a>`, `<control1>` and `<control2>` which all have x and y attributes for recording each coordinate.

Once information for all of the anchors is stored in the XML string, we close the tag for this particular shape element and move on to the next one.

Once we've gone through all the shapes, we close the `<illustration>` tag and create the new XML object so that we can send this XML string to the server:

```
shapesXML += '</illustration>';
var shapesFile = new XML(shapesXML);
shapesFile.xmlDecl = "<?xml version=\"1.0\" ?>";
```

To actually transmit our XML data to the server, we use the `saveAndLoad` method of the XML object to send data when we expect data in return – in this case we want a confirmation from the server that the file was saved correctly.

> The `XML.sendAndLoad` *method requires not only the URL of the server-side processing page, but an XML object into which it can load any returned data.*

We create our result XML object as follows:

```
var resultXML = new XML();
resultXML.ignoreWhite = true;
resultXML.onLoad = verifySave;
```

Here we specify that the `resultXML` object will ignore any white space in the incoming XML, and when it has fully received and parsed the incoming data, to call the `verifySave` function. Finally we can save our file to the server:

```
var URL = "http://localhost/saveDrawing.aspx?";
URL +=   "filename=";
URL += escape(fileFolder + saveSeperator);
URL += escape(filename + fileExtension);
// shapesFile is the completed XML file
shapesFile.sendAndLoad(URL, resultXML);
    }
  }
```

When the ASP.NET page processes the file, it will send back a success or failure message to this object.

So, there are now just two steps left in the save process: writing the data into a file on the server, and reporting back to the user. This is where we move into server-side territory, and take a look at the file called `saveDrawing.aspx`.

Storing data in the file

As you'll recall from earlier chapters in this book, the basic process of saving data into a file on the server is fairly painless. We create a new file with the name supplied by the user, dump all the XML data into it, and close the file.

However, we need to take things one step further. Should a user enter a filename that already exists, ASP.NET will throw its hands in the air and complain – known technically as **throwing an exception**. We're going to trap that exception – independent of any other problems that may arise – and let the user know what's gone wrong.

Inside the page_load function for this ASP.NET page, we have the following C# code:

```csharp
string error_type = "";
string file = Request.QueryString["filename"];
file = Server.UrlDecode(file);
file = Server.MapPath(file)

try {

  FileStream oFS = new FileStream(file,
                              ➡   FileMode.CreateNew,
                              ➡   FileAccess.Write,
                              ➡   FileShare.Write);
  StreamWriter oSW = new StreamWriter(oFS);
  oSW.Write(Server.UrlDecode(Request.Form.ToString()));
  oSW.Close();
  oFS.Close();
  error_type = "none"; // assume it saved without error
}

catch (IOException) {
  error_type = "exists";
}

catch {
  error_type = "error";
}

finally {
  Response.Write("<server_response><error>");
  Response.Write(error_type);
  Response.Write("</error></server_response>");
}
```

We use a **try..catch..finally** block to trap errors, which works in much the same way as the name suggests – we **try** to run the code, **catch** any errors that occur, and **finally** execute whatever code he have that depends on the outcome.

When we create the FileStream object oFS, we pass it the filename that was set in Flash, along with parameters specifying how we want to access the file.

Assuming the filename was unique, we create a new StreamWriter object oSW, and use it to dump the contents of the Flash request (the XML object data, accessed from Request.Form) in the relevant file. We can then close up both the StreamWriter object and the FileStream object, and set the error_type string variable to show that we've not received any errors.

If the file already exists though, the line defining oFS will throw an IOException, and cause us to jump straight on to the first catch block, where error_type is set to show that the file exists.

If some other exception is raised, we jump to the second block, where error_type is set to show that we've received a generic error.

We close with the finally section of our try..catch..finally block. Error or no error, the code in this section gets called after everything else in the block is done, and we use it to send data back to our Flash movie. Since we're returning data to an XML object, we create a tiny snippet of XML, using our error_type variable as the main data.

Verifying the save operation

Our final step in the save operation is to reporting back to the user. You'll remember that when we saved our data to the server, we specified an XML object (resultXML) to hold the response. We also specified that when the movie received data from the server, it should call the verifySave() function.

Back in our Flash movie, we need to add the verifySave function right where we left off – immediately below the saveXML() function (in the save & load layer).

```
verifySave = function(save_success) {
```

As this function is called from the onLoad method of an XML object, a single parameter is passed in – a Boolean (true/false) value called save_success to indicate whether the incoming data was parsed successfully.

If everything went to plan, and the XML was saved successfully, this will be true. If there was a problem communicating with the server, or if the data sent back was malformed XML, this will be false. However, if we trapped an error on the server, and sent back error details as valid XML, Flash will assume everything's gone okay, and save_success will be true again.

So, we use this information (carefully!) to display an appropriate message to the user:

```
if (save_success) {
  var server_error = this.firstChild.firstChild
                  ➥ .firstChild.nodeValue;
```

If we received a `true` value from `save_success`, we store the text of the error message (`error_type` variable from our C# page) in the Flash variable `server_error`. We can then decide what to do based on its value.

If the error string was "none" we pop-up a message letting the user know the file was saved without error, and `break` out of the `switch` block:

```
switch (server_error) {
  case "none":
    canvas.openErrorPopUp("File saved successfully.");
    break;
```

If the error string was "exists", we tell the user that the filename's already there, and to try using a different one:

```
  case "exists":
    canvas.openErrorPopUp("File already exists\nwith
      ➥     that name.\nTry a different\nfile name.");
    break;
```

Should the error string be "error" (a generic error from our C# page) or completely empty (some other problem that we've failed to account for), we let the user know the file was not saved correctly:

```
  case "error":
  case null:
  case "":
  default:
    canvas.openErrorPopUp("Error saving file.\nFile not saved.");
    break;
```

We close up this function by handling what happens should the `save_success` parameter be `false`. Again, this would be caused by a communication error with the server, or an error in the syntax of our XML response:

```
  }
} else {
  // report communication error
  canvas.openErrorPopUp("Error saving file.\nFile  not saved.");
```

continues overleaf

```
        }
    }
```

Loading what's been saved

The process of loading an existing drawing requires no special server-side programming – everything we need to load a drawing already exists inside Flash. To start, we first need to set up our Load button with the following code (in the Save & Load layer again):

```
loadButton.useHandCursor = 0;
loadButton.onRelease = function() {
 var props = {};
 props._x = stageWidth/2;
 props._y = stageHeight/2;
 props.type = "type-in";
 props.padding = 20;
 props.inputWidth = 250;
 props.message = "Type in name of file to load:";
 props.callBackHandler = loadXML;
 props.textFormatting = popUpTF;
 props.draggable = 1;
 this._parent.attachMovie("popUpSymbol", "popUp",1500, props);
 }
```

You'll notice that it generally looks very similar to the equivalent function for the Save button. We start by disabling the hand cursor, create an object to hold the properties of a new pop-up window, specify a handler function that is called when the user clicks a button in the pop-up, and attach and show the new window.

In this case, we call the loadXML() function when the user presses either the OK or Cancel button in the pop-up window. Let's see what's in that function.

Just like saveXML(), two parameters are passed in from the pop-up window: the user's button response, and the filename they typed in.

```
loadXML = function(option, filename) {
    if (option == "OK") {
      if (filename == undefined || filename == "") {
        canvas.openErrorPopUp("A filename must be
                    ➥ provided\nin order to load.");
        return;
      }
```

Should the user have clicked OK but not typed in a filename, we let them know they need to enter a filename before we can load a file.

Now, to prepare for loading of the data, we cleared out any existing shapes on the canvas:

```
canvas.selectAll();
canvas.deleteShapes();
canvas.shapes = [];
```

Next, we set up a new XML object to load the drawing into, specify that it should ignore any whitespace in the file, and tell it to call fillCanvas() on receiving the data:

```
var shapesFile = new XML();
shapesFile.ignoreWhite = true;
shapesFile.onLoad = fillCanvas;
```

We use the load() method on shapesFile, passing in a filename that's built up from the fileFolder variable, the loadSeparator character variable, the filename (as entered by the user), and our application's fileExtension:

```
shapesFile.load(fileFolder + loadSeparator
           ➥   + filename + fileExtension);
```

Now, while the user is waiting for the drawing to load, we open a new pop-up window with some brief "loading" text:

```
var props = {};
props._x = stageWidth/2;
props._y = stageHeight/2;
props.type = "status";
props.padding = 40;
props.message = "loading " + filename + "...";
props.textFormatting = popUpTF;
this._parent.attachMovie("popUpSymbol", "popUp", 1500, props);
```

Should there be any communication errors or computer errors that would cause the loading process to take an exceedingly long time, we set a function to be executed after 10 seconds (10000 milliseconds).

```
loadWait = setInterval(loadAbort, 10000);
```

We close the function by handling the case that the user clicked the Cancel button instead of the OK button. Here, we simply remove the pop-up window from the screen, and return to our app:

```
      } else {
        popUp.removeMovieClip();
      }
    }
```

Hang ten

We've provided for the possibility that the loading of the drawing may take more than ten seconds. This delay might be caused by network traffic, a server going down, or any number of server communication scenarios. In this case, we've specified that the loadAbort function be called if this situation arises.

This function is small, but very useful:

```
    loadAbort = function() {
      clearInterval(loadWait);
      canvas.openErrorPopUp("File could not be found.");
    }
```

We never want a user left wondering what happened. In the case of a communication delay, it's best to let the user know there was a generic error, and let them get back to drawing, or trying to load the file again.

Fill it up

In our loadXML() function above, we've specified that once shapesFile has received the XML data, the fillCanvas() function should be called. This function works by iterating through the XML drawing data, and recreating the previously drawn objects:

```
    fillCanvas = function(load_success) {
      if (load_success) {
        clearInterval(loadWait);
```

If the data was successfully loaded and parsed, we start by clearing out the interval we set earlier, which calls the loadAbort function after ten seconds. After all, we don't want that happening once the drawing has been loaded!

We've already cleared the screen of any current drawings, but now we remove any pop-up windows from the screen:

```
        popUp.removeMovieClip();
```

We create a reference variable (illustration) to hold the root node of our incoming XML object, and another (shapes) to hold its child nodes. Each of these represents one of the shapes that make up the saved drawing:

```
var illustration = this.childNodes[0];
var shapes = illustration.childNodes;
```

We now loop through all the shapes in the drawing, create a new object for each one, and attach properties based on the incoming XML, just as if we'd created it using the interface tools:

```
var newShapes = [];
for (var i = 0; i < shapes.length; i++) {
  var loadShape = shapes[i];
  var newShape = {};
  newShape.fill = {};
  newShape.stroke = {};
  newShape.anchors = [];
  newShape.closed = loadShape.attributes.closed
              ➥     === "1" ? 1 : undefined;
  var fill = loadShape.childNodes[0];
  newShape.fill.color = fill.attributes.color
    fill.attributes.color == "null" ? null :
              ➥       fill.attributes.color;
  newShape.fill.alpha = fill.attributes.alpha;
  var stroke = loadShape.childNodes[1];
  newShape.stroke.thickness = stroke.attributes.thickness;
  newShape.stroke.color = stroke.attributes.color
              ➥     == "null" ? null : stroke.attributes.color;
  newShape.stroke.alpha = stroke.attributes.alpha;
```

Since each shape is defined in terms of anchors, we now loop through all the child nodes of the current shape to find them all. We then push each newAnchor onto the anchors property of newShape:

```
var anchors = loadShape.childNodes[2];
for (var j=0; j<anchors.childNodes.length; j++) {
  var loadAnchor = anchors.childNodes[j];
  var newAnchor = {};
  newAnchor.type = loadAnchor.attributes.type;
  var a = loadAnchor.childNodes[0].attributes;
  var cp1 = loadAnchor.childNodes[1].attributes;
  var cp2 = loadAnchor.childNodes[2].attributes;
  newAnchor.anchor = {x:Number(a.x), y:Number(a.y)};
  newAnchor.control1 = {x:Number(cp1.x), y:Number(cp1.y)};
  newAnchor.control2 = {x:Number(cp2.x), y:Number(cp2.y)};
```

continues overleaf

```
        newShape.anchors.push(newAnchor);
    }
```

Once we're done with each shape, we push it onto the end of the newShapes array:

```
    newShapes.push(newShape);
```

Once we've parsed the incoming shapes and their respective anchors, and added them all to our newShapes array of shapes, we can delete the XML object, and send newShapes to the canvas.populate() method:

```
    }
    delete this;
    canvas.populate(newShapes);
```

Again, we finish by handling the case that there was an error. Maybe Flash was unable to find the file, or there was an error in parsing the incoming data. Either way, we let the user know that an error occurred, but let them return to the application to continue as normal:

```
    } else {
    clearInterval(loadWait);
    popUp.removeMovieClip();
    canvas.openErrorPopUp("File could not be loaded.");
    }
}
```

Summary

Well that's it for our study of the PenPad application. In the last forty or so pages, we've seen how PenPad hangs together, and examined a few particular areas in detail. While we've not had time to look at every little detail, you've seen a whole stack of ideas and code techniques that you can take and apply to your own interface development.

Along the way, we've covered some fairly advanced ground: extending movie clips as new classes to handle very specific functionality, creating custom events that can be heard throughout the Flash movie, adding interface feedback tools such as tooltips and pop-up dialog windows.

We also looked at how the app's internal organization helps us to describe PenPad's drawings in terms of a simple, predictable XML document, which we can store on the server and call back up whenever we like.

Now that you have a better idea of how the application works, go back and have another play with it. You might even think of ways to build on what's there already, and maybe add some brand-new features of your own – just don't be afraid to have a go!

Index

The index is arranged hierarchically, in alphabetical order, with symbols preceding the letter A. Many second-level entries also occur as first-level entries. This is to ensure that you will find the information you require however you choose to search for it. Index entries relating to the .NET framework are listed under 'N'.

friends of ED particularly welcomes feedback on the layout and structure of this index. If you have any comments or criticisms, please contact: feedback@friendsofED.com

If you're serious about Flash design, and if you want to push your ideas to the very limits of possibility in Flash MX, then this book and CD are your indispensable companions.

This book and CD package combines two vital elements:

- The most comprehensive and in-depth reference resource for Flash MX ActionScript

- Rich, practical tutorials on using ActionScript effectively in your Flash movie design

We've packed in twenty chapters of tutorials, hundreds of detailed reference entries, and hundreds of example FLAs and SWFs. The CD reproduces and expands the complete ActionScript dictionary, providing you with a comprehensive and portable reference tool.

Our aim has been to make this book the best Flash MX ActionScript resource, bar none – the book that you'll keep on your desk and never exhaust.

With the release of Flash MX, scripting in Flash has moved from being a desirable asset to an essential skill in the world of web design. ActionScript is, quite simply, the center of power in Flash, and it's no surprise that most of the advances in Flash MX are Script-centric.

Flash is a design tool, and ActionScript can easily scare designers. This book is for anyone who has ever looked in awe at a cutting-edge Flash site, then taken a look at some code, and run in the other direction. Learning ActionScript with friends of ED will not turn you into a boring programmer, it will turn you into someone who finally has the power to achieve what they want with their web design.

This book will take you from knowing nothing about ActionScript to a firm knowledge that will allow you to exercise a previously unimaginable amount of power over your flash movies. It does this with fully worked examples throughout, and a case study that will leave you with a cutting-edge Flash site by the end of the book.

Advanced PHP for Flash is the follow-up to the hugely popular Foundation PHP for Flash.

The main aim of this book is to extend the reader's knowledge of using PHP and MySQL to produce dynamic content for Flash. Essentially, it picks up the baton from the first book and runs with it until there's no more road.

The book takes the reader from being an intermediate to an advanced PHP/Flash developer, and to help them create some awesome Flash-based web applications along the way. It covers the core PHP features, as well as some exciting extras, that follow on directly from the knowledge gained in the first chapter, and show the reader how to use them in real-world applications.

This book covers:

- Sessions
- File Uploading
- Advanced MySQL
- Socket Functions
- PHP and XML
- Ming
- Plus fully functional case studies

This book is aimed squarely at those readers who want to create dynamic Flash-based web applications, and especially at those who have finished the first book and are hungry for more.

As this book is pitched at those with an intermediate knowledge of PHP (and a decent grasp of MySQL) it has the advantage of being useful to both programmers and those coming over from the first book.

friendsof

DESIGNER TO DESIGNER™

friends of ED writes books for you. Any suggestions, or ideas about how you want information given in your ideal book will be studied by our team.

Your comments are valued by friends of ED.

For technical support please contact support@friendsofed.com.

Freephone in USA	800.873.9769
Fax	312.893.8001
UK contact: Tel:	0121.258.8858
Fax:	0121.258.8868

Registration Code: | 4089XP53TV46IO01

Flash .NET – Registration Card

Name ....

Address ....

City ....State/Region ....

Country ....Postcode/Zip ....

E-mail ....

Profession: design student ☐   freelance designer ☐
                     part of an agency ☐   inhouse designer ☐
                     other (please specify) ....

Age: Under 20 ☐ 20-24 ☐ 25-29 ☐ 30-40 ☐ over 40 ☐

Do you use: mac ☐ pc ☐ both ☐

How did you hear about this book?...

Book review (name)...

Advertisement (name) ....

Recommendation ....

Catalog ....

Other ....

Where did you buy this book? ....

Bookstore (name) ....City.............................

Computer Store (name)..

Mail Order..

Other..

How did you rate the overall content of this book?
Excellent ☐   Good ☐
Average ☐   Poor ☐

What applications/technologies do you intend to learn in the near future?...
....

What did you find most useful about this book? ....
....

What did you find the least useful about this book? ....
....

Please add any additional comments ....
....

What other subjects will you buy a computer book on soon?
....
....

What is the best computer book you have used this year?
....

Note: This information will only be used to keep you updated about new friends of ED titles and will not be used for any other purpose or passed to any other third party.

ISBN: 1904344089

friendsof ED

DESIGNER TO DESIGNER™

NB. If you post the bounce back card below in the UK, please send it to:

friends of ED Ltd.,
30 Lincoln Road,
Olton,
Birmingham.
B27 6PA

NO POSTAGE
NECESSARY
IF MAILED
IN THE
UNITED STATES

BUSINESS REPLY MAIL

FIRST CLASS   *PERMIT #64*   *CHICAGO, IL*

POSTAGE WILL BE PAID BY ADDRESSEE

friends of ED,
29 S. La Salle St.
Suite 520
Chicago Il 60603-USA